THE INFORMATION
WEAPON

THE INFORMATION WEAPON

Winning Customers and Markets with Technology

WILLIAM R. SYNNOTT

JOHN WILEY & SONS

New York · Chichester · Brisbane · Toronto · Singapore

This publication is designed to provide accurate and
authoritative information in regard to the subject
matter covered. It is sold with the understanding that
the publisher is not engaged in rendering legal, accounting,
or other professional service. If legal advice or other
expert assistance is required, the services of a competent
professional person should be sought. *From a Declaration
of Principles jointly adopted by a Committee of the
American Bar Association and a Committee of Publishers.*

Library of Congress Cataloging in Publication Data:

Synnott, William R.
   The information weapon.

   Bibliography: p.
   Includes index.
   1. Management—Communication systems.   2. Management—
Data processing.   3. Information resources management.
I. Title.

HD30.335.S96   1987   658.4'038   86-32393
ISBN 0-471-84557-4

Printed in the United States of America

10 9 8 7 6 5 4 3 2 1

To Mark and Amy

PREFACE

A profound change is occurring in the business world; the competitive power of technology has been discovered! After 25 years of relegating computers and information technology to the back office as a cost cutting productivity tool, the business community has discovered that technology has an exciting untapped potential as a competitive force in the marketplace. Leading companies such as Citicorp, American Express, American Hospital Supply, Sears Roebuck, Merrill Lynch, American Airlines, and others are gaining a significant competitive advantage through smarter use of their information resources. How these and other excellent companies are turning technology to competitive advantage has become an issue of considerable interest to business and information managers alike.

This book addresses this new and exciting trend by looking at how successful companies are using information technology as a competitive weapon, what new strategic planning methodologies are working for them, and what management initiatives are needed to put a firm's information resources to work successfully in today's information society.

In most companies, a huge gap between corporate strategy and information technology strategy prevents the vision of competitive technology from being realized. This book was written to help bridge this gap. It shows how leaders in the leading edge companies are sharing the vision of information technology as a competitive weapon and are seizing the opportunity to put their information resources to work innovatively to beat the competition. They are doing it through strategic planning that truly integrates business and information technology planning, through technology architecture that assures a responsive and supportive technology infrastructure, and as technological engines of change. These four forces— *vision, strategy, architecture, change*—combine to create *the information weapon.*

Vision. The vision of information resources as a competitive force is the primary requisite for gaining competitive advantage through technology. Part I discusses the transformation occurring today in information resource management and the new role of the chief information officer (CIO), working closely with top management, to achieve the information weapon vision.

Strategy. Corporate and information systems strategy must be effectively merged if the vision of competition through technology is to be achieved. Part II examines strategic planning methodologies and also reviews a powerful competitive planning model useful in the continuing search for innovative information weapons. A number of case examples and strategies provide insight to how leading firms are using technological innovation, new information services, and productivity strategies to gain advantage in the marketplace.

Architecture. Part III zeroes in on the difficult and complex problem of ensuring a responsive and facilitating technology infrastructure in the face of the increasing decentralization of information resources. Just as the CIO needs to be involved in strategic business planning, the chief executive officer (CEO) needs to provide direction and support to technology architecture. An architectural framework is described to drive architectural planning to assure a consistent and coordinated technical foundation capable of responding quickly to business needs and competitive initiatives.

Change. Change must be added to death and taxes as inviolate certainties. Nowhere is this more true than in technology. Technology is one of the most potent forces of change in business today. Yet, it has only scratched the surface. In the next decade, we will see technology move into the mainstream of business as this maturing industry slowly but inexorably transfers from control of the technocrats into the hands of business managers. Part IV suggests four major engines of change that are impacting the business landscape today, changes that can be channeled into opportunity by alert change agents who share the information weapon vision.

This book is not a technical treatise, it is a *management* book. that deals with the application of information technology from a management perspective, equally useful to CEOs and CIOs and to anyone bent on using technology as a growth and profitability lever. If only one or two ideas result in furthering this goal for the reader, then this exercise will have been well spent.

Finally, my thanks to the friends and colleagues who contributed to the ideas and strategies used in this book; to the careful typing of the manuscript by my secretary, Joyce FitzGerald-Galloway, to the able guidance and editing of John Mahaney and the staff at John Wiley & Sons, and to my wife Suzanne whose patience tolerated the weekend retreats and early morning writing that led to this work.

W. R. SYNNOTT

Wellesley Hills, Massachusetts
March 1987

CONTENTS

THE INFORMATION
WEAPON

PART I

INFORMATION RESOURCE MANAGEMENT

1

THE INFORMATION WEAPON

> The information society is an economic reality,
> not an intellectual abstraction.
> JOHN NAISBITT (1)

The information age is upon us. The first "megatrend" reported in Naisbitt's book of the same name was, in fact, the change from an industrial to an information society. According to Index Systems, a management consulting firm: "The transition from the industrial era to the information era is evident by looking at the shifting numbers of workers from the farm (now 3% of the workforce), to the factory (now 12%), to the office (now 65%)"(2).

There is no question that we are no longer an industrial society; we are an information society, and one that is growing rapidly. In 1985 the information industry made up 3.3% of the Gross National Product (about as much as the auto industry). It has been predicted that in 1995 the information industry will constitute 6% of the Gross National Product, making it the largest industry in the world. Moreover, data processing and communications, a $300 billion industry today, is expected to reach $1 trillion by the early 1990s.

What does all this mean to business? The information society is having a profound impact on business and competition. The need for information has created an unparalleled growth in the demand for information systems and technology to support business and customer services. A great wave of information technology and electronic delivery of services is engulfing the business world and bringing new meaning to *winning customers and markets with technology.* Consider these developments:

- *Customer Terminals.* In the 1970s, employees were put online; in the 1980s, customers are going online. The trend to put terminals in customer spaces is accelerating. When American Hospital Supply (3) first put terminals into their customers' spaces (in this case, hospitals) in 1978, it was basically a ploy aimed at moving their back-shop opera-

3

tions to the customer; in other words, it was a cost-cutting strategy. However, by doing their own order entry, the hospitals soon found they could lower expensive inventory costs. The more they used the system, the greater the savings and likelihood of expanded use. As a result American Hospital Supply's sales soared as their competition became "locked out" of the hospital supply business. What started as a cost-cutting measure became a powerful new *information weapon*, so powerful, in fact, that American Hospital Supply was sued by their competition for unfair advantage. Competitive advantage is obvious when the competition sues.

Since then hundreds of companies have turned to the competitive strategy of putting terminals in customer spaces. Banks have terminals on midtown and business district street corners; retailers put terminals in stores as sales aids; the airlines even put terminals in their competitors' locations. *Customer terminals* have become one of the most potent competitive strategies of the information age.

• *Electronic Data Interchange.* In 1984 General Motors instructed their suppliers to install terminals to conduct their business with GM electronically or face the prospect of losing future business (4). All four major U. S. automakers (GM, Ford, American Motors, and Chrysler) have since notified suppliers of their intention to fully implement an electronic data interchange (EDI) network. The suppliers have overwhelmingly gone along. The EDI network today is putting intercompany transactions online, linking suppliers, manufacturers, distributors, and retailers in an "electronic chain" that eliminates paper processing and speeds up business transactions. More and more, players in the chain do not have a choice. They either go online or lose the business to their competitors who do so.

• *Electronic Funds Transfer.* The Sears *Discover* card, introduced in 1985, has already become one of the largest money-card systems in this country. Not only is it accepted on bank automated teller machine (ATM) networks throughout the country, but major national companies such as American Airlines, Holiday Inns, Budget Rent-A-Car, and Hospital Corporation of America extend discounts of 20–50% to Discover cardholders (5).

Businesses (e.g., Sears, American Express, and Merrill Lynch) have discovered that the movement of money electronically can be done by anyone, not just banks. As a result, a whole new financial services industry has emerged, which is almost entirely focused on the use of "electronic" money. Debit and credit cards can be used to obtain cash and conduct financial transactions at automated teller machines and point-of-sale (POS) terminals everywhere. And almost all of the major U. S. banks are competing fiercely today to sell their cash management services to corporate customers via personal computers (PCs) located in the corporate Treasurer's offices. Dozens of pilot tests of "home banking" (banking from home over a PC) are under way all around the country. The bulk of all money movement in the United States today is not by cash or check, but by electronic transfer, and every indication is that this trend will continue in the rapidly growing service economy.

What these developments have in common is *electronic delivery*. As the use of communications networks and terminals grows and computers become ubiquitous, it will be the electronic delivery systems that serve the information age, provide competitive force, and create major changes in the way business is conducted, managers manage, and products and services are sold. In a recent issue of the *Harvard Business School Bulletin*, Nancy O. Perry summed it up well:

> . . . IS [Information Systems] now touches every business activity of a company offering a product or service—from conceptualization, design, and production, to marketing, distribution and support. As a result: IS has become a critical component of corporate strategy planning and competitive advantage. (6)

Information systems, or information technology (IT), as it is referred to in this book, is truly a competitive force—an *information weapon*—that is opening up new ways of doing things better, faster, and cheaper. The firms that are able to grasp and exploit these new information technologies will excel and lead the competition as we move into the 1990s.

THE SERVICE INDUSTRIES

As noted, fully two-thirds of the U. S. population is now engaged in information services of one kind or another. The information sector is huge. It includes government, education, health and medicine, financial services (banking, insurance, brokerage), transportation, entertainment, travel and leisure, information, management, professionals (doctors, lawyers, accountants, engineers), and so on. Because IT tends to be applied heavily to the services sector (government and the financial services industry are the largest users of information technology), this book focuses primarily on the service industries. Also, because this author's background and experiences are in banking, the reader may find a liberal number of allusions to banking examples. This is not to suggest that manufacturing and other industries cannot benefit from the information weapon; on the contrary, we are seeing increasing growth in computer-integrated manufacturing (CIM), the imbedding of information services within manufacturers' products, and the increasing use of communications networks by multinational corporations to promote global markets. But the phenomenal growth in the services sector is driving the increased need for information services. *Nation's Business* recently reported the following statistics on growth:

- Services now account for nearly 70 percent of the gross national product.

- Of 25 million jobs created since 1970, 22 million, or 88 percent, were in the services sector.

- Nine out of 10 jobs created between now and 1995 are expected to be in services.

- The service sector is given principal credit for pulling the nation out of the 1982–83 recession, the worst economic downturn since the 1930s depression. (7)

The service industries' rapid growth has resulted in a tremendous need to move information, transactions, and money in an accurate and expeditious manner, thus fanning the growth of electronic delivery and information systems. As we seek new ways to develop and implement these information weapons, we need to focus on the transformation that occurred as we moved from an industrial to an information society.

Dr. Stanley Davis of Stanley M. Davis Associates (Brookline, Massachusetts) provides a useful model for thinking about product/services planning in a service-oriented information society (8). Dr. Davis suggests that in an industrial economy we strive to produce standardized goods for mass markets (e.g., Ford's mass-produced black passenger automobile of the 1930s), whereas in a service economy, the focus shifts to the development of customized services for mass markets (e.g., PC spreadsheet programs that can be tailored to a wide variety of users). Davis's model compares the differences in these two economies in terms of four dimensions: scale, time, mass, and space (see Figure 1.1). An industrial economy typically looks for economy-of-scale (EOS), involves long lead times, deals in tangible goods, and is bounded (by the factory, the home, or the office). A service economy seeks flexible scale (serving both large and small simultaneously, i.e., EOS at the individual level) and fast turnaround time, deals in intangible services, and is unbounded (electronic delivery, for example, has no bounded space).

From a technological perspective, the Computer Era of the past was characterized by centralized processing (scale), traditional project life cycles were long (time), the focus was on hardware (mass), and physical delivery was bounded [e.g., stores (space)]. The Information Era of the future will see processing decentralized (scale), systems development automated to effect fast turnaround (time), a focus on less tangible software

	Industrial Economy	Service Economy
Scale	EOS	Flexible
Time	Lagtime	Realtime
Mass	Tangible	Intangible
Space	Bounded	Unbounded

Figure 1.1. The Davis model. Adapted from Stanley M. Davis, 2001: **Management,** *forthcoming, 1986 Stanley M. Davis Associates, Boston, Massachusetts.*

and information "assets" (mass), and unbounded services [e.g., electronic delivery (space)]. A case in point is the trend toward "electronic" banking today. Electronic banking aims to provide customized services through self-service banking, for a mass market that is serviced individually and distributed globally through distance-insensitive electronics. It serves consumers and corporations alike (scale), online service is instantaneous (time), it deals in intangible services (mass), and it delivers the bank to the consumer (space).

Davis's model thus provides a useful way to think about forging new information products and services that fit an information economy.

To business, the rapid gains in technology offer opportunities for innovating new technology-driven services; lowering production costs, thereby leading to lower prices; and utilizing new electronic delivery systems that provide a competitive edge. The explosion in end-user computing is providing management with information access and use never before possible. There is belated recognition that global communications networks offer opportunities to break into new worldwide markets. The enormous power of technology as a strategic weapon is just beginning to dawn on most senior managers. Information technology (IT) is still a baffling phenomenon for those who are being overtaken by the tidal wave of technological change. Many have tried to avoid these changes, because their experience is rooted in a different time, an age of intuitive-based management rather than the research-based management style of the information age. But technology is here, like it or not, and businesses will be information-driven in the future, giving rise to major cultural, political, and structural changes in the organization.

THE INFORMATION ERA

Information managers are also feeling the impact of the transformation to the information society. Consider these trends:

- Data processing (DP) is rapidly changing from centralized data-center management to decentralized computing with the trend toward multiple data centers, business-unit data processing, and distributed minicomputers and microcomputers spreading across the organization.
- Traditional systems development life cycles are being made obsolete by the new fourth (and fifth) generation languages and tools which speed up development and information access and allow users to "do-it-themselves."
- The need to link distributed information resources is making communications and data management the chief challenge of information managers, rather than the management of computers and systems as in the past.
- The old-style DP manager is being replaced by a new breed of senior information executive, the Chief Information Officer (CIO), who understands both business and technology and, operating at an executive policy level, can effectively integrate the two for greater business growth and profitability.

The metamorphosis from the Computer Era of the 1960s and 1970s to the Information Era of the 1980s and 1990s, as shown in Figure 1.2, represents profound and permanent changes in the way technology serves business, in the business manager's involvement with IT, and in the role of the information manager within the business.

In the Computer Era, technology served the business as a back-office productivity tool by automating clerical processes and saving jobs, and performing record-keeping and accounting chores faster and more accurately; in other words, it generally attacked the cost side of the business. In the Information Era, technology will continue to do that but, in addition, will be used more creatively and innovatively to invent new information services and products designed to attack the *revenue* side of the house.

In the Computer Era, the business manager's information needs were served through batch processing. Transactions were processed overnight and detailed reports were printed daily and distributed to managers. Since DP managers did not know what information would be needed, they simply printed it all. Managers' needs were never served by this "information overload." In the Information Era, managers selectively access the

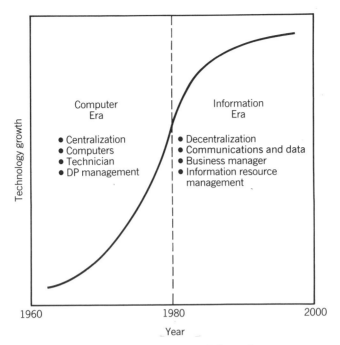

Figure 1.2. Computer era versus Information era.

information they need directly, through terminals or computers at their desks, served by Information Centers with user-friendly interfaces.

In the Computer Era, technology was typically seen as a centralized data processing function, focusing on computer hardware management, and run by what management viewed as a mystical technocrat whose business was *data processing* management. In the Information Era, technology is characterized by decentralized computing, connected through a centrally managed communications and data utility, and overseen by a business manager schooled in technology, whose business is *information* management.

If data processing is a business, information is an industry! The magnitude and scope of this transition forms a monumental challenge to business and information managers alike, not only because of the rapid pace of the changes taking place, but also because the old and the new must coexist during the transition period, a phenomenon that Richard Nolan called a "period of discontinuity."

There is an old law of wing-walking which says: "Don't let go of what you've got until you've got hold of something else." We have gotten hold of something else—Information Era technology—but we can't just let go of Computer Era technology. We must, in fact, hold on to both at once—

at least during the transition period. While we are decentralizing computing, with the spread of minicomputers and microcomputers across the organization, we must still maintain mainframe data centers, and provide interconnectivity as well. While we concentrate on interconnection through communications and data management, we must still manage computers. Internal operating systems must continue to be supported while we also build management information systems and invent new competitive systems. During the period of discontinuity, information managers must manage diffused technology resources and end-user computing, and integrate diverse technologies, all while striving to convert technology from a back-office tool to a front-office weapon. In the face of it all, information managers must deal with those who want to preserve the status quo as well as those who are impatient with slow progress and/or have unrealistic expectations of the new technology. To get through the transition from the Computer Era to the Information Era, to apply technology in new and better ways, to control what otherwise could be decentralized chaos, information managers need planning, management involvement (at all levels of the organization), and vision. Let's talk about *vision!*

THE NEW VISION

Vision is needed to see our way through the period of discontinuity and to manage information resources to best serve the needs of Information Era businesses. Vision is not just understanding trends; it's seeing what isn't yet there. It represents an image of future direction. Vision articulates a view of a future that is different and, hopefully, better than what now exists. Vision is the link between dreams and actions. It begins with a clear vision of where one is going and follows with the steps needed to move in that direction. Information managers need be on top of the changes swirling around them, while simultaneously working toward a clear technological direction. Vision is direction: a mission, not a map. Horace Greeley's dictum "Go west, young man, go west!" was a vision, a direction, not a map on how to get there. The vision must be broad, flexible, and simple enough for everyone to remember and follow. Technology is changing too fast to be specific. One must be able to adjust to find the best path. Like climbing a mountain, the closer we come to the vision, the clearer we see it. Each step clarifies the vision; we see all that there was before, and a little more. But it isn't enough to have vision. Vision must be shared or it is useless. *Management must share the vision.* Without shared vision, either nothing will change, or change will occur randomly, haphazardly, without a cohesive plan or sound management, and without garnering the potential that technology promises. What is this new vision?

- Is the vision that information must be managed as a vital resource of the firm? Information resource management (IRM) is an important concept for realizing the potential of information technology within a company, but this in itself is not the vision. Managers must ask why managing information as an asset is important.
- Is it that a new breed of information manager, a CIO, is needed to lead IRM? A new leadership might, indeed, be needed to carry out the vision, but the leader of the vision is not the vision itself.
- Is the integration of business and information systems planning the vision? The integration of business and technology is certainly an important goal but, again, managers must ask why it is important.
- Perhaps the vision is the integration of diverse technologies in the firm to form a synergistic information force? This is certainly important, even mandatory, but it is a task, not a vision.

All of these are part of a bigger vision, *the vision of using information as a competitive weapon!*

IW 1—THE NEW VISION
The exploitation of information technology as a competitive weapon.

Strategic vision should be simply put and easy to remember and reinforced constantly. "Information as a competitive weapon" is such a strategic vision. By focusing information technology on the bottom line—PROFITS—companies can reach the apex of their true potential. In this way, senior management will share the vision. Information technology never entirely made it as a back-shop productivity tool. But by focusing on information as a revenue generator rather than a cost reducer and as a competitive tool rather than just a productivity tool, information managers have the opportunity to "mainstream" systems technology into the business, thereby integrating business and technology as an important competitive strategy.

Information resource management is needed to harness the full potential of information technology for competitive advantage. And an information resource manager, a Chief Information Officer, is needed to lead IRM toward that vision. Business and information systems planning must be integrated to exploit technology for competitive advantage. Technology must be integrated to facilitate the use of information within the firm and to support new competitive information products and services.

A recent survey conducted by the Diebold Group revealed that in firms where the IRM concept is real, it is primarily because top management views information as a competitive weapon. They have the vision! Typically, their companies tend to be in service industries (like the financial services industry), are market-driven, have strong strategic planning programs, and the Information Manager is part of the top management team (9). These "information companies" invest heavily (5–6% of sales compared with 1–2% average) in IT and constantly seek new innovative uses of technology in customer markets. These companies understand that computers can be used for more than number-crunching, and that information can be used as both an offensive (competitive) and defensive (productivity) weapon.

In the past, the use of technology did not attract investors or raise stock prices. This is now changing, as technology-driven companies like American Express, Sears Roebuck, Merrill Lynch, Citicorp, and others use the "information weapon" to gain new customers, new markets, and bigger profits. Information is not just an asset or even a business. It is an *industry.*

Information Is Profit!

Promoting the vision of information as a competitive weapon requires a little "Show and Tell." For example, monthly management briefings can be used to *tell* management what is happening in the industry, how IT is being used by leading companies and/or competitors, and what the potential value of information is to the firm. These briefings with senior executives need not be long to be extremely valuable communications for users to review technology issues, trends, and forecasts, and new technology-driven competitive products and services. Whether developed in-house or with the help of outside consultants, a carefully prepared monthly briefing of 1½ hours consumes only 18 hours, less than 1%, of an executive's time annually. This is little to ask considering the size of the investment in technology (certainly more than 1%) and its potential to the firm.

We can also *show* what is happening through competitive examples. For example, when Merrill Lynch announced their Cash Management Account (CMA) product a few years ago, banks could quickly see the advantages of having an integrated technology infrastructure. Merrill Lynch used theirs to bundle together a number of financial services (deposit account, brokerage, money market fund) covered by a single combined financial statement. Many banks with diverse and unrelated systems had a difficult time following suit because they did not have the necessary underlying and supportive integrated technology infrastructure to quickly create a competing product.

New technology-driven products and services can be developed working with product managers and marketing people. For example, PC-based "prototypes" can be used to put something together quickly to test the market or respond to competitive initiatives. An information manager can develop productivity measures to show management how their investment in technology leads to being the low-cost producer. He/she can also develop valuable management information systems, for example, information on products, performance, or competitive analysis. The objective of the firm should be to build a value-added technology track record, to impact the bottom line with new technology-driven products, and to mainstream information systems out of the back office to the front office, as a competitive weapon. By doing so, managers everywhere will come to share the vision of the *information weapon.*

INFORMATION RESOURCE MANAGEMENT

> **IW 2—INFORMATION RESOURCE MANAGEMENT**
> The concept of managing information as a vital corporate asset.

In 1979 John Diebold stated that "the organizations that will excel in the 1980s will be those that manage information as a major resource."(10) In my previous book (coauthored with W. H. Gruber), *Information Resource Management: Opportunities and Strategies for the 1980s* (11), a great deal of attention was paid to the new concept of managing information as a vital asset of the firm. We talked about the changing roles for information and business managers in the management of distributed processing. We presented strategies for managing the various components of IRM, such as human resource management, hardware and software management, telecommunications, office automation, and information systems. In all, 68 strategies for IRM were presented.

Since 1981, when the book was published, the IRM concept has received a great deal of attention. Many companies have adopted the conceptual notions advanced in our book, and many others are actively working on implementing IRM programs.

Progress in IRM has been slow, however, for a variety of reasons. By itself, IRM is an abstract concept that is pervasive (corporate-wide) and requires major cultural, political, and structural changes. Here are some of the hurdles to be overcome:

- *No Vision.* Many organizations simply do not have a clear vision of the information weapon. They still see data processing as a back-shop bookkeeping operation run by white shirt-sleeved managers walking around with punch cards in their pockets. The asset value and the competitive use of information are simply not envisioned.
- *No Involvement in Strategic Planning.* Many information functions report several layers down in their hierarchy and are, consequently, too far removed to be involved, or influential in, the strategic planning process. In "vision" companies, the information exective reports di-

rectly to the top and is heavily involved in corporate policy and planning matters.

• *No Architectural Plan.* Without a plan, one has only a hope, a dream. Few organizations have actually drawn up a technology architectural plan to guide and support the technology infrastructure needed to support corporate objectives.

• *Corporate Culture Barriers.* To mainstream technology into the business requires not only vision, but also linking systems planners with marketing. Business managers must be involved in information systems, and information managers must understand business needs. Many companies still have information systems reporting to Finance, focusing on accounting systems and not customers.

• *New Data Processing Role.* Many information managers are "techies" who find the transition to the new information resource manager role, that of the CIO, difficult, if not impossible. They have no tradition in business or management and consequently feel ill at ease in the executive arena. As a result, many companies are putting managers from the business side of the house over the information resource function.

• *Resistance to Decentralization.* Some data processing professionals resist the decentralization of information resources. Business managers, as a consequence, go and do their own thing. As a result, IRM, as a coordinated function, simply does not exist.

• *The Politics of Territorialism.* The converse to the problem described above is the tendency of users to resist perceived attempts of information managers to "control" what is theirs. They will defend their territories as fiercely as a dog defends his. Political suasion and influence is needed to make IRM work, not control or mandates.

• *Inertia.* Business managers, information managers, or both may suffer from inertia, the tendency to maintain the comfortable status quo and not make waves. Information resource management requires considerable change—which many are simply not ready or able to make.

• *Difficulty.* Information resource management is a long and incremental process that requires top management support, and involves significant cultural and organizational changes. It is difficult to get initial support for the vision, difficult to change the organization, and difficlt to implement.

Information resource management is a management approach that treats the management of information as a value-added asset of the firm.

That simple definition is hard for many to embrace. Information has been around forever. It is not thought of as an asset. It is considered a free resource, like air and water. To think of managing it like one manages people, machines, or money is a foreign notion to most managers. Man-

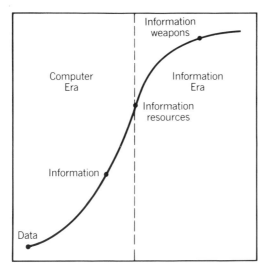

Figure 1.3. Information vision.

agers need to make the conceptual transition from data to information, to information as a resource, to information as a competitive weapon, as depicted in Figure 1.3. The Computer Era saw the production of raw data massaged into information. The Information Era first aggregated information into an information resource and is now employing that resource as an information weapon. Most business managers are just beginning to understand this Information Era concept of the value and potential of the information resource weapon.

To manage information as an asset, we need to understand that the information asset is composed of two parts: the information itself and the information resources.

Information management is the process of identifying, defining, collecting, storing, processing, protecting, and distributing information. It deals in information *content*, which is a business issue; that is, understanding the need, use, and value of information. One addresses information content with software (data bases, information systems, software languages).

Information *resource* management is the process of architecting and managing the technological infrastructure of the firm. It deals with information *conduit*, which is a technical issue. One addresses information conduit with hardware (computers, communications networks, office systems).

Of the two concepts, information is more important; without it, information resources are not needed. Nonetheless, an IRM program must necessarily embrace both information content and conduit to be effective.

In his well-known "Stages Theory of Computer Growth" (12), Richard L. Nolan described six stages of data processing growth. The first three stages—Initiation, Contagion, and Control—belonged to the Computer Era. The last three—Integration, Architecture, and Demassing—fit the Information Era.[1]

Organizations that are falling behind today are still in the Control stage. The vast majority of companies are in the Integration stage. The leaders are in the Architecture phase. And a few are Demassing, that is, decentralizing information technology. Information resource management deals with the latter three Information Era stages.

INFORMATION WEAPONS

Two powerful forces are combining today to cause companies to embrace the IRM concept: (1) information technology is being utilized strategically in more and more organizations as a way to achieve competitive advantage; and (2) information technology is being decentralized through microcomputers and communications networks, making integration increasingly difficult.

Both of these developments require the close cooperation of business and information managers. The information weapon vision cannot be achieved without the integration of business and information planning. Likewise, a coordinated technology infrastructure cannot be achieved without an integrating architecture that orchestrates business information needs and information resources into a working "system."

Tomorrow's information weapons will probably be mainly driven by business managers with help from information managers. Conversely, technology architecture will probably be driven by information managers with policy direction and business needs coming from business managers.

Part II of this book deals with the search for and development of these strategic information weapons. This entrepreneurial effort can be led by almost anyone: business managers, information managers, CIOs, strategic planners, marketers, product managers, or consultants. We are not concerned with where the leadership and direction comes from at this point, only in the strategic process itself. Therefore, the term *information weapon (IW) planner* is used broadly to refer to the person or persons carrying out these activities in the enterprise. The IW planner is an innovative manager who focuses on the best use of resources in the constant search for competitive advantage. In most cases, this involves the collaboration of the business and systems sides of the house. This suggests a strong opportunity for the CIO to play a strategic role in tomorrow's information intensive companies. Chapter 2 looks at this new emerging role and its place in the

---

[1] Nolan's original stages IV–VI were Integration, Data Administration, and Maturity. These have since been redefined as Integration, Architecture, and Demassing.

organization as an IW leader. However, before we get to that, a word about the Information Weapons presented in this book.

In my last book, *Information Resource Management,* I compiled all of the management strategies presented into a single listing which could be used by the reader as a reference source for information management solutions that could be applied to specific business problems. Because that technique was so well received by readers, I decided to use it again in this book. As each information weapon strategy is presented, *in this book* it is identified by a distinctive box:

```
IWn—Name
Explanatory sentence.
```

The first two such information weapons, "The New Vision" and "Information Resource Management," are presented in this chapter. These are the first of 63 such information weapon (IW) strategies presented throughout the book. A complete inventory of these IW strategies is compiled in Chapter 11 for the reader's convenience. By referring to this inventory of information weapons, IW planners can return again and again to review strategies that have been used by others to successfully achieve competitive advantage through technology. Information weapon planning is continuous, not a one-time occurrence. Therefore, one of the values of this book is its utility as a reference handbook of IW strategies that can be utilized in the ongoing process of strategic systems planning, which is first addressed in Chapter 3. As noted, Chapter 2 focuses on the new role of the CIO as a key member of the senior executive team and IW planner. The emergence of this role as the firm's chief information architect has only come about in the last 5 years. Information managers, CIOs, and would-be CIOs will be interested in examining this role further. Business managers and others outside the information management field may want to skip to Chapter 3 and dig right in to the challenge of integrating business and systems planning to achieve competitive advantage.

Notes

1. John Naisbitt, *Megatrends,* Warner Books, New York, 1982.
2. "The Strategic Role of Information Technology in the Information Era," *Indications,* a publication of Index Systems, Inc., Summer, 1984.
3. *Fortune,* 7/26/82 pp. 56–61.
4. E. W. McFarlan, HBS Bulletin, ———.
5. *American Banker,* 1/8/86, p. 1.

6. Nancy O. Perry, "Managing the IS Power," *HBS Bulletin*, Feb. 1986, p. 38.

7. *Nation's Business*, 4/86, p. 27.

8. Dr. Stanley Davis, *2001: Management*, 1986 (in preparation).

9. "The Chief Information Officer Concept," Report of preliminary research, The Diebold Group, Dec. 1984.

10. John Diebold, Foreward to the Diebold Group Special Report, "IRM: New Directions in Management," *Infosystems*, Oct. 1979, p. 41.

11. W. R. Synnott and W. H. Gruber, *Information Resource Management*, Wiley, New York, 1981.

12. Richard L. Nolan, "Managing the Crises in Data Processing," *Harvard Business Review*, March–April, 1979, pp. 115–126.

2

THE EMERGING CHIEF
INFORMATION OFFICER

Wanted: Chief Information Officer. Prerequisite: General
management experience and ability to implement the
latest in technologies. Technicians need not apply.(1)

> IW 3—CIO
> The emerging role of the top computer executive as an
> engine of technological change.

The CIO, as the information resource manager, has the opportunity to
preside over the firm's information weapon arsenal. In this chapter, we
examine this emerging role on the information management scene.

There have been many definitions of the CIO. Simply put, *a CIO is
the highest ranking executive with primary responsibility for information management.*

The CIO is responsible for the planning and architecture of the firm's
information resources, for promoting information technology throughout
the firm, and for looking after the corporation's investment in technology.
The CIO manages information resources as a vital corporate asset.

This is not a new name for the same old thing. An information manager
does not become a CIO simply by calling himself a CIO. He or she must
have the new responsibilities that go with Information Era management.
It is senior management that provides the form and substance (and authority) of the new position, not the information manager.

THE CIO TREND

In 1981 when we introduced the CIO concept in our book, *Information Resource Management,* we said:

> The CIO role does not yet exist except in the minds of imaginative leaders
> today. It remains to be created by information managers committed to har-
> vesting the management of information as a resource in the years ahead.(2)

Since then, the CIO concept has taken hold and has spread throughout the country in both large and small firms. Articles on the subject appear almost every day in trade papers and magazines, Here are some excerpts:

> [The CIO is] a new designation to match a fast-changing era. Information executives are beginning to take their places among the most senior executives of major corporations. This rise coincides with the recognition of information as a powerful competitive force. (3)

> At some companies, a new position is emerging—the "chief information officer"—with the responsibility of seeing that the company is making effective, innovative use of information technology . . . The CIO reports to top management, will be the prime source of information policy, is a person who "knows the business," and who is not viewed as primarily a technical person. (4)

> Clearly, the business rationale exists to establish the Chief Information Officer. Not to do so seems tantamount to allowing departments of the same organization to operate with differing accounting or personnel practices . . . lack of coordination will produce incompatibility and inaccuracy . . . an information "Tower of Babel." (5)

> [The CIO] is much like any member of the top management team. And to be effective he must be a working member of that team. He is a professional, who like the chief financial officer or vice president of research and development, should be a candidate for the position of managing director or chief executive officer. (6)

According to John Diebold and Associates, roughly one-third of the nation's major corporations now have a CIO—in function if not in title (7). Trade conferences are devoted to the CIO movement. For example, the 1985 national conference of the Associated Information Managers in New York centered around the theme: "AIMing at CIO." The Center for Information Systems Research (CISR) at MIT has explored the concept in its seminars and publications. And in 1984 the Society for Information Management commissioned a research project to investigate this changing role for information managers.

The CIO concept has stirred much interest and enthusiasm in the information community itself. Why? Because information managers perceive the position as an opportunity, a further step up their career ladder, a step that goes beyond the top job in the information function today. Those who reach the top data processing or information systems position today often reach the end of the road. Unless they move into the business as a manager of another function, or leave the company for a similar (but bigger) job elsewhere, they are often pretty much at a dead end. They occupy a comfortable position, are generally well paid and respected, but they are confined (pigeon-holed?) to their technical specialty.

The CIO role offers information managers a new opportunity to contribute at a higher level of the organization, to be part of the mainstream of the business, to be a member of the top management team, and to do so without giving up their specialized skills in technology. To the contrary, they become top technical advisers to management and promote, plan, and manage technology from a corporate-wide perspective. Small wonder that information managers are excited about the prospect.

It is not just the information community that has picked up the CIO notion, however. The business community has embraced it as well, as evidenced by the growing number of companies naming CIOs to preside over the management of information resources in the firm.

Where there has been resistance it is usually because business managers misunderstand the role. They sometimes fear another level of management is being imposed. Not so! It is a broadening and an expansion of an existing management function. Or they feel a technology "czar" is being created that threatens to take over information resources under their control. Not so! The CIO does not control resources in users' hands. The CIO architects the functional use of information resources. The architect that designs a house doesn't also own it!

The Diebold Group, in a survey of 130 major corporations, found that whereas in 1979 only 5% of the companies surveyed had what we now call a CIO reporting to the top level of the company, by 1984 about a third had CIOs reporting to the top. In a separate survey of 15 CIOs in top *Fortune* companies, Diebold offered these findings (8):

1. There is a growing awareness of information as a critical resource.
2. IRM is often initiated by top management.
3. The CIO has to be a strong executive, with both business and technical skills.
4. Data must be accessible as information in the organization.
5. The CIO must be perceived as having a corporate viewpoint.
6. The CIO should be separated from daily responsibilities.
7. The CIO must have a strong track record.
8. A CIO is needed to consolidate decentralized resources.
9. The CIO must be part of the top management team.
10. The CIO is the custodian of information, not the owner.
11. Information technology can impact both expense and revenue.
12. Information systems must be integrated with business strategic planning.

The bottom line is that the need for a CIO is rapidly gaining acceptance. As information resources continue to decentralize, the CIO trend will continue to accelerate. This is because CIOs are needed most in decentralized companies where coordination needs are greatest. Often, these companies are prime targets for "information weapon" opportunities because decentralized companies are often market-driven growth companies with strong strategic planning programs.

The CIO is of course a functional, not an actual, title, much as a CFO (Chief Financial Officer) is a functional title for the top financial person in the firm, whose actual title may be Vice President of Finance or Vice President and Treasurer. Similarly, the CIO's actual title may be Director of IRM, Vice President of Corporate Systems, or Senior Vice President of Information Systems. Regardless of the actual title, if the role and responsibilities as assigned by senior management fit the CIO definition, the person is performing as a CIO. (See Figure 2.1 for one functional job description of a CIO.) The CIO concept has piqued widespread interest because business and information managers alike see the change from the Computer Era to the Information Era, understand that technology is becoming vital and pervasive to business, and recognize that a new brand of leadership is needed to manage increasingly decentralized and complex information resources. The skills needed to manage the centralized data processing shop of the past are very different skills from those necessary to manage distributed information resources. Technical skills have to be supplemented with solid business, organizational, political, managerial, and interpersonal skills to integrate business and technology effectively.

The CIO will have to be a technology "generalist," not a specialist, who can effectively bridge the gap between top management and technicians while applying technology to the solution of business problems and the promotion of competitive advantage. Information technology cannot be just left to happen. Chaos would result. Technology is moving too fast and too furiously.

Computers continue to experience quantum jumps in power and capacity, growing at a rate of 40% or more per year. Communications (both voice and data) is, likewise, growing rapidly with alternative options (microwave, fiber-optics, and satellites) obliterating geographic boundaries and opening up new competitive opportunities and markets. Previously separate technologies are converging upon one another (mainframe computers, office systems, and personal computers).

Information resources are mushrooming all over the firm as minicomputers and microcomputers spread decentralized computing. The need to integrate hardware and software from different vendors is forcing industry standards to enable information flow between incompatible systems. The sophistication, complexity, and rapid growth of the technology revolution in the Information Era are mandates strong leadership to plan the implementation and integration of distributed information resources. This, together with the growing awareness on the part of senior managers of the potential for using information technology as a competitive force, is validating the concept of information resource management and the establishment of the CIO position to manage these resources in more and more companies.

Mission

As a Senior Staff Officer, spearhead corporate-wide maximization of the company's investment in information systems and technology, both internally and for long-term competitive advantage.

Responsibilities

o With reporting duties to the Office of the Chairman, establish and maintain the direction of the corporate information architecture at continuing high levels of efficiency consistent with vigorous standards of quality to be formulated by him/her.
o Optimize use of advanced information technologies throughout the corporation and issue appropriate overall policies for compatibility, control, integrity (security and backup) and functionality, while respecting the decentralized environment of its component businesses.
o Shape awareness and vision among senior corporate and business unit managers concerning the gathering, processing, and delivery of information as vital tools toward improved productivity, superior management decisions and achieving competitive gains.
o Participate in all decisions involving significant resource allocations for new and enhanced information systems and technologies as well as for related management and professional staff.
o Help assure a sufficient supply of professional quality human talent to carry on these and follow on responsibilities in case he/she is unable to do so.

Personal Characteristics

  Required

o Strong experience (minimum 10 years) and proven success in all areas of information resource management (data processing, systems, data management and telecommunications).
o Continuing drive to remain abreast of evolving information technologies and applications, management processes, and technical staff development.
o Good record of leadership and communication abilities demonstrated in business environment of comparable size, complexity and diversification, with emphasis on progressive use of state-of-the-art technology for enhanced efficiency and new business support.
o Flexibility in choosing approaches to complex problems, while aiming at finding effective solutions quickly.
o Established links with professional contacts and leading vendors of hardware/software.

Figure 2.1. Sample Job description of a chief information officer.

There is simply no comparison between the DP manager of the Computer Era and the CIO of the Information Era. Let's take a closer look at this new position in the firm.

THE CIO ROLE

The new breed of information managers, the CIOs, are businessmen first, managers second, and technologists third—in that order.

The Businessman

As businessmen, they wear business suits. They are articulate, good communicators, educated, and knowledgable about the business enterprise they represent. The people they deal with on a day-to-day basis are business managers, strategic planners, marketing people, and customers. They spend a great deal of their time learning the business and its information needs. The business skills and areas of knowledge that they must possess in this dimension of their role include the following:

- Strategic planning.
- Production management.
- Marketing and market Research.
- Financial planning and management.
- Corporate strategy formulation.
- Product knowledge.
- Government relations.
- Business ethics.
- Competitive analysis.
- Organizational development.
- Customer relations.
- Communications skills.

The CIO's personal libraries include books like *Competitive Strategy, In Search of Excellence*, and *Megatrends* alongside the information technology books. They read the *Wall Street Journal*, the *Harvard Business Review, Fortune*, and *Business Week*, as well as the technical trade magazines. There is an old saying: "If you act like a duck, talk like a duck, and walk like a duck, then you're a duck." CIOs understand that if they act, talk, and walk like businessmen, then they are businessmen. More importantly, they will be perceived by management as businessmen, a necessary prerequisite for membership on the executive team.

The Manager

As general managers, CIOs, first of all, run a business within a business. They manage people, budgets, and projects just as other general managers do. A large corporation can have a CIO overseeing 1000 people and a $100 million budget. Any person who can manage that successfully is certainly a *manager.* The general management tasks performed by a CIO include:

- Financial planning and budgeting.
- Human resource management.

- Project management.
- Technology planning and management.
- Communications.
- Decision analysis.
- Control systems.

All the typical management skills—planning, organizing, staffing, directing, and controlling—are practiced every day as part of their job. But the able CIOs see to it that these management skills are not buried behind technical "cloaks." Technical cloaks are dropped in favor of business suits. Technical jargon is dropped in favor of business English. Management must perceive a manager, not a technician.

The Technologist

Third, and finally, CIOs are technologists, staff professionals skilled in managing information technology. They must understand diverse technologies and how they interact with one another. They need to be on top of technological trends so that they can translate their potential and likely impact on the enterprise. They must surround themselves with the necessary technical experts to manage sophisticated technologies. However, it is most important that they do not try to keep themselves at an in-depth level of technical expertise. They are technology "generalists." They bridge the gap between management and technology specialists. Those who keep their hands too close to the technical nitty-gritty lose their ability to balance the business and managerial aspects of their job. They are too buried in technology. Here are some of the technology "generalist" areas covered by CIOs:

- Data center management (e.g., capacity planning, hardware acquisition, security, contingency planning).
- End-user computing planning and support.
- Systems planning and management.
- Telecommunications planning and management.
- Data resource planning and management.

Notice the word "planning" in all of these categories. If there is one word that characterizes what CIOs do it is PLANNING.

The CIO's priorities, then, are: (1) concentrate on the business; (2) be a general manager; and (3) keep up with technology at the planning and managerial (not the technical) level.

The CIOs who succeed in balancing the three roles—businessman, manager, technologist—will be seen by senior management as general managers whose specialty happens to be information technology, much as other managers are perceived to be specialists in finance, marketing, engineering, and sales. They will be like any other member of the top management team. To be effective they must, in fact, be a member of that team, preferably reporting to the top of the organization.

In the past, information managers most often reported to the CFO because computers were first applied to the accounting functions of the business. As more and more internal operations were automated, many began to report to Operations Vice Presidents. Today, with computers being applied to operations, management support, and competitive systems that effect virtually every area of the business, more and more CIOs are reporting directly to the top. In many cases, they delegate the daily running of the data processing function to others in order to concentrate on their primary role as a planner.

INTEGRATION PLANNING

The CIOs have a responsibility to manage information resources into an *integrated* information system. Therefore, their role is not just that of a planner, but more specifically, an "integration planner." This involves two primary responsibilities: *strategic* systems planning and *architectural* planning.

- *Strategic* systems planning involves working with strategic planners and business managers to create an integrated business and systems plan to support internal operations and external products.
- *Architectural* planning involves integrating the company's various information technology resources into a supportive technology infrastructure. Narrow DP planning shifts to corporate-wide technology architecture planning.

Strategic systems planning's contribution to the firm is essentially adding VALUE through the optimization of information technology. It is business-oriented and therefore requires that the CIO be involved with business issues to plan value-added technology. Architectural planning's contribution to the firm is to bring STRUCTURE to the enterprise; that is, to oversee the technology infrastructure needed to flow and manage information throughout the firm. Although it is technology-oriented, business input and direction is needed by the CIO for structure to be accomplished successfully.

To be successful, the CIO must bring both VALUE and STRUCTURE to the organization. This is not easy. In companies where top management shares the vision of the information weapon it will be easier, because the CIO will be involved in strategic planning (the VALUE goal) and top management will provide direction to architectural planning (the STRUCTURE goal). This blending of business and technology is key to achieving IRM's vision of "winning customers and markets with technology."

Many other roles are carried out in the performance of the CIO's VALUE and STRUCTURE responsibilities. These include being a strategic planner, an architect, a proactive change agent, a business manager, a politician, an integrator, an information controller, a staff professional, and a futurist. The key to success is the CIO's ability to manage and form information resources into a cohesive whole, while not necessarily having direct control over the resources themselves. As computers, systems, and systems professionals become more and more decentralized in the future, information resources will be in the hands of the users. The CIOs must then become *facilitators* of information services rather than the *owners* of the information resources. They will have responsibility over the information *function*, not necessarily the resources. Therefore, CIOs must carry out their mission through persuasion and influence, not control and mandate.

Think of CIO as an acronym for

<u>C</u>oordinator
<u>I</u>ntegrator
<u>O</u>rchestrator

and you have the essence of the facilitator role performed by a CIO. Let's examine this facilitator role:

- *Coordinator.* As systems and computers spread across the organization, the coordination of different systems, equipment, and information needs between applications and between people must be carefully thought out and planned. The CIO must work with the "owners" of information and information resources to bring about the necessary interfaces to pull together information and help systems "talk" to one another. The CIO is a corporate facilitator, a coordinator of decentralized technologies.

- *Integrator.* Whereas the coordinator role concentrates on organizing the information resource functions of the organization, the integrator role focuses on the integration of planning, people, and technologies. Planning integration involves bringing business and systems planning together as a single effort, not systems responding to the business plan. People integration means bringing together top, user, and systems management to share the vision of the "information weapon," and working together to apply technology to business and competitive goals. Technology integration requires merging the "islands" of technology into an infrastructure that supports the organization's information and information services needs.

- *Orchestrator.* The CIO "orchestrates" the owners and users of information in harmony to deliver information where and when it is needed in the form desired. Systems need information from other systems. Management needs consolidated information. Employees and customers need to access information located in different parts of the organization. Information "discipline" is needed to insure fast access to timely and accurate information. That discipline is provided through the CIO's orchestration role. Peter Drucker said the following:

> The information-based system . . . resembles the symphony orchestra. All instruments play the same score. But each plays a different part. They play together, but they rarely play in unison. . . . What makes a first-rate conductor is the ability to make even the most junior instruments at the last desk way back play as if the performance of the whole depended on how each one of those instruments renders its small supporting part. (9)

In this sense, CIOs are like symphony conductors. They do not play themselves (do not own all the resources), but they have the "score" (the architectural plan), and they orchestrate the players (users) and their parts (systems) into a symphony. Whereas the score spells out what every player is doing and how it relates to the whole, technology architecture spells out where the information pieces are and orchestrates them into a whole.

Figure 2.2 summarizes the marked differences of the transition from the Computer Era to the Information Era. The CIOs clearly have a higher role

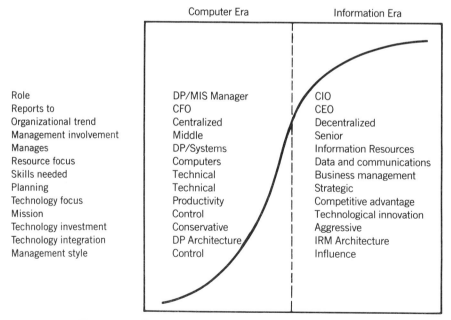

	Computer Era	Information Era
Role	DP/MIS Manager	CIO
Reports to	CFO	CEO
Organizational trend	Centralized	Decentralized
Management involvement	Middle	Senior
Manages	DP/Systems	Information Resources
Resource focus	Computers	Data and communications
Skills needed	Technical	Business management
Planning	Technical	Strategic
Technology focus	Productivity	Competitive advantage
Mission	Control	Technological innovation
Technology investment	Conservative	Aggressive
Technology integration	DP Architecture	IRM Architecture
Management style	Control	Influence

Figure 2.2. Differences between computer and information eras.

in the Information Companies of the 1980s and 1990s than did their counterparts of the 1960s and 1970s. They also have a more difficult and broader role to play as technology moves inexorably into the front office. But the new CIO is an exciting and challenging position that spells career opportunity for today's bright and aspiring information managers.

TRANSITION MANAGEMENT

Not every company is in step with the transition from the Computer Era to the Information Era. Some are still in the Computer Era, and some are in the Information Era, but the majority are in transition between the two.

The two extremes in company management today are as follows. The old management still views data processing as a back-office tool supporting internal operations and providing little management support and no competitive systems. The new management has the information vision and uses information technology strongly for productivity, management support, and competitive advantage.

There are also two extremes of information managers today. The old breed is the shirt-sleeved punch-card carrying DP manager who may run an efficient back shop supporting internal systems, but has little (if any) association with senior management. The new breed is an executive level business manager, a technology generalist who works closely with upper management to integrate business and technology.

Figure 2.3 illustrates the possible combinations of these management styles, which I describe as Punch Card Mentality, Transitional Mismatch, and the Information Company.

- *Punch Card Mentality.* This company is definitely "out of it." They will not survive in the Information Era. Sooner or later their competitor's use of technology will put them at such a disadvantage that they will either fold, shrink, be bought out, or change management.

	Punch-card mentality	Transition mismatch		Information company
CEO	Computer Era	Information Era	Computer Era	Information Era
CIO	Computer Era	Computer Era	Information Era	Information Era

Figure 2.3. Management style combinations.

- *Transitional Mismatch.* The first condition has an enlightened management but an old-style DP manager. This usually results in a new information manager. The second condition has an enlightened information manager with a "backwoods" management. The CIO will usually try in vain to push technology. When he finds he can't get out of the back office, he leaves. The company turns over a lot of information managers, not knowing why.
- *The Information Company.* This company has it all together, a strong management team, which includes a CIO, focusing on advanced uses of information technology for competitive advantage. A winner. The most successful are the information companies that are driven by top management vision.

Successful transition management requires a clear vision of where one is going and a transiton plan to get there. The CIO's main mission (vision) is to leverage information technology as a competitive weapon. This requires *strategic (value) planning* and *architectural (structure) planning;* that is, the integration of (1) business and technology through participative strategic planning and (2) the company's technology resources through technology architecture planning. Part II of this book focuses on the strategic planning goal and Part III covers technology integration through IRM architecture.

The organization of this book directly addresses the most important issues facing information managers as reported in a 1984 research study sponsored by the Society for Information Management (SIM) and the University of Minnesota (10). The survey ranked the top three issues as:

1. Improved information systems planning.
2. Facilitation and management of end-user computing.
3. Integration of data processing, office automation, and telecommunications.

Improved systems planning. Chapter 3 deals with the integration of business and systems planning. Chapter 4 follows on with planning information "weapon systems," and Chapters 5–7 bring together a number of strategies and case examples of strategic systems planning.

End-user computing. Chapter 10 focuses in part on the end-user computing revolution and discusses architectural strategies to manage and lead these decentralized information resources.

Technology integration. Integration of the diverse technologies that make up IRM architecture is the subject of Chapters 8–10.

By successfully managing these important issues, the CIO will have the opportunity to help move the company forward through technology leverage, thereby joining the ranks of the information companies that will be the competitive leaders of the 1990s.

WHO GETS THE JOB?

The role of the CIO is clear; however, the choice of who gets the job is not. One would assume that the most likely candidate would be the top data processing or information systems manager. In fact, this would seem to be an excellent career path for the head of the information function, because the CIO notion suggests an elevated rank, a top reporting relationship, broader responsibilities, and probably greater financial reward. Yet, of the CIOs interviewed in the Diebold survey reported earlier, less than half had spent their careers in data processing. Diebold observed:

> The CIO offers information systems executives a management position to which they can aspire. But it requires a new viewpoint—one that will not be familiar to many. This job is not for the DP manager who is still the classic computer jock, the machine room honcho, the software closet-type. The CIO will know technology, but he must know business. The CIO can talk to technicians, but he must talk to executives. (11)

The problem is that many information managers came up the technical route to the top and have no tradition in either business or management, two critical ingredients of the CIO role. Their ability and/or opportunity to acquire the business and managerial knowledge and skills necessary to make the transition may be limited. Many information managers will have a difficult time crossing over the "bridge" from technician to business manager. Figure 2.4 shows the transition from the old-style DP manager to the new breed of CIO using the paredo principle (the 80–20 rule). The old-style DP manager's job skills were 80% technical and 20% management. The CIO is just the opposite: he or she needs 80% business and management skills and 20% technical skills. The old job was oriented around things (machines); the new job is oriented around people. The old job was logical; the new is political. The old was precise; the new is amorphous. These polarities are such that if the DP manager's education, background, and experience has been primarily technical, the transition to a business manager CIO could be extremely difficult and, in some cases, impossible.

There are a variety of ways to gain business and managerial knowledge and experience:

- *On-the-Job Training.* The best way to learn about business management is to become a business manager. Some companies provide rotating assignments into various areas to help potential managers learn the

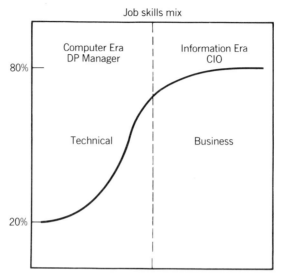

Figure 2.4. Job skills mix.

business. Systems people participating in these can gain valuable business experience. This may be too late for the top information manager, but not for more junior managers. Swap programs can sometimes be arranged; that is, a systems person goes into a business unit for a year in exchange for a business person in that unit going to systems. This is especially useful for the business and systems people who will eventually work together on business systems projects.

• *Management Development.* Many companies have formal management training programs that run anywhere from 6 to 18 months and cover short stints in a variety of areas. The problem is that these programs often do not include the systems organization. Even if they do, entry level programs such as these may not be practical for veteran systems managers.

• *MBA Programs.* Getting an MBA by attending night school is a possibility for the aspiring CIO willing to put in the time, effort, and money. Having finished the program, however, there is a high likelihood that the recipient may opt to go into another area of the business other than the information systems function. Although this is beginning to change, few MBAs go into systems work, yet this is the very training needed for the CIO role.

• *University Courses.* If an MBA is too demanding, numerous business and management courses can be taken individually in continuing education programs (night schools) at many colleges and universities. The point is: take management courses, not technical courses.

- *Graduate School Programs.* A number of schools offer special executive management programs. The Harvard Business School, for example, has a variety of such programs that run anywhere from 1 week to 3 months. For example, the Advanced Management Program which is aimed at high level managers generally over age 40, and the Program for Management Development, aimed at up and coming managers under age 40, both run 13 weeks.[1] Columbia University's Master's Degree Program for Executives is being populated by an increasing percentage of MIS managers. According to Thomas P. Ference, director of the program:

  > . . . ambitious information managers have begun to use such degree programs to leverage themselves out of MIS departments and up the career ladder. They are obviously trying to overcome what one management development expert feels is a certain bias against systems people. A background in technology has yet to take its place alongside finance, marketing, and other fields as a springboard to the top. (12)

  A list of some of the current executive management programs is shown in Figure 2.5.
- *Company Executive Programs.* Some companies, such as GE, run their own in-house executive programs. The GE program is a partnership with Purdue's Graduate School of Management. All candidates are information managers within GE. Students spend six 2-week sessions on campus, studying subject matter that is similar to that found in regular MBA programs. (13)
- *Industry Programs.* Some industries, such as banking, run executive courses for managers to broaden their understanding of the business itself. The Stonier Graduate School of Banking at Rutgers University, for example, is a 6-week program run over 3 summers, supplemented by assignments between each summer session. Students have the option of preparing a thesis on any banking subject or substituting additional case problems in their final year. The subjects taught are all banking, not general management (e.g., lending, credit analysis, financial analysis, investment management, trusts, and estate planning).
- *Conferences.* Information managers can (and should) attend periodic management conferences such as those held by the American Management Association or the Conference Board. Even more specialized

---

[1] In 1972, the author attended the 13-week Advanced Management Program at the Harvard Business School. The subjects covered (largely through the case study method) were as follows: strategic planning, organizational development, finance (budgeting, control, and external financing), economics (business, government, international), marketing (sales, competitive analysis), human resources (organizational behavior, management succession, human resource management), and management control systems (including information systems).

School	Program Name	Length (wk)	Management Audience	Approximate Cost ($)
Harvard	Advanced Management Program (AMP)	13	Upper	22,500
Harvard	Program for Management Development (PMD)	13	Middle	22,500
Stanford	Stanford Executive Program	8	Senior	16,000
University of Michigan	The Executive Program	8	Upper middle	7,500
Columbia	Managing the Enterprise	4	Upper middle	9,500
Dartmouth	Tuck Executive Program	4	Upper middle	9,000
Northwestern	Institute for Management	4	Upper middle	7,000
Penn State	Executive Management Program	4	Upper middle	6,900
University of Illinois	Executive Development Program	4	Middle	6,800

Figure 2.5. Executive management programs.

conferences such as those sponsored by the Financial Executives Institute of the American Marketing Association can be excellent learning experiences. Most information managers keep abreast of their field through attendance at one or more information industry conferences each year, but seldom do they attend conferences outside their field, even though this is where they need the most help to better understand business. (I often ask how many of my technology seminar attendees have ever taken a sales course. The absence of raised hands says it all.)

- *Self-Education.* Self-education is a process of learning from other people's experience. This can take the form of on-the-job mentors, attendance at seminars, or reading. Reading is, of course, a form of learning from others.

Timeplace, Inc. (Waltham, Massachusetts) has a service called "Edvent," which is a time-shared data base of educational offerings useful to managers seeking to broaden their business skills. Edvent provides a comprehensive listing of seminars, conferences, workshops, and continuing education programs. It contains such information as the program title, description, date, length, location, cost, educational credits, instructors, and sponsors.

Today's Information Manager basically has three options for advancement, which might be categorized as "Up, over, or out."

1. Move up. If the CIO position is at the same level as other senior corporate positions reporting to the top, he or she has an opportunity to work up to that position (expanded role). Alternatively, a number of information managers have moved up to other corporate positions in the firm (new role). Examples include CFO (Paul Daverio, SVP, Owens Corning Fiberglass), head of Consumer Operations (Joseph Ryan, Vice Chairman, Chase Manhattan Bank), head of Strategic Planning (Paul Strassmann, Vice President, Xerox Corp.).

2. Move over. Sometimes lateral moves can be made instead of upward moves. Many information professionals make this career change *before* reaching the top information management position.

3. Move out. Unfortunately, more often than not, the top information manager either finds no opportunity upward in the firm (dead-ended) or finds a similar (but bigger) position elsewhere and moves out.

The data processing industry is now 30 years old. Many who entered the business 25 or 30 years ago are now in their fifties. Those mature information managers are concerned with final career path options. Many do not want to change jobs or move out of the information management business. The CIO role and the opportunity to manage information resources for competitive advantage offers these top information managers a chance to contribute at the senior level of the organization, as part of the executive management team.

If the CIO position does not go to the top information officer, who then gets the job? The answer is whoever can best integrate business and technology in the firm. This could be a variety of people:

- *The CFO.* The chief financial officer is often viewed as an information officer, at least for financial information. However, the information resource extends to vast amounts of internal operating, textual, competitive, and other information which does not generally fall within the CFO's domain.
- *The Strategic Planning Officer.* Corporate planners certainly deal with a lot of information about the company. Strategic, competitive, financial, and product data are their tools in trade. Marrying strategic planning and information management would certainly help to integrate the business and systems planning process.
- *Business Managers.* The Harvard Business School teaches the universality of management; that is, good managers can manage anything, be it tire manufacturing, a hospital, or an information company. Therefore, any experienced (universal) business manager could, theoretically, be the CIO. Companies that have named business managers to head the information management function include: (1) FMC Corp., a chemicals and construction equipment conglomeration based in Chicago, which named a former line manager and business planner to the post; (2) IDS Financial Services (an American Express subsidiary), which picked a specialist in financial planning to head systems, (3) and Southern Companies, a utility based in Atlanta, which promoted a manager to the slot who had previously held human resource and line management jobs (14). The disadvantage, however, is that business people usually do not have the technical background and experience needed to manage technology. Just as the information manager needs to acquire business knowledge, so the business manager must acquire a knowledge of technology to perform the CIO role. One without the other weakens the job. Is it easier for an information manager to learn the business, or a business manager to learn the technology? It depends on the business and how it uses technology, of course, but generally speaking, the most important thing is to select someone who has *management* capabilities, the "universal" manager type, who might be found on either side, technology or business. Either way, one without the other is going to need a lot of support.

The ideal candidate, therefore, is a person with a background in both business and technology. How does one acquire such a background? Generally it is acquired serially; that is, a person starts out as a technical manager and later moves into the business, or starts as a business manager and ultimately moves into the information management function. After several years experience in both, the individual has the requisite background for the CIO[2] role. There are not a lot of people who fit this mold because it requires many years of exposure to both business and technology. However, more and more companies are beginning to include the information systems function in the career path of business executives and/or are moving information managers into line business operations. Over 25 years ago, computers became a part of the business world. As a result, we are now seeing more people with both solid business and technical experience.

Why Companies Need a CIO

The CIO role is still evolving, and its state of evolution differs from company to company. Some information companies are at the vanguard of the CIO movement. Others are still in the Computer Era. The trend, however, is real and growing because the *need* for the CIO is growing. In the 1990s, the traditional MIS manager will be obsolete and will have been replaced by the CIO, in this author's opinion. There are five reasons for this eventuality:

1. A CIO is needed to forge and carry out the vision of managing information resources as a vital corporate asset. In 10 years, when the information industry is the largest industry in the world, the information weapon will be used for increased productivity and for better management support. But more significantly, it will routinely be used for competitive advantage—a role that is only now beginning to be fully understood by business managers.

The CIO will be responsible not only for creating this IRM vision, but also for persuading other top managers in the company to share it. Without someone to play that missionary role, the potential of the firm's information resources will not be harnessed fully, and the company will lag behind the competition.

2. A CIO is needed to bring systems out of the back shop and into the competitive marketplace. Technology must be applied to gain competitive advantage, not just to run internal operations. Thus, information systems in the future must be allied not with operations or finance (as they have traditionally been), but with strategic planning and marketing. To become part of the mainstream of the business, information systems must attack the income side of the house, not just the cost side. Bringing leadership to the integration of business and systems planning is probably the most important responsibility of a CIO.

3. A CIO is needed to manage and coordinate increasingly decentralized information resources. The decentralization of computing, coupled

---

[2] As an example, I started my own career in banking as a management trainee, then moved successively through a variety of banking assignments before going into the systems and data processing end of the business. Thus I had 12 years of general banking background, followed by over 20 years of data processing and systems experience in the banking business.

with the cornucopia of advancing technology, will make planning for sound IRM the second most important responsibility of the CIO. Integrating the technologies and fitting the distributed bits and pieces into an appropriate infrastructure will be a monumental challenge.

A sound IRM program has two fundamental building blocks: (1) integrating business and systems planning into a foundational business plan, and (2) integrating technologies into a coordinated, integrated architecture that assures effective information flow and use throughout the organization.

4. A CIO is needed to manage the explosion in end-user computing and to leverage managerial productivity. The movement of data processing and systems management away from centralized departments of information professionals to end users constitutes an information "revolution." But end-user computing uses business computers and business data to facilitate business decisions. As such, it is part of the firm's architecture and must be managed and led in a way that makes sense to the organization.

By 1990 most all managers will use some sort of electronic workstation and probably half or more of a firm's data processing will be end-user computing. This is a profound force that cannot be just left to happen. A CIO can provide the imagination, skill, and leadership to manage end-user computing intelligently and to integrate it as a vital part of the firm's overall information management plan.

5. A CIO is needed as a driving "engine of change." Technological change is dramatic—its pace is increasing, as is its overall impact on every company, both internally (in terms of its potential for improving productivity and management support) and externally (competitively). To be the driving engine of technological change, the CIO must be a person who possesses a rare blend of business and technical skills, and a member of the senior management team, skilled in harnessing the full potential of information resources technology for company profit and growth.

These five reasons why companies need a CIO also serve as the CIO's own critical success factors. If these functions are performed well, the CIO will succeed as a valuable member of the top management team. The question then is not whether companies need a CIO. Clearly, they do. The question is: "Who will it be?" Will it be the traditional information systems professional, or someone from the business side of the house? If today's information managers don't become the CIOs, other business managers will. The information managers may then find themselves looking at each other saying (to paraphrase Pogo): "We have met the CIOs, and they are not us!"

The Final Challenge

In this chapter, we have been examining the emergence of the CIO in organizations as an executive-level policymaker, promoting his/her tool in trade, information technology, as a "mainstream business" of the future information company. I have suggested that applying technology to competitive advantage is the key to moving from the Computer Era's backshop mentality to the Information Era's strategic application of the *information weapon*.

The CIO's challenge is to lead the company's competitive technology push in an age when the size, complexity, sophistication, and pace of change is almost overwhelming. I am convinced that the CIOs who succeed will not only occupy a seat on the top executive team but they may even have a chance at the final challenge, the CEO position. In my last book, I suggested that historically the people who controlled information rose to the top. In the 1960s, we saw marketing managers ascend to the top. In the 1970s, financial managers had the inside track (see Figure 2.6). The 1980s has seen the emergence of the CIO as a senior executive reporting directly to the top. This evolution has coincided with the growing impact and importance of technology to the enterprise. In the 1990s, it may well be the company's most critical resource in terms of competitive potential. The CIOs who do their job well could have an excellent chance at the top. Striking evidence of this potential exists in one of the country's largest institutions. When John Reed (an MIT graduate and technologist) succeeded Walter Wriston as chairman of Citicorp in 1984, it represented a big win for technology. It was a statement to the world about how Citicorp viewed the importance of technology. Even though he has had many business roles, John Reed has been the technology driver at Citicorp throughout his career. His promotion to CEO showed that those who manage technology in a way that puts their company on the leading edge can rise to the top. Other CIOs that have risen to the top include Robert Crandall, President of AMR Corp., parent of American Airlines, the nation's second largest domestic carrier, and Donald Kelly, Chairman of Beatrice Companies, the well-known conglomerate. Both had previous backgrounds in information systems and technology.

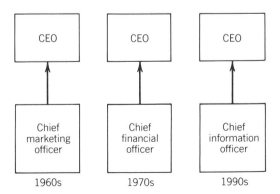

Figure 2.6. Top management succession.

The final challenge for CIOs is to make a bid for the top slot by demonstrating the kind of leadership and ability that brings information technology into the mainstream of business—as a competitive force, as an engine of growth, and as a major contributor to profit, the bottom line! The place to start is by successfully achieving the total integration of business planning with information technology planning, the subject of Chapter 3.

Notes

1. John Rymer, "Chief Information Officer," *Computer Decisions,* Sept. 1983.
2. W. R. Synnott and W. H. Gruber, *Information Resource Management,* Wiley, New York, 1981.
3. Rymer, *Computer Decisions,* Sept. 1983.
4. "The Chief Information Officer Role," *EDP Analyzer,* Nov. 1984.
5. Jack Borbely, "Chief Information Officer—What's in a Title?," *ONLINE,* May 1985.
6. Leslie D. Ball, "Information Systems Management: A Profession Whose Time Has Come," Working paper series WP85-05, Babson College, Apr. 1985.
7. *The Wall Street Journal,* 9/16/85, p. 47C.
8. "The Chief Information Officer Concept," Diebold Research Group, Dec. 1984.
9. Peter F. Drucker, "Playing in the Information-Based Orchestra," *The Wall Street Journal,* 6/4/85.
10. Gary W. Dickson et al., "Key Information Systems Management Issues," *Spectrum,* a publication of SIM, Sept.–Oct. 1984.
11. Michael Weiner and John Girvin, "Chief Info Officer Interviews," *Computerworld,* May 13, 1985, ID/7.
12. Thomas P. Ference, as quoted by Warren Kalbacker in "How GE Turns Techies into Skilled Executives," *Management Technology,* May 1985.
13. Ibid.
14. *Information Week,* 2/3/86 p. 23.
15. Ibid., 12/2/85, p. 28.

PART II

PLANNING THE INFORMATION WEAPON

INTEGRATING BUSINESS AND INFORMATION PLANNING

Ready! Fire! Aim!

There are 5 types of Planning.

A great deal has been written about the importance of integrating information systems planning with the business planning process. Yet few companies do it. It's not that planning does not take place. Some plans may be less formal than others, but planning does take place in most companies. However, in most cases, systems planning is done as a reaction to business planning, rather than proactively with it. A 1982 planning survey of 40 of the most successful U. S. companies, conducted by A. T. Kearney, Inc., a management consulting firm in Chicago, indicated that only 11% of the companies surveyed had no formal plans, 14% had a business plan only, 5% a systems plan only, and 70% had both a business and a systems plan. However, only 19% of those who had both a business and a systems plan reported that these plans were *integrated* (1). Even though these figures might be somewhat different today, if only 1 in 5 of the most successful companies are integrating their business and information planning, one can only speculate that the less successful companies must do almost no integrated planning.

THE PLANNING SPECTRUM

Before we examine the possible reasons for such a low percentage of companies doing truly integrated planning, let us review what is meant by "integrated" planning. Figure 3.1 illustrates five levels of planning that a company could adopt, ranging from no planning to totally integrated business and information planning.

No Plan

Some smaller companies still do not engage in any planning process, but few large companies are in this category today. Where planning is not a

Type of Planning	Description	Degree of Integration
1. No planning	No formal planning takes place, either business or information systems.	No plan
2. Stand-alone planning	The company may have a business plan or an information systems plan, but not both.	Business or system plan
3. Reactive planning	A business plan is prepared and the information systems function reacts to it—a traditional, passive systems role.	Business plan ▷ System plan
4. Linked planning	Business planning is "interfaced" with information systems planning. Systems resources are matched against business needs.	Business plan / System plan
5. Integrated planning	Both business and information systems planning occurs simultaneously, interactively. They are indistinguishable.	Business and system plan

Figure 3.1. The planning spectrum.

formal process, informal planning generally takes place at the top levels of the organization—few companies are "shooting from the hip," or reacting day-to-day to whatever comes up. Those who do will simply not be able to adequately respond to competitive pressures in the Information Era.

Stand-Alone Planning

These companies are generally in the "Transition Mismatch" stage described in Chapter 2. In the first instance, management is doing business planning without considering information systems, either because they do not understand or appreciate the potential value of information technology to the firm, or they have a Computer Era DP manager who is not "tuned in" to applying technology to business needs (other than back-office processing). In the second instance, information systems planning is taking place in a vacuum, with no business plan to relate to, or with little or no business input.

Reactive Planning

Most companies, as found in Kearney's survey, are in this planning category. They prepare business plans and then ask the information systems function to react to those plans in terms of what is needed technologically to support them. Sometimes this takes the form of a support capability review, or audit, of the adequacy of the supporting technology infrastructure. In any event, information systems has had no input to the business planning process—they are an after-the-fact responder.

Linked Planning

In this planning stage, the business plan is linked, or interfaced, with the information systems plan. Through interviews with business managers, information systems managers pull together business plans and objectives to identify information systems projects and management information needs required to help business units meet their objectives. Linked planning focuses on traditional project amalgamation, priority setting, and resource allocation.

Integrated Planning

When business and information planning is truly integrated, there is no distinction between the business and systems plan. They are one because they are done together. Most companies are a long way from achieving this objective. As business plans are formulated, the information manager looks for "targets of opportunity," suggesting technology support alternatives, weighing the impact of technical trends on business plans, and suggesting likely competitive technological responses. As information systems plans are devised, business managers suggest priorities, evaluate alternative investment levels of different technology options, and decide resource allocations.

An example of why iterative feedback is important in integrated planning can be illustrated by examining the trend toward electronic banking. Electronic banking, or electronic funds transfer systems (EFTS), refers to the growing use of online terminals in the public domain to conduct banking transactions, rather than through banking offices per se. Banking offices require capital backing, staff, and considerable support overhead. Terminals can provide a ubiquitous low-cost delivery system based on "self-service" banking. Industry forecasters predict that the nation's 15,000 banks will probably shrink through mergers to several thousand in the next 5–10 years, following expected banking deregulation. A dozen or so superbanks (assets over $200 billion), a dozen major regional banks (assets over $25 billion), and a few hundred "niche" banks will probably dominate the banking scene. The remainder will be small rural banks that are outside major banking centers. As this deregulation occurs, and nationwide banking spreads, electronic banking will be the "enabler," not branch banks. Bank of America will not spread across the country with branches; they will do so with terminals.

Consider a hypothetical retail banker who produces a business plan without information sytems involvement and without an understanding of the EFTS movement. Let's say our banker decides (plans) to open 10 new offices in the next 3 years. His competitors, meanwhile, are planning to install low-cost automated teller machines and POS terminals in such places as retail shopping centers, airport terminals, supermarkets, and gas stations. They will even bring banking right into their customer's homes through PC or "black-box-to-TV" hookups providing home banking services. Without integrated planning, without technology forecasts, without input from the information manager, our banker could very well go down a completely wrong path—building expensive brick and mortar branches while the competition pursues EFTS. In 3 years, our banker friend will have 10 new customer-service facilities (branches) at a cost of millions of dollars, while the competition has brought the bank to the customer with hundreds of terminals located everywhere, at a fraction of that investment. That's why integrated (interactive) planning is important in the Information Era, and is the key to competitive success.

PLANNING THE FOURTH RESOURCE

Planning is simply employing a company's resources optimally. Traditionally, business managers have thought of resources as *capital, manpower,* and *plant and equipment,* or as the accountants think of it, men, machines, and money (the three M's). However, we are now in an information society; 90% of new jobs are information-related. This requires that managers consider a fourth resource in their planning activities—*information.*

Information is a resource just like capital, manpower, and equipment. As such, information has value, (productivity, management support, and competitive value), costs money (to collect, store, process, and disseminate), has qualities (timeliness, accuracy, form), and is controllable (can be accounted for and managed). Therefore, if business managers include information as a fourth resource in their planning, the potential contribution of information technology to the organization will be built into the planning process and the integration of business and information planning will be automatic.

Failure to include information resources in the strategic planning exercise will likely result in a poor allocation of resources, with too much going into poor businesses that should be getting little or no support (the "squeaky wheels"), and too few devoted to good businesses that should be getting the lion's share of development resources. Strategic systems planning will be ineffectual because the planners will not know which businesses to focus on, or will use the wrong support strategies to support those businesses (e.g., focusing on an efficiency strategy when he/she should be going after competitive systems advantage). Finally, business managers will be unhappy because instead of seeing value-added information services supporting their business goals, they will see only high costs, slow responsiveness to needs, and poor communications between business units and the information organization.

Think of information as a fourth resource. Conduct strategic planning around capital, manpower, equipment, and *information*—and integrated planning will be assured. Time spent on integrating business *and* information planning will be worth many times over the time spent on business planning alone. The investment in technology will then provide a high payoff to the organization—as an *information weapon*.

STRATEGIC PLANNING METHODOLOGIES

> IW 4—A PLANNING METHODOLOGY
> Adopting one or more methodologies as a strategic systems planning catalyst.

A number of strategic planning methodologies have surfaced in recent years to address the problem of appropriately integrating information systems planning with business planning. Since all affect business linkage in a different way, it is useful to briefly review six of these well-known planning methodologies. These are:

1. Business Systems Planning.
2. Critical Success Factors.
3. Stages Analysis.
4. Portfolio Analysis.
5. Management by Strategies.
6. User Needs Survey.

Business Systems Planning

Business Systems Planning (BSP) is the strategic planning process developed and used extensively by IBM to assist businesses to match up their information resources with business needs (2). This technique is a combination of top-down analysis and bottom-up development strategy. The top-down analysis identifies the firm's information needs through extensive executive interviews to determine their business plans. Priorities are defined based on those interviews. Current systems support resources are assessed and additional resource needs (if any) are identified. The bottom-up process focuses on identifying information needs, developing information systems solutions, and establishing implementation goals (task scheduling) and resource needs. The steps of BSP are:

1. Determine the scope of the planning process to be undertaken.
2. Put together the BSP planning team.
3. Conduct business manager interviews to learn business plans and identify information support needs.
4. Establish priorities and select the top-priority projects to be undertaken.
5. Develop functional specifications and costs/benefits for the selected projects.
6. Turn over the selected projects to systems development for implementation.
7. Begin planning the next priority group of information systems needs.

The business linkage focus of BSP is the identification of needed information systems through heavy *user participation;* that is, information and business managers work together to develop information support needs. A new automated version of BSP is now available to speed up this process. Called Information Quality Analysis (IQA), it uses a set of simulation programs to capture, manipulate, and analyze the data used in the planning process.

Critical Success Factors

The Critical Success Factors (CSF) method was developed at the Center for Information Systems Research at MIT by Dr. John F. Rockart (3). Whereas BSP focuses on identifying needed information systems projects, CSF aims at identifying *executive* information needs, that is, information needed by a manager to manage. This technique depends on the use of short interview sessions with senior executives to focus on the 6–8 key areas of the business where things must go right. Having identified these factors, measurements are devised and reports produced to provide the executive with a control process for his/her critical success factors. The steps involved in CSF are:

1. Identify the objectives of the organization.
2. Determine the critical success factors necessary to assure those objectives.
3. Develop measurements of those factors.
4. Produce reports of those measurements.
5. Institute follow-up activities to improve on the results.

The linkage focus is *top management* information needs rather than information systems projects as in BSP.

Stages Analysis

Nolan-Norton and Co.'s planning methodology is based on Nolan's well-known "stages of growth" theory (4). Stages Analysis examines the degree of automation in a company, by organizational, or strategic, business unit (SBU), relative to automation's potential in the organizational unit. The types of systems employed—operational, control, or strategic—also indicate what automation stage they are at versus where they ought to be. Finally, a "report card" is prepared on existing systems indicating their general efficiency (design, maintainability, and operating efficiency) and effectiveness (quality, reliability, and satisfaction of information needs), which pinpoints candidates for update or replacement. The focus of Stages Analysis is *automation penetration*, or how well information technology is serving the business.

Portfolio Analysis

A number of Portfolio Analysis planning methodologies have been developed. Some of the more well-known are the Boston Consulting Group model, the GE/McKinsey model, and the model developed by Michael Porter at the Harvard Business School (5). These models are discussed further later in the chapter; for now it is sufficient to understand that the Portfolio Analysis methodology segments a company's businesses into a "portfolio" of strategic business units (SBUs), and then examines these in light of their competitive status in the marketplace. The SBUs are divided into categories according to their relative position in the market (share of market, profitability, technological state, strengths and weaknesses) and according to their future potential in the market (size of market, industry profitability, market growth, expectations, competitive advantage). Current information technology support to the portfolio of businesses is then assessed in terms of its appropriateness to the contribution and potential to the company. Where appropriate, resources are reassigned or added to correct obvious imbalances between business potential and information support strategy. Business linkage is achieved through information *resource allocation* according to business potential.

Management by Strategies

In my last book, I described the Management by Strategies (MBS) methodology as a planning process aimed at complementing Drucker's Management by Objectives (MBO) strategy by "fitting" information systems strategies to business objectives in a customized fashion (6). Although

MBO can be a very effective strategy for developing business objectives, MBS recognizes that specific information strategies to meet those business objectives are often missing. The MBS method uses a process called "environmental analysis" to recognize that corporations and business units are all different. Each has different objectives and each needs different strategies to meet those objectives, strategies that are uniquely fitted to each business. "Fit" means: (a) understanding the business environment, its objectives, and its information needs; (b) developing appropriate information plans designed to attain business objectives; and (c) developing specific strategies to ensure successful implementation. What is successful for business A may not work for business B. Strategies must be tailored to the environment, that is, management style and culture, competitive strategy, posture towards technology (conservative, aggressive), political organization, and individual personalities. These factors influence how information planning is done, what implementation strategies will work best in the environment, and how management acceptance and support is gained. The MBS technique links to business strategy through *environmental analysis*, custom-tailoring information solutions to fit the specific business environment.

User Needs Survey

Dr. Robert Alloway developed his User Needs Survey (UNS) technique while at MIT in 1981 (7). The aim of UNS is to correlate what user managers and information managers think are the most important things to do well versus what is actually being done well. This is correlated by surveying user and information managers in the organization utilizing a set of criteria developed by Alloway over a period of time as a consultant in the field. Managers are asked to rank a criteria list of 26 on a scale of 1–7. Tabulations are made of both users' and information managers' responses. These are then merged to determine the relative correlation between the two factions. The survey thus allows a company to correctly perceive what they are doing well or not well and to focus on where improvement is needed. In other words, it helps a company to do the "right things right." Linkage is achieved by bringing consensus between information users and information providers as to the correct *priorities* to focus on in information planning.

STRATEGIC PLANNING MODELS

> **IW 5—A PLANNING MODEL**
> **Planning models as frameworks for identifying information weapons.**

Earlier I noted that only a small percentage of companies have truly integrated their business and information planning processes. One reason is that information is not thought of as a resource that requires planning, because many business managers still view information technology as a back-office productivity tool rather than as a potential competitive weapon. The way in which business managers view the role of information technology in the firm is crucial to how these resources will be deployed.

Systems Relevance Model

A useful model to consider in this regard is one suggested by McFarlan and McKenney in *Corporate Information Systems Management* (8). They classify information technology support to a company as falling into four broad categories, as shown in Figure 3.2*A*:

SUPPORT. Businesses where the computer resource is important to support accounting and record-keeping activities but is not critical to the mainstream of the business.

FACTORY. Currently automated operations are vital to continuing successful business operations, but where current research and development may be light, such as in an established airlines reservation system. The accent is on efficient, low-cost operations rather than on new development.

TURNAROUND. There may be an opportunity to revitalize the business by implementing a new state-of-the-art system that could help increase business growth and profitability.

STRATEGIC. Businesses where the computer support resource is critical to success or may even be the driving engine of the business, such as electronic banking (EFTS) in the retail banking industry today.

The authors state that the degree of systems support that a business gets, and the amount of corporate support that the information function receives, is relative to how the information organization is perceived according to their model. For example, a support role will likely not result in a strong link between corporate and systems planning, whereas a strategic role would.

A number of other factors will be affected by how management views the information function role. In a support role, for example, information systems will report to a CFO. The information steering committee will be composed of middle managers, top management exposure will be nonexistent, information systems will be focused on productivity, the investment in technology will be conservative, technological innovation will be

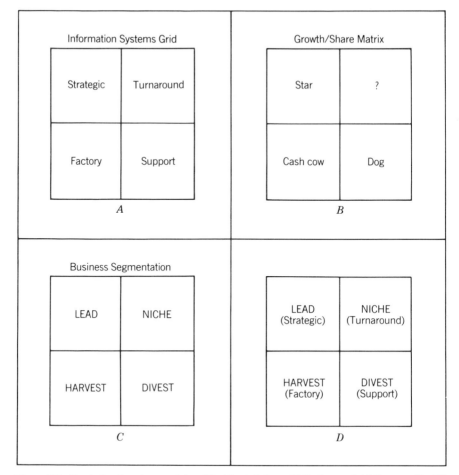

Figure 3.2. Strategic planning models: (A) Adapted from McFarlan and McKenney (8). (B) Adapted from the Boston Consulting Group. (C) Adapted from Porter (5).

low (only proven technologies will be used), and willingness to assume risks will be conservative. In a strategic role, the information systems function will report to the CEO, its IRM (steering) committee will be composed of senior level managers, top management involvement will be heavy, information technology will be focused on competitive systems, the investment in technology will be aggressive, technological innovation will be encouraged, and management will be much more willing to assume risks (through technological innovation).

The key question the CIO must ask is: "Is the role I am playing appropriate?" How does senior management view information technology in the organization—as a support function or as a strategic function? And is this the right role?

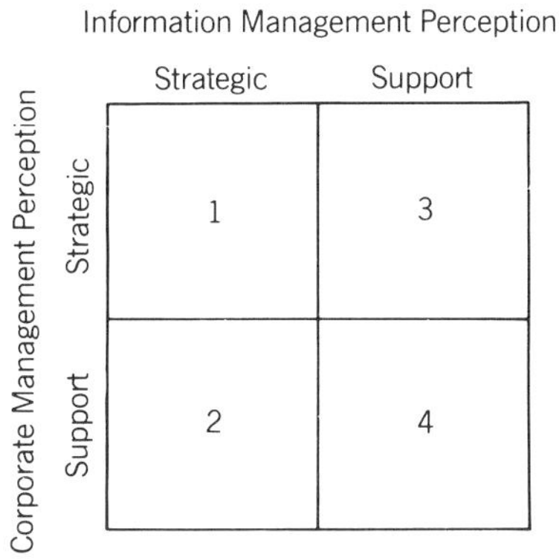

Information Management Perception

Figure 3.3. Information management perception.

If senior management views information technology as simply a support organization (doing the bookkeeping, processing the transactions, keeping the back office records straight) when in fact it should be a strategic force, some education and awareness has to be directed toward correcting their improper "vision" of what technology could mean to the firm. Conversely, if senior management views technology as a strategic weapon, but it is in fact only performing a support function (running internal operations), some change is probably needed in the management of the information function. Having the proper role in the organization requires that both the CIO and the CEO be on the same wavelength and share the same perception (vision) of how technology should be employed. Figure 3.3 illustrates four possible perceptions.

Zone 1 is where both corporate management and information management share the vision of information technology as a strategic weapon. This is the information company. Zone 2 is a mismatch because senior management sees information as a support resource, whereas information management sees it as strategic. If senior management is correct, the information manager is going to be a frustrated individual. If the information manager is correct, management education is needed. Either way, the misperception must be corrected. Zone 3 is the opposite: senior management thinks information should be strategic, but it is actually being applied by the information manager as a support function. As discussed in Chapter 2, this "transitional mismatch" is likely to result in a new information manager. Zone 4 is where both agree that the proper role of information in the organization is as a support function. If both are right, the information function role is proper and it will never be part of the strategic planning process. If both are wrong, the company has a "punch-card mentality" and will likely be rudely awakened by its competition in due course.

Having the proper perception does not mean that information resources should always be strategic. On the contrary, in some businesses, such as small manufacturers, the information function may properly be a support function. In others, such as airlines, the airline reservation system may run like an efficient factory. In still others, such as banking and insurance, the information function is strategic to the business. Probably the best test of whether the information function is strategic or just support is to have the computer go down. How long will it be before the business grinds to a halt? If hours or days, it's probably strategic; if never, it's support.

The proper role for the information function does not only depend on the importance of information systems to the business. It also depends on the importance of the business to the company. That is, the role of technology to the company will vary by business unit. For example, a strong and growing business may need strategic information services, while a mature business unit may only need support services. It is important, therefore, to list all business units and to determine with senior and user management the proper role of information technology—support, factory, turnaround, or strategic—for *each business unit.* By listing the business units within the grid shown in Figure 3.1*A,* the planners will have a clear picture, on one page, of how and where information resources should be employed in the company. The company's investment in technology can then be properly balanced within the company, allocating information resources to the businesses that all have agreed need them the most.

Business Segmentation Models

A number of models have been developed for categorizing a company's "portfolio" of businesses. One of the oldest and best known is the growth share matrix developed by the Boston Consulting Group (BCG)(9), as illustrated in Figure 3.2*B.* The four quadrants of this model are labeled Dogs, Cash Cows, Question Marks, and Stars.

Dogs. Businesses that have a low share of a low-growth market are considered Dogs because of their weak competitive position.

Cash Cows. Businesses that have a large share of a low-growth market are Cash Cows because they produce heavy cash flows which can be "milked" to produce cash for other businesses (especially the Question Marks).

Question Marks. These are the businesses that have a low share of a high-growth market. The Question Mark means the company must decide whether to stay in this "niche" or pump money in, in an attempt to increase market share.

Stars. The "stars" of the portfolio are those businesses that enjoy a high market share in a high-growth industry. These are the businesses that should get resources for they offer the highest growth and profit potential.

The BCG model is a marketing view of a company's business units and is, therefore, useful for determining business relevance in competitive analysis and planning.

A similar business relevance model is that produced by Michael Porter of the Harvard Business School (10). Porter's model also divides businesses into four categories, which he labels Divest, Harvest, Niche, and Leadership, as shown in Figure 3.2C.

DIVEST. These businesses are unprofitable and declining in competitive position. If they cannot be boosted into the Niche category, they are candidates for divestiture.

HARVEST. Harvest businesses rely on past strengths to optimize cash flow by cutting costs and/or raising prices until profits have been "milked." (Ultimately the business is sold or liquidated.)

NICHE. The niche business seeks to identify and focus on a segment of the market where it can compete successfully in a small niche either through product or cost advantage.

LEADERSHIP.. Leadership businesses are strong and profitable in a good market. They are the high potential growth businesses.

The BCG and Porter models use quite similar techniques for dividing up a company's "portfolio" of businesses according to competitive strength or weakness in the marketplace. Both analyze SBUs from an external market-driven view.

An Integrated Model

Combinations of the models discussed thus far can be used to create an integrated model for business and information planning, as shown in Figure 3.2D. This model says that if the company can break down its businesses according to competitive position into LEAD, NICHE, HARVEST and DIVEST business categories, the information support role appropriate to each (the McFarlan/McKenney model) can be easily determined. LEAD businesses will receive STRATEGIC support in terms of systems development resources and competitive information systems. NICHE businesses will also get development resources to help TURNAROUND and/or maintain or find niche positions through competitive products and services in segmented markets. HARVEST businesses will be supported as efficient FACTORIES, minimizing costs through efficient data processing and systems, but no new development resources will be devoted to them. DIVEST businesses will also get no development resources. Existing systems will merely be SUPPORTED until the business is liquidated. The bottom line is that the LEAD and NICHE businesses get the firm's development resources, and the HARVEST and DIVEST businesses do not. Having determined what is strategic and what is support from a *business* viewpoint, we can now allocate information resources and technology investment according to identified business potential.

PORTFOLIO ANALYSIS REVISITED

IW 6—PORTFOLIO ANALYSIS
The six stages of portfolio analysis for business and systems integration.

I have selected the Portfolio Analysis methodology discussed earlier to illustrate an integrated business and information systems plan because it is based on an *external* view of the business; that is, the planning process looks outward at the competitive marketplace, not inward at the budgeting process. Thus, it is particularly useful as a "competitive" planning tool. Planning that is based on budget aggregations is not planning, it is forecasting. Even when it extends beyond 1 year, it is still a forecast, only less certain. Planning that begins with external competitive analysis is far superior. Strategic planning has this external focus. Strategic planning is part of strategic *management*. To understand how Portfolio Analysis theory fits in with strategic management, let's consider the elements of strategic management:

1. Strategic management uses strategic business units (SBUs) as the key building blocks of the planning process. (SBUs are profit centers. Staff support units are cost centers that allocate their costs to the profit centers.)

2. Each SBU is given a specific and discriminate *mission* (e.g., LEAD, NICHE, HARVEST, DIVEST).

3. Forecasts (balance sheets and profit and loss statements) are then prepared which are tied to the missions.

4. Finally, managers are rewarded based on achievement of the forecasts.

When I taught a course on corporate finance some years ago, the opening sentence of the textbook I used was that the purpose of business is to maximize shareholder wealth. That means that the primary objective of a business should be to maximize stock price, the market value of its shares. What drives market value up is profits, or return on equity (ROE). High

ROE, in turn, results from competitive advantage. Competitive advantage is achieved by competitively positioning the companies' individual business units (SBUs).

Strategic planning, therefore, concentrates on ways to achieve competitive advantage in the SBU's products and services. If the purpose of business is to maximize shareholder return, the purpose of information resource management should be to maximize the business impact of information technology. The Portfolio Analysis methodology is a means toward this end. The aim in Portfolio Analysis is to categorize SBUs according to their position and potential in the marketplace and then to allocate information resources (as well as other resources) to the advantaged SBUs, or potential (targets of opportunity) SBUs. A variety of analyses are possible to arrive at the SBU missions, but they generally revolve around relative profitability, share of market, and future potential. Figure 3.4 illustrates a six-step Portfolio Analysis process.

STEP 1: PROFITABILITY ANALYSIS. Businesses are coded by number and graphed according to dollar sales and relative profitability. This assumes that profitability numbers can be obtained by business units. If not readily available, the strategic planner may have to start by allocating the company's financials (fully loaded with overhead) to product lines to produce balance sheets and profit and loss statements by product line. (This can be complicated by the fact that a product can have costs in several organizational units. In such cases, percentage allocations must be made through agreed-upon estimates, time surveys, etc.) Once financials are arrived at by product lines, all products within a SBU are aggregated into SBU financials.

The sales volume is useful to compare the amount of resources needed to produce a given level of profitability (or loss). Zone 1 SBUs, for instance, have high profits to go with high sales, as expected. Zone 2, however, has high sales generating low profits—a problem. Conversely, Zone 3 businesses are high-margin businesses with low sales and high profits.

STEP 2: RETURN ON CAPITAL. Next, businesses are graphed (and coded) according to their individual return on capital (ROC) and the cumulative ROC. The vertical line represents the SBUs ROC and the horizontal axis is the amount of the company's capital invested in each business. This chart shows the businesses with the high returns that are contributing to higher stock prices. It also shows the negative contributors. Clearly, those below zero are candidates for divestiture unless it can be demonstrated that they have a reasonable chance of being turned around. The dotted line represents the company's desired "hurdle rate;" that is, the after-tax rate of return which the company has set as an overall business goal. Each SBU's goal should be to meet or exceed that hurdle rate.

STEP 3: COMPETITIVE POSITION. The Boston Consulting Group's Growth/Share matrix is used next to create a "bubble" chart of all SBUs according to their share of market (SOM) and future potential. Each coded bubble

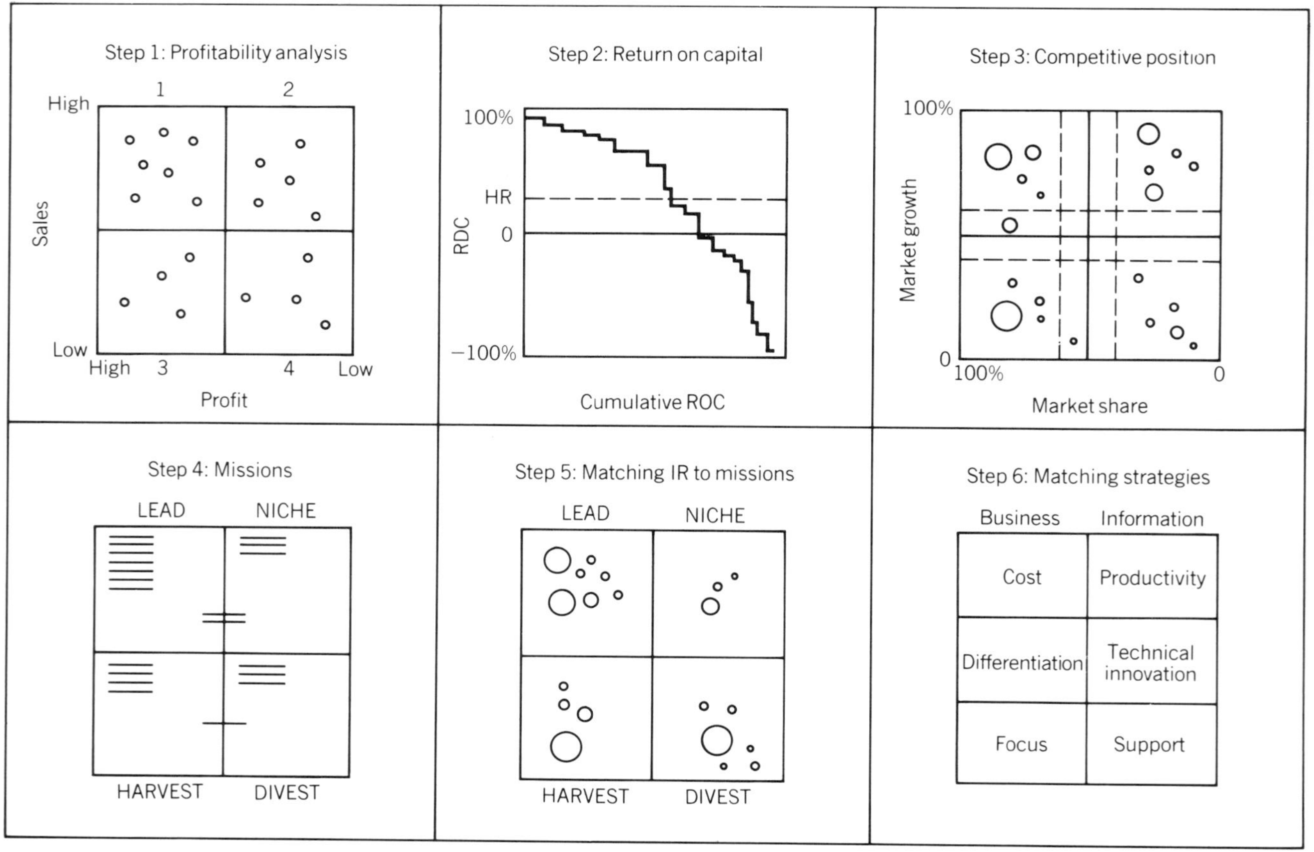

Figure 3.4. Portfolio analysis.

tells three things about the business it represents: (1) the size of the bubble represents its relative profit contribution (% of total); (2) the horizontal scale represents the SBUs share of market (%); (3) the vertical positioning indicates its future potential within the market. The dotted lines represent a "grey" area to help further categorize businesses into 9 groupings instead of only 3. Thus, in *one* chart, all of the company's businesses are represented, and management can see at a glance what the company's overall health and condition is—as well as where it is sick.

STEP 4: MISSIONS.   The next step is to assign missions to SBUs as a result of the analysis done in the first three steps using one of the Portfolio Analysis models. Mission assignments generally center around ROE and growth rate expectations. As missions are assigned, each business is written into the appropriate box. The businesses that are strong, competitive, and profitable become the LEAD (or Star) businesses. Those that are strong enough to maintain a profitable position in the market become the NICHE businesses. (These could become LEAD businesses, or they could ultimately fall into the HARVEST or DIVEST categories.) The HARVEST businesses are those with some strength left but not enough to grow. They are the Cash Cows, generally mature businesses that will ultimately fade out. Finally, the loss businesses with little chance to grow become the last category of DIVEST (Dog) businesses. Sometimes a business may be put into the NICHE instead of the DIVEST category for a time to give it an opportunity to find a niche if that is felt to be a reasonable gamble. Others may have conditional missions and thus rest on the line between their two possible missions. For example, a current NICHE business with a mission to try to become a LEAD business in 2 years.

STEP 5: MATCHING INFORMATION RESOURCES TO MISSIONS.   Having completed the business planning process of segmenting business units into their appropriate competitive mission categories, we are now ready to prepare an information technology support plan that "fits" the business plan; that is, integrates the business and information planning process. In general, the goal is to see that the LEAD and NICHE businesses get the bulk of the systems development resources, while the HARVEST and DIVEST businesses are simply supported as efficiently as possible until they are ultimately sold or divested. In more specific terms, each business must be examined in light of the reasonableness of its information resource support relative to its mission.

Information technology support needs for the LEAD and NICHE businesses are studied, systems projects are identified and prioritized, and the total investment in technology (money, people, machines, and information systems) for the LEAD/NICHE businesses is determined. Next, the support needs (data processing, systems maintenance and enhancements, and package programs) are calculated for the HARVEST/DIVEST business so that the total resources needed in those areas can also be examined and summed. (Note that new development is avoided. If necessary, package programs are acquired to ensure needed support, but the use of scarce systems development resources are avoided for these businesses.) The total investment in information support needs is determined, by SBU, and coded bubbles representing that investment are inserted in each quadrant of the grid according to that SBU's mission. The larger bubbles (larger investments) should appear in the LEAD box and the smaller bubbles in the DIVEST box. Anomalies between a SBU's mission and its information support resources are immediately evident, enabling management to take appropriate action relating to priorities, to reallocation of existing resources, or to add new resources or investments.

STEP 6: MATCHING INFORMATION STRATEGY TO BUSINESS STRATEGY. It is not enough to identify the businesses that should get the information resources. *Information strategy* must also be in tune with *business strategy.*

Each business unit is unique in terms of what it offers to the market. Thus business strategies may (and likely will) differ from one business to another. According to Porter, there are only three basic business strategies (11). Although it is possible for a business to pursue more than one simultaneously, one is usually primary. The three competitive business strategies are:

1. Cost leadership.
2. Product differentiation.
3. Market focus.

Cost Leadership. The first strategy is to be a low-cost producer in the industry. This generally requires experience and maturity in the business, heavy up-front investments in "plant" to get economies of scale, heavy management attention to cost control, and large share of market. The idea is to make it extremely difficult for competitors to be able to match your costs. The lowest-cost producer, of course, has the lowest price potential. Given reasonable quality and service, such a strategy can result in strong competitive advantage.

The information strategy that best supports this business strategy is one that focuses on efficiency of operations, or *productivity,* to drive costs down and, therefore, prices.

Differentiation. The second strategy is to create a unique product or service, to differentiate it in the marketplace. Differentiation can be achieved in a variety of ways: brand identification, superior quality or service, technological innovation, a vast dealer network, and so on. Again, combinations can also be used to produce a unique product. Sometimes, differentiation results in a premium price for perceived quality; in other cases, both low price and uniqueness is possible.

The information strategy supporting product differentiation is to create uniqueness in product through *technological innovation.*

Focus. The third strategy is to focus on finding a niche in a narrow marketplace (small share of market) where one can compete favorably. This could be a product niche, a customer segment niche, or a geographic niche. Either cost advantage or product advantage (or both) could be used in a niche market.

Information strategy might be a strategy mix of product or information support (i.e., increased productivity, technological innovation, or just support). It is interesting to note that in Porter's first book (*Competitive Strategy*), published in 1980, the use of information technology as a competitive strategy is not even mentioned. In his second book (*Competitive Advantage*), published 5 years later, one chapter is devoted to "Technology and Competitive Advantage." In July 1985, in a *Harvard Business Review* article co-authored with Victor Millar (Arthur Anderson & Co.), Porter finally acknowledges the importance of information technology to competitive advantage:

> The information revolution is sweeping through our economy . . . Most general manageres recognize that the revolution is under way, and few dispute its importance . . . As they see their rivals use information for competitive advantage, these executives recognize the need to become directly involved in the management of the new technology. (12)

The authors go on to suggest that the information revolution affects competition in three important ways: by changing industry structure (through impacting on the competitive forces that shape company structure), by giving companies new information services to outperform competitors, and by spawning new information-driven businesses.

The potential of information technology for gaining competitive advantage, however, was not focused on in Porter's earlier work, probably for the same reason that business managers often do not include information resources in their business planning: information is not usually thought of as a competitive weapon. It takes time for this *vision* to take hold. But, as the authors noted in their conclusion,

> Companies that anticipate the power of information technology will be in control of events. Companies that do not will be forced to accept changes that others initiate and will find themselves at a competitive disadvantage. (13)

In Chapter 4, I will develop the concept of matching information and business strategy further in the context of competitive strategy frameworks. The strategic planning models discussed in this chapter, however, clearly illustrate that planning methodologies exist to integrate business and systems planning. The tools are there. What is needed is the shared *vision* of using information as a competitive weapon. Given the *vision*, strategic planning can proceed as an integrated process, and the CIO can be instrumental in marshalling information resources to competitively support business objectives. The companies that have successfully integrated business and information planning may be in the minority today, but their ranks are growing. They are the companies with the *information weapon systems.* We look at how they are winning the "electronic battle" for market share in the next four chapters.

References

1. Planning survey, A. T. Kearney, Inc., Chicago, 1982.
2. IBM, *Business Systems Planning: Information Systems Planning Guide.* July 1981.
3. John F. Rockart, "Chief Executives Define Their Own Information Needs," *Harvard Business Review,* March–April 1979 p. 82.
4. Richard D. Nolan, *Managing the Data Resource Function,* 2nd ed., West Publishing, St. Paul, Minn. 1982.
5. All three models are described in Michael E. Porter's *Competitive Strategy,* The Free Press, New York, 1980.
6. W. R. Synnott, W. H. Gruber, *Information Resource Management,* Wiley, New York, 1981, Chapter 2.
7. Robert M. Halloway and Judith A. Quillard, "Top Priorities for the Information Systems Function," CISR paper # 79, MIT Sloan School of Management, Sept. 1981.
8. F. Warren McFarlan and James L. McKenney, *Corporate Information Systems Management: The Issues Facing Senior Executives,* Richard D. Irwin, Inc., Homewood, IL, 1983.
9. Gerald B. Allan and John S. Hammond, Note on the Boston Consulting Group Concept of Competitive Analysis and Corporate Strategy, Harvard Business School, Boston 1975.
10. Porter, *Competitive Strategy.*
11. Op. cit.
12. Michael E. Porter and Victor E. Millar, "How Information Gives you Competitive Advantage," *Harvard Business Review,* July–Aug. 1985.
13. Ibid.

4

INFORMATION WEAPON SYSTEMS

Vision is the art of seeing things invisible

JONATHAN SWIFT

The Portfolio Analysis planning methodology described in Chapter 3 showed how to segment SBUs as the building blocks of a strategic (competitive) planning process. The SBUs were segmented into four categories: LEAD, NICHE, HARVEST, and DIVEST businesses. The businesses that have valuable cash flow potential to the firm (LEAD, NICHE, HARVEST) versus those that are drains on capital and thus candidates for sale or liquidation (DIVEST) were identified.

However, Portfolio Analysis does not determine what businesses we might or should be in and are *not*. It only deals with the businesses in which we are already engaged. The question for managers then is: "What businesses *should* we be in?" Management needs to consider if there are "holes" that need filling in the portfolio, or where selective additions could provide synergism to an existing business.

This is also true of technology. One can often find technological synergism through the merging of technologies, or by creating new technology businesses that better support corporate objectives. Competitive unions are the opposite of competitive rivalry. "If you can't lick 'em, join 'em," so the saying goes. Driven by high entry costs of communications, software, or new market penetration, many companies are joining with competitors or customers as a faster way to achieve competitive advantage than going it alone. Hence we begin our search for information weapon systems with a look at new technology business opportunities.

NEW TECHNOLOGY BUSINESSES

Competitive technological advantage can often be created quickly and effectively through the formation or acquisition of new information businesses. Let us examine five areas of possibility:

63

- Mergers and acquisitions.
- Joint ventures.
- Licensing.
- Shared resources.
- Selling internal technology.

Mergers and Acquisitions

> IW 7—MERGERS AND ACQUISITIONS
> Horizontal and vertical unions to provide competitive synergies.

Acquisitions come in two forms: stand-alone and related. Stand-alone acquisitions are businesses that are acquired primarily for diversification purposes. These can reduce portfolio risk because diversified businesses provide protection from declines in certain industries which might be offset by gains in others. This is known as "horizontal" integration. (Information systems in the form of data base searches, industry and company analyses, and decision support models can help in the quest for acquisition candidates.) Some conglomerates, like ITT, make a business out of looking for LEAD companies that might be added to their portfolio.

Related acquisitions are businesses in the same or allied industries that are acquired to increase a company's share of market or strengthen the overall position of the company in the industry. This is "vertical" integration. Buying a supplier, for example, is an example of backward vertical integration, while buying a value-added reseller is an example of forward vertical integration.

Business consolidations are often used to increase competitive advantage through horizontal or vertical integration. Such competitive unions can result in better product integration, improved distribution channels, new uses for products, or new information services that complement "in-house" information resources.

The merger of Burroughs Corp. and Sperry Corp., which would displace Digital Equipment Corp. as the number 2 computer company in the United States, is an obvious merger to achieve instant size and market dominance. The merger brings synergistic benefits to the combined enterprise because the two companies basically serve different markets (government vs. private business) and bring different technical and marketing strengths to bear on the marketplace.

The IBM and AT&T rivalry is another example. Each has tried to get into the other's business, with IBM buying into communications businesses (Rolm, MCI) and AT&T buying into computer businesses (Olivetti, Convergent technologies). Likewise, Wang Laboratories made significant progress in its plans to become a fully integrated office systems supplier by acquiring interests in two PBX manufacturers, InteCom and Telenova. Telenova supports small installations (100 lines or less) while InteCom supports larger installation switches (600 lines or more). Not all are hardware company mergers. Ashton-Tate, for example, is an example of a software company that has pursued innovation through acquisition rather than product development. Its three main product lines—dBase management systems, Framework, and Multimate—were all acquired through acquisition, making Ashton-Tate the third largest independent microsoftware house (behind Lotus and Microcroft), with sales up from $3.6 million in 1982 to $145 million in 1985 (1). Cullinet Software is another example of a major software company that has grown through acquisition (See the discussion on Licensing below).

An example of nonrelated business acquisitions is the auto industry's foray into financial services. The "Big 3" auto companies have already spent $1.5 billion on financial services companies, picking up a consumer finance business, an equipment leasing firm, two mortgage servicing operations, and even a savings and loan association (2). General Motors also purchased EDS (Electronic Data Systems, Dallas), the highly successful facilities management and remote data processing business. General Motors did not buy EDS just to run their internal data processing; they also wanted to diversify into the data processing business.

In a reverse twist, FIserv Inc., a large financial data processing firm, acquired a bank, First Trust Corp. of Denver. Banks have often bought data processing firms, but this was claimed to be the first case of a data processing firm buying a bank. Again, its purpose was to permit FIserv to add such new services as trust and retirement plans, thus enabling it to expand its DP services to other banks. Bankers Trust, in New York, bought a 49% stake in ADS Associates (Woodland Hills, California), a producer of treasury workstation software, in order to become an instant leader in the corporate "cash management" business.

To aid in prospect hunting, there are even information services that provide data on mergers and acquisitions in the technology industry. For example, *The Cerberus Report* (an annual publication containing acquisition offer prices and other statistics covering the computing industry) and its companion, *Cerberus OnLine* (a monthly acquisition transaction monitoring service), are publications of Charles Varga (Frenchtown, New Jersey) in cooperation with W. T. Grimm & Co. (Chicago).

Joint Ventures

> **IW 8—JOINT VENTURES**
> Joining forces with others for mutual advantage.

Rather than actually acquire another company, many simply enter into joint ventures (agreements between two or more parties) where each brings something that synergizes the other.

In addition to its acquisitions, IBM, for example, has entered into a variety of joint ventures. One of the earliest was the joint venture with Aetna Insurance Co. and Comsat General Corp. to form Satellite Business Systems (SBS) which, unfortunately, did not work out. Comsat and Aetna ultimately sold their interests to IBM, which in turn sold it to MCI Communications in exchange for an 18% interest in MCI. While that particular joint venture may not have worked out, it ultimately got IBM an interest in MCI, the second largest communications company (behind AT&T).

Later, IBM joined with CBS and Sears Roebuck to announce a planned nationwide videotex service. Then they joined Merrill Lynch to develop and market a brokerage information system. This was followed by an agreement to distribute Stratus (fault-tolerant) computer systems. The list goes on.

In yet another example, Manufacturers Hanover Trust Co. in New York and Wells Fargo in San Francisco, along with eight other banks, joined together to form a lockbox-based cross-country network using simple PCs and standard asynchronous communications. A lockbox service enables customers to send payments to a local bank, which credits the seller's account immediately, wiring the funds to its chief clearing bank, thus saving the company one or more days of "float" (lost time in collecting accounts receivable checks). The joint venture established that payments would be sent to the nearest bank in the network. A customer need only sign up with one bank in the network instead of having to establish 10 bank accounts in 10 cities (saving considerable fees in the process).

Sears Roebuck entered into a joint agreement with The First National Bank of Atlanta to enable its customers to use their new combined credit/financial services card, Discover, to get cash advances on their credit line through the bank's network. A few weeks later, they announced that they had joined a similar network run by Mellon National Bank (Pittsburgh). This was quickly followed by an introduction of the card in California in the San Diego Trust & Savings Bank. To promote the card nationally, they signed up retail outlets and chains around the country to accept the Discover card. Major companies such as American Airlines, Budget Rent-A-Car, Denny's Restaurants, Holiday Inns, and Hospital Corporation of America signed up to accept the Sears card, offering discounts to card members. It is Sear's announced intention to add other services from the Sears Financial Network, such as loans, deposits, investments, and insurance, to those already provided by the card. Sears, in fact, expects the number of retail and other business outlets accepting the Discover card to eventually exceed those that now have the American Express card. Again, joint ventures were used to get it off the ground (3).

Companies in seemingly different lines of business sometimes join forces to advantage—Citicorp, Nynex Corp., and RCA Corp. formed a joint venture to study home banking, home shopping, and similar *videotex* services. The venture is not actually marketing products or services, but is engaging in marketing research. AT&T, Chemical Bank, and Time, Inc. formed a new videotex service called New York Pulse, serving the greater New York metropolitan area with excerpts from the New York Times, restaurant reviews, film and theater reviews, news, and weather.

As industry lines have blurred, we have seen companies adding businesses or entering into joint agreements in allied industries to broaden their lines of business, not just for diversification. For example, the banking, insurance, and brokerage businesses have merged into a financial services industry, with increased competition between all three. Similarly, computers, communications, and office systems are rapidly merging into a broader information services industry. With regard to the IBM/AT&T rivalry mentioned earlier, *The New York Times* quoted Robert Conrads, of McKinsey and Co. (a management consulting firm), as saying:

> IBM has not taken major share from AT&T except where it has bought. And AT&T has not taken share from IBM because it has not bought. (4)

The *Times* article noted that the two giants continue to lock-step each other around the world with competitive alliances. For example, when IBM teamed up with Merrill Lynch to offer brokerage information services, AT&T entered into an agreement with their rival, Quotron. In Japan, IBM joined with Mitsubishi to offer data communications services; AT&T followed suit with rival Mitsui. And in Italy, IBM has an alliance with the state-owned telephone equipment company STET, while AT&T has a piece of Olivetti, a computer company (10). Both companies have used acquisitions and joint ventures to broaden their hold on the information industry. (However, the expected clash of the titans is as yet turning out to be a non-star wars encounter.)

To these giants, technology *is* their business and such alliances would be expected. But, as the Sears Roebuck, Bankers Trust, General Motors, and other cases show, many companies in other industries are also using such strategies to gain technological strength and, in turn, competitive advantage, through expanded technological depth.

Licensing

IW 9—LICENSING
The buying and selling of software licenses.

Licensing arrangements are similar to joint ventures except that rights to products are given in exchange for royalties or fees. For example, Cullinet Software, Inc. (Westwood, Massachusetts) originally acquired the rights to what is now their IDMS flagship data base system from Goodrich Tire. IDMS has since been completely revamped, with considerable functional capacity added, for example, data dictionary, online query, and online screen generators (ADS/O). But their line also was filled out through the licensing of software products such as Artificial Intelligence's Intellect (added as On-Line English) and Computer Pictures (Trendspotter) graphics software. Application software has also been added, including the personnel/payroll system (from Insci), the banking system (from Bob White software), manufacturing modules (from Rath & Strong), and financial modules (from McCormack and Dodge) (5). Through selective acquisitions and licensing arrangements, Cullinet has succeeded in building a broad and integrated product line around its IDMS product, and even through its enviable earnings growth has dropped of late, Cullinet is still the second largest (behind IBM) data base vendor in the country.

Electronic Data Systems (EDS) in turn, obtained the rights from Cullinet Software and Hogan Systems to offer their data base and integrated applications systems, respectively, to EDP customers serviced by regional data processing centers. Each party to the agreement gains because the alliance extends software resources normally available only to large users to a new market of smaller customers using shared systems (10).

Of course, licensing is a two-way street. Just as the licensee gains from acquiring rights, the licensor also gains revenues from the granting of licenses. Chemical Bank in New York, for example, licenses several technology products to others as a source of new revenue. Two examples are Chemlink (a cash management service) and PRONTO (a home banking system), which Chemical licenses to other banks, especially smaller banks seeking to avoid the high costs of developing such services on their own.

From the beginning, software has traditionally been licensed rather than sold because of the greater potential for revenue from a continuing stream of fees, as well as to prevent buyers from reselling the package in competition with the original developer. Software can usually be purchased at a fraction of the cost of developing one's own so, once again, licensing can be beneficial to both licensor and licensee.

Shared Resources

> **IW 10—SHARED RESOURCES**
> Achieving economy of scale through the sharing of resources.

Economies of scale can be achieved through the sharing of resources. Data processing service bureaus serving smaller businesses, such as Electronic Data Systems (facilities management), Automatic Data Processing (financial and personnel services), First Data Resources (credit card processing), and Computer Processing, Inc. (mortgage processing) all bring economies of scale to customers sharing resources they would otherwise not be able to afford. PLUS and CIRRUS are two competing organizations of banks that have agreed to share ATMs across the country, and even abroad.[1] Banks that sign up with either organization add the PLUS or CIRRUS logo to their own ATMs. Individual banks, of course, could not afford to have a nationwide network of ATM locations. The sharing of machines broadens every participating member's geographic base.

Another recent development is the provision of shared telephone services by property managers who have wired their buildings during construction to offer a competing service to the Bell Operating Companies (BOC). Building owners supply a shared centralized telephone switchboard much the same as they have always supplied common elevators, heating, and air conditioning. "Wired" buildings can get by with fewer local telephone lines, providing lower telephone bills to tenants as well as a profit on the shared resource. Some of the major buildings in New York City, for example, that have or will be wired for shared computerized telephone switches include Rockefeller Center, the World Financial Center, Park Avenue Atrium, 245 Park Avenue, and 1290 Avenue of the Americas. Older buildings being retrofitted with shared telephone services include the World Trade Center, Empire State Building, One Penn Plaza, and 230 Park Avenue (7).

The development of back-up computer sites (so-called "hot sites") are another example of shared resources. Here, companies share the cost, or pay a stand-by fee, for use of a back-up computer facility available to subscribers in the event of a disaster. The high cost of a "hot" back-up site prevents many companies from being able to afford such a contingency except on a shared basis. Some of these contingency back-up sites are developed as joint ventures and some are licensed from third parties (e.g., Sun Guard). An example of the former is a group of nine banks in Maine that obtained permission from the Federal Reserve Bank of Boston to install an IBM mainframe computer in the federal Regional Check Processing Center in Lewiston, Maine. The computer is used by any of the nine banks that require emergency back-up. All costs are shared among the banks equally.

Selling Internal Technology

> **IW 11—SELLING INTERNAL TECHNOLOGY**
> Leveraging internal technology through outside sales.

[1]A recent partnership between Bank of Hawaii and the Japan Credit Bureau, Tokyo (a consortium of Japanese Banks), has now extended PLUS to Japan.

Many companies have come to the realization that technology developed internally can often be sold externally.

In the early days of computing, many companies began selling off excess computer time. In the banking industry, only the large banks could afford computers. Capitalizing on systems developed for themselves, many began to offer data processing services to smaller correspondent banks which could not afford their own computers. To this day, some 10,000 small banks (two-thirds of the nation's banking institutions) are still dependent on these "Big Brother" banks and other suppliers (EDS, ADP, NCR, Burroughs, etc.) for their data processing and other information products and services. Although very few companies have successfully turned their internal DP capabilities into successful revenue generation, a few have demonstrated that it can be done. In 1970, the Boeing Co. spun off its DP group as a subsidiary designed to service both its own computer needs and outside customers. By 1986, Boeing Computer Services employed 12,000 people serving more than 1500 outside customers (as well as Boeing itself), which would rank it among the Fortune 500 if it were a separate company (8). Other companies that have successfully spun off DP as a revenue business include Security Pacific Automation Co. (SPAC), General Electric Information Service Co. (GEISCO), and McDonnell-Douglas Automation Co. (McAuto).

The whole software industry was basically spawned from software originally developed for a single company and then generalized and marketed as "turnkey" packages. Hundreds of software companies were formed in this way. Many companies spun off software subsidiaries to sell their internally developed software. Florida Software, for instance, sellers of a broad line of banking software, was formed as a spin-off from a Florida bank that developed the original software applications for its own use and then decided to capitalize on its investment. Citicorp formed a subsidiary to sell several internally developed products, including their Letters of Credit system, an operational accounting settlement system called AIM (for automated information management), and others.

Weyerhauser Co. formed a profit center called Weyerhauser Information Systems (WIS) to sell a variety of internal services such as mainframe and microcomputer software developed for in-house applications and disaster recovery services including a "hot" site, systems planning, telecommunications consulting, and educational programs. Although only comprising 10% of Weyerhauser's revenue currently, WIS says it hopes to generate 50% of its revenue from outside sales within 5 years.

Some companies, taking advantage of in-grown technical expertise, have gone into the business of managing data processing for others (the facilities management business). Wells Fargo Bank and Bank of Boston are two that come to mind. Still others are utilizing their in-place communications networks to generate new revenues. J. C. Penney, for instance, offers its nationwide network to several oil companies to service purchases made at gasoline stations scattered throughout the country. And GTE Telenet (a subsidiary of GTE Corp.) introduced the first public electronic mail network by allowing multiple companies to share the same lines through their Telenet packet-switched network. By using its in-place packet switching network, GTE was able to provide a natural base for an electronic mail service. The Security Pacific Bank in Los Angeles decided that the potential gain from selling their technology services was so great that when they reorganized the bank recently they established data processing as one of four main lines of business. (The other three are retail and wholesale banking and nonbanking services such as financing and mortgages). The Security Pacific Automation Co. was formed in September 1984 as a separate subsidiary to offer new computer-related services to banks and others.

Banks are not the only companies following this strategy. McDonnell-Douglas, the aerospace company, did the same when it formed the McDonnell-Douglas Automation Co. (McAuto) in the early 1960s, as General Electric did with its timesharing business, the GE Information Services Co. (GEISCO), at about the same time (9).

A number of companies are recognizing the value of technology not only for internal consumption, but also as a potential revenue-producing service. This has certainly been the case with the recent rash of microcomputer-based services offered by companies seeking to lock in customers to their business offerings. A number of examples are presented in Chapter 5.

New technology businesses have one thing in common: *entrepreneurial management*. Before one can begin to look for information weapon systems, one needs to think about whether the management culture is supportive of this vision. Both business and information managers need to have "Information Era" thinking—that is, the use of technology in the firm in ways that are creative, strategic, and entrepreneurial.

TECHNOLOGICIAL ENTREPRENEURSHIP

> **IW 12—TECHNOLOGICAL ENTREPRENEURSHIP**
> Boldness in promoting technological innovation in the firm.

ENTREPRENEUR: One who assumes the risk of business.

Entrepreneurship, of course, normally refers to people who are in business for themselves. It suggests invention, individualism, smallness, high potential reward, and high risk. "Intrapreneurship" (a term coined by Gifford Pinchot, III) refers to corporate entrepreneurship, the strategy of trying to promote entrepreneurship within a large organization; that is, to encourage entrepreneurial individuals in big business to run a piece of the business as a small entrepreneurial "business within a business." To be effective, intrapreneurs must have free rein to spend money and make mistakes, and be driven by incentives (bonuses tied to profits), which is a general break from traditional corporate bureaucracy. In other words, intrapreneurship requires converting from a bureaucratic, control-oriented management practice to an individualistic, innovative, loosely-controlled style. Intrapreneurship entails risk. There will be successes and failures. The pattern of earnings growth in an entrepreneurial organization is likely to be much more volatile (ups and downs) than a traditional management organization (the steady, consistent rise which shareholders like to see). Intrapreneurship is needed to run pieces of the corporation like entrepreneurial companies, providing autonomy, risk, and reward for searching out and successfully implementing new and innovative information products and services.

According to Pinchot, the main advantages of entrepreneuring are the economy of scale resources provided by the corporation. These include financial resources (especially in ventures not of interest to venture capitalists), manufacturing resources (tapping unused capacity to develop prototypes cheaply), technology (research and development resources), people (the valuable information base of a people network), and marketing (e.g., if IBM is stamped on it, a product is off to a fast start) (10).

Even IBM, steeped in its traditional management style, is looking to entrepreneurship to compete more effectively, as *The New York Times* reported:

> . . . . the remaking of IBM has turned of late into a precarious balancing act—between entrepreneurship and central control: IBM needs its creative spark, but it does not want to abandon the tough management style that has made the company such a fearsome competitor. . . . The most dramatic and far-reaching example of IBM's new commitment to risk has been its creation of the independent business unit. These IBUs are specifically designed to operate completely outside Armonk's orbit, unencumbered by the slow and sometimes stifling corporate bureaucracy. The goal is to give the small units the freedom to experiment, to bet their capital and talent on new and untried solutions—in short, to be entrepreneurs. (11)

The *Times* went on to point out that one of the first IBUs was the PC group set up in July 1980 near Boca Raton, Florida. A small group of a dozen people came up with the prototype of the IBM PC in just four short months. The PC did not represent a technical breakthrough. It was, in fact, put together with existing off-the-shelf components bought from other manufacturers, a break in IBM tradition. Another break with tradition was to open up the software market for the PC to small software houses by making available the test specifications of the PC. This spawned thousands of programs for the PC, giving it a giant lift-off. The result was that within 2 years, the IBM PC dominated the business office![2]

Technological entrepreneurship represents a new Information Era way of putting technology to work competitively in ways unimagined a decade ago. Technological entrepreneurship is needed to encourage experimentation because innovation means risk, and management has to encourage the taking of risks if new information products and services are to be "invented" and brought to the competitive marketplace.

Leaders vs. Managers

Entrepreneurship implies leadership, but management and leadership are different. With managers, actions come out of strategies, that is, actions are an aftermath of planning; with leaders, strategies come out of actions, that is, they see new insight to innovation. The search for leadership traits has gone on forever, but traits have not proved to be a very reliable criteria for leadership. Rather than look at leadership traits, perhaps we should look at what leaders do. Leaders inspire, innovate, and motivate. Leaders create, invent, and are idea-oriented. When a leader appears in an organization, an entrepreneurial culture replaces managerial culture. Leaders are proactive risk takers. They develop fresh approaches, new options. Leaders invent; managers solve problems. Leaders relate to ideas; managers relate to people and roles. Abraham Zaleznik at Harvard had this to say about leadership:

> In considering the development of leadership, we have to examine two different courses of life history: 1) development through socialization, which prepares the individual to guide institutions and to maintain the existing balance of social relations; and 2) development through personal mastery, which impels an individual to struggle for psychological and social change. Society produces its managerial talent through the first line of development while through the second leaders emerge. (12)

Zaleznik suggests that for corporations to consciously develop leaders as compared with managers requires developing one-on-one relationships between junior and senior executives and fostering a culture of individualism, even "elitism." Technology innovators working with business "leaders" can be extremely prolific, creating new and innovative information weapon systems that can give the company a giant lead in the competitive "information wars" of the information age.

---

[2]The PC Junior, by contrast, was a failure. It was not innovation, just a smaller (and more limited) version of the PC with not enough memory to run the popular spreadsheet and word processing programs. The popularity of IBM in the office was not matched in the home.

Efficiency vs. Effectiveness

As we strive for competitive advantage in information services, what should be the focus—efficiency or effectiveness? Consider the difference in meaning. Efficiency is productivity (output over input); it is cost-oriented; it is concerned with internal performance, action without waste, doing things right. Effectiveness is value (benefit over cost); it is results-oriented; it is concerned with doing the right things. It is perfectly possible to be efficient without being effective. Information managers are accustomed to efficiency because in the Computer Era, systems and data processing efficiency was the primary focus because of the high cost of resources. Systems were described in terms of equipment utilization, throughput efficiency, run times, "tight" coding, rather than in terms of the system's *value* to line managers and customers. With advances in the price/performance of hardware and with the widespread use of fourth-generation languages and tools, the pendulum has swung in recent years to effectiveness as the goal. If the customer values the benefits received more than the price paid, value will have been created—that's effectiveness. That is the essence of competition. The customer will choose the product perceived to offer the best value for the dollar. Hence in developing competitive Information Weapon systems that depend on product differentiation, it is effectiveness that counts, not efficiency. In this strategy, the technology innovator needs to focus on creating *product innovation* (effectiveness). (Technical efficiency is important when *productivity* is key to a low-cost product, however, as we discuss in Chapter 7.)

Entrepreneurial Strategies

Peter Drucker in *Innovation & Entrepreneurship* suggested that there are four classes of entrepreneurial strategies (13). These I interpret as: leadership, followership, finding niches, and being innovative. He calls his strategies: Fustest with the mostest. Hit them where they ain't, Ecologicial niches, and Changing values and characteristics.

"Fustest with the mostest" (of "Stonewall" Jackson fame) is a leadership strategy, getting there first with a new and innovative product. Visicalc was such a breakthrough in generalized business software.

"Hit them where they ain't" is a followership strategy, designed to improve on the original with what Drucker calls "creative imagination" or "entrepreneurial judo." That is what Lotus Development Corp. did to Visicalc with their "follower" Lotus 1-2-3 product. And it's what IBM did with their PC, which followed Apple Computer by several years. Leaning on their reputation in the business office and by opening up the market to thousands of people to write software for their PC, IBM (as a follower), quickly dominated the business PC market.

Ecological niches aim at achieving control (even a monopoly) over a niche market. For example, a market may be so small that one product fills it, thereby making it unattractive for anyone else to come in. Or a company might develop a specialty skill or knowledge of a market that is hard for anyone else to duplicate.

An example of this might be EIC Intelligence in New York City, a firm whose specialty is "information brokering." Their staff of PhDs cull information on specialty subjects, creating unique information data bases of highly summarized and valuable information out of what otherwise could be "electronic junk mail." To the businessman or researcher interested in the subject, the service has great value. But the business is unique enough to also have few competitors (so far).

The niche strategy aims at analyzing a trend, inventing an innovative new product (or enhancing an existing one) to fit the trend, and then continually adding "bells and whistles" to keep it unique and valuable to the buyer while making it unattractive for competitors to try to match.

Changing values and characteristics is a strategy aimed at creating product innovation, either through pricing strategy, greater product usefulness, adaptation to buyers' needs, or delivering better value than the competition. An example of pricing strategy is Xerox's early introduction of copiers. Xerox decided not to just charge for the copiers, but to charge on a per copy basis. This made the price sound small, but experience has taught us the insidiousness of this pricing strategy, as copying costs soared when the convenience factor caused everybody to start copying everything. Time-shared computer services is another example of "use" cost that rose rapidly with escalating computer use (until the microcomputer came along and all but killed the traditional time-share business). The Gillette company's strategy of giving away razors in order to sell blades is yet another example of such a pricing strategy.

An example of innovative competitive strategy that provides greater *product usefulness* is the American Express Company's traveler's checks business. By utilizing their existing worldwide network of offices, American Express added value by providing a ubiquitous travelers check replacement service for lost or stolen checks. Through their worldwide computerized information data base, they are able to verify the serial numbers of checks issued to a customer at any location, determine that they are still outstanding, place "stops" on them in the computer file, and issue replacements, all in a matter of minutes. This turns out to be such a valuable service to travelers far away from home that it is the backbone of their advertising program: "If they are American Express traveler's checks, no problem; there is an American Express office just around the corner," says the cab driver in Bombay, India, reassuringly to the hapless tourist who has just lost his traveler's checks. Replacement checks can now even be obtained from traveler's checks machines located in airports and other convenient locations, so the tourist doesn't even have to go into town to replace his lost checks. American Express has few competitors, because not many companies can match their worldwide network of service outlets and online computer network. (Don't leave home without them.)

These cases illustrate not only the use of different strategies to achieve competitive advantage, but that several strategies can sometimes be combined to create even greater product differentiation. The innovator looks for something the customer needs and creates a useful product that provides greater value to the customer than competing products, hopefully at lower cost.

The entrepreneurial strategies of leadership, followership, niche identification, and product innovation apply equally to technology when searching for competitive advantage. The information weapon can be a leadership strategy when it takes the form of a new and unique technology-driven product (Visicalc). It can also be equally effective as a followership strategy, if one can learn from the leader and improve on the product (Lotus 1–2–3). Niche technologies can be product, market segment, or geographically focused (information brokering). Product innovation can take the form of finding and filling customers' needs (the IBM PC). It might also provide greater utility (usefulness) to the customer, give value that exceeds the price paid (and exceeds the competitor's product as well), and/or offers imaginative pricing.

The key to developing information systems for competitive advantage lies in closely allying information systems with marketing and product management; for as Drucker says:

> . . . anyone who is willing to use marketing as the basis for strategy is likely to acquire leadership in an industry or a market fast and almost without risk. (14)

COMPETITIVE SYSTEMS PLANNING

> IW 13—IW SYSTEMS
> Competitive systems opportunities exist in three classes of systems: operations, management, and customer.

Many factors contribute to the success of leading companies today, but one common factor seems to stand out: they all use their computer resources to advantage. As Nolan Norton and Co., the management consulting firm, points out:

> Successful companies are developing and implementing business strategies that are yielding far more than the traditional target of 10% ROI (Return-on-Investment): Some of these companies are exceeding tenfold returns (1000%) on their investments! While many factors are involved in these companies'

business strategies, they all include a featured role for the computer. It is an integral element of their business strategies. In contrast, the computer is conspicuously absent from the business strategies of less successful companies. (15)

Not only are successful companies using computers, but they are going well beyond the traditional use of computers as back-office productivity tools. They are forging strategic (competitive) systems to gain competitive advantage. But when it comes to transforming the computer into an Information Weapon, most companies are at a loss. Even if they recognize its strategic value, they don't know how to go about using it to exploit new market opportunities. Most companies simply have no strategy to identify competitive uses of technology. In Chapters 5–7 I attempt to address this gap.

Building strategic (competitive) systems requires four things:

1. Sharing of the "information weapon" vision with top management and line management. (Chapter 1 discussed the information vision.)
2. Involvement in the corporate strategic planning process in order to understand the business unit's missions and strategic objectives. (Chapter 3 covered integrated planning.)
3. Knowledge of the company's information resource architecture, infrastructure, and support capabilities. (Chapters 8–10 focus on the building blocks of IRM architecture.)
4. *A strategic approach to search for, identify and, create competitive systems.*

This last item is covered now. But before discussing a planning model for searching out competitive systems, we must first review the different types of systems that have evolved over time (Figure 4.1), because these form the foundation for the creation of Information Weapon systems.

Systems Evolution

The first generation of systems concentrated on automating the internal operations of the company. I call these operations support systems (OSS). The second generation of systems were aimed at supporting management information needs, or management support systems (MSS). The current generation of systems focus on customers. These are customer support systems (CSS). There is some overlap between generations; that is, the first generation (past) focused on OSS, but also produced some MSS by-products. The second generation (present) produces both OSS and MSS, with CSS in an embryonic state. The third generation (future) produces all three types, but with primary focus on CSS.

These classifications represent not only three different types of systems, but the planning process, the development tools, the staff resources sup-

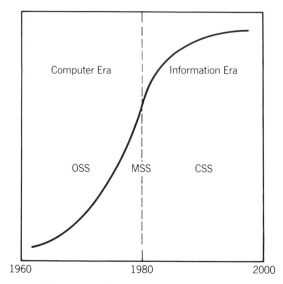

Figure 4.1. Information system evolution.

porting them, and the methodologies used are all different. Operating systems tend to be large, structured, high-level language (e.g., COBOL) systems; management systems may be small, unstructured, fourth-generation language prototypes; Customer systems could be either or both. These three systems types serve as options for achieving competitive advantage through productivity, information services, and innovation as follows:

- *OSS.* Operating support systems are aimed at reducing costs, saving jobs, or increasing quality; they are productivity systems. The CIO can use productivity-driven systems projects to drive costs down and give the company a competitive edge as a low-cost producer in the marketplace.
- *MSS.* Management support systems are information services that have been developed to give managers faster access to better information for decisionmaking, business control, competitive analyses, risk analyses, performance measurement, and so on. The CIO can support these important information needs with MSSs that provide highly responsive and flexible data base systems, information centers, and fourth-generation languages and tools. But information can also be a value-added service to customers. If information is important to your own managers, it is also important to customer managers. Therefore, there are opportunities to turn information services to customer advantage as well. Thus, information services has a double-edged potential, depending on whether it is inwardly (self) or outwardly (customer) directed.

Hardware resources

Software resources		Mainframe	Mini	Micro
	OSS	EOS	Dedicated	Task automation
	MSS	IC	DSS	SS
	CSS	Super systems	Product innovation	Customer terminals

Figure 4.2. Hardware and software resources.

- *CSS*. Customer support systems are technology-driven products and services aimed at increasing market share and revenue generation. The strategic planning of these technologically innovative systems represents the third level of opportunity for the IW planner.

By focusing on these three systems categories, IW planners can draw on three different strategies to achieve competitive advantage. Moreover, as Figure 4.2 illustrates, by applying the different systems to different computers, a variety of competitive opportunities open up. The horizontal and vertical axes represent hardware and software architecture, respectively, whereas the cells represent strategies to create *value* from information technology. For example, the value to the corporation of a *mainframe* OSS might be economies of scale (EOS). An MSS on a mainframe becomes an information center (IC). A CSS could be a Super System (see Chapter 7 for explanation). On *minicomputers,* an OSS can also provide a cost-effective dedicated system, an MSS can take the form of a management decision support system (DSS), and a CSS can be a new minicomputer-based customer service. On *microcomputers,* an OSS can leverage productivity through automation of managerial tasks, a MSS can take the form of a spreadsheet package (a micro-based DSS), and a CSS might be the placement of terminals (PCs) in customer locations (see Chapter 5 for examples). All of these strategies represent competitive advantage opportunities to use technology architecture to create value.

The strategies derived from the three types of systems are not mutually exclusive. Some systems projects present opportunities to achieve all three simultaneously. Each can often be added one on top of the other, achieving cumulative benefits as competitive information weapons. This is because not all systems fall neatly into only one category. Some systems fit more than one. However, one is usually primary. In my definition, if the target is information for competitive advantage, then it's a CSS; if it's to satisfy management information needs, it's a MSS; if it's to support internal operations, it's a OSS. An airline reservation system serving customers is primarily a CSS, even though it also automates record-keeping operations and provides marketing and management information. An in-house information center is an MSS, even though it may provide customer information (unless it is meant to be accessed directly by customers, in which case it is a CSS). An accounts receivable system is a OSS, even though it provides customer and management information.

In Chapter 3, I reviewed a number of strategic planning methodologies that can be used to link business and information planning. All have value for this purpose, but some fit the three systems types better than others. The OSS is served well by BSP (Business Systems Planning) because of its concentration on identifying internal systems projects. The MSS probably fits best with CSF (Critical Success Factors) because CSF zeroes in on management information needs. The CSS can be matched with PA (Portfolio Analysis) because of its market-driven competitive focus.

Although we are concentrating on competitive systems planning, we should not forget that an efficient internal operating system (OSS) can be extremely valuable to a business with a low-cost producer strategy, and a management system (MSS) can provide valuable marketing and management information to both management and customers. Thus, there is a place for all three in planning.

Having identified the evolution of systems types and the competitive strategies they can bring to bear on competitive products and services (productivity, information support, innovation), let us now consider a framework for thinking about competitive advantage.

The Competitive Strategy Model

> **IW 14—THE COMPETITIVE STRATEGY MODEL**
> Linking the three business and technology strategies.

In Chapter 3, I showed how Michael Porter's model divides up the strategic missions of businesses into four categories—LEAD, HARVEST, NICHE, and DIVEST (Figure 3.2C). Porter has also suggested that the three primary business strategies are product differentiation, focusing on market niches, and low-cost producer. Figure 4.3 shows how appropriate IT strategies can be used to complement these business strategies as follows:

Business Strategies
- *Product differentiation* is probably more closely aligned with LEAD businesses. This is not always true, of course, as some LEAD businesses will have "low-cost producer" as a primary thrust. Some will have both. But product uniqueness or differentiation is probably the prevalent strategy in most growth businesses.

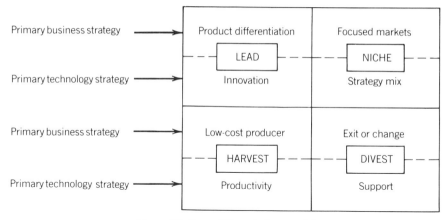

Figure 4.3. Competitive strategy model.

- *Low-cost producer* is the appropriate business strategy for most HAR-VEST businesses, since their primary aim is to throw off cash to other businesses. As the product matures, the goal is to reduce costs and maximize revenue so as to be a cash generator to other businesses as long as possible.
- *Focused markets* is the strategy of NICHE businesses that are trying to carve out or maintain a market in a particular customer, product, or geographic segment. Product differentiation and/or low-cost producer could be appropriate strategies to such businesses. The strategy for DIVEST businesses is to either get out of them or try to change their mission, usually to a NICHE mission.

Technology Strategies

- *Technological innovation* is usually most appropriate as the primary technology strategy serving LEAD businesses. In other words, a prod-uct differentiation business strategy is best matched with technology innovation. Again, this is not always exclusive. If the LEAD business strategy is to be a low-cost producer, the appropriate technology strat-egy might better be productivity. The primary technology strategy should always be matched to the primary business strategy; hence differentiation suggests innovation.
- *Productivity* is usually the best technology strategy for HARVEST busi-nesses that are the "Cash Cows" of the enterprise. Again, a low-cost producer business strategy invites a productivity-oriented technology strategy.
- *Strategy mix* fits NICHE businesses; that is, depending on the market focus, the technology strategy could be innovation, productivity, or simple support.

• A *Support* strategy could fit either a NICHE or a DIVEST business. Support entails no new development, no new initiatives, no additional staff; base level support only is provided until a new direction is indicated.

The Competitive Strategy model thus provides the IW planner with a framework for matching technology strategies with business strategies. It would be just as inappropriate to introduce innovation into all business units as it would be to focus on productivity for all businesses. Usually, one strategy dominates, and that one best aligns with the dominant business strategy.

The IW planner needs three things to create a Competitive Strategy model for his/her own company: (1) segmentation of all SBUs into the four mission categories, a process that only comes from a company-wide strategic planning effort; (2) determination of the prime business strategy to be pursued by each SBU and a general understanding of the reasons behind that choice; and (3) assignment of the most appropriate technology strategy to fit the business missions and strategies so that information resources are used to best advantage in support of each business unit.

The Information Weapon Model

IW 15—THE INFORMATION WEAPON MODEL
A framework for searching out competitive advantage through technological innovation, information services, and productivity.

It has been suggested that CSS, MSS, and OSS also produce three different kinds of IW: those that focus on technological innovation for competitive advantage; those that use information itself as a weapon; and those that lower the cost of production, marketing, or distribution through increased productivity. These, then, form the three primary strategies of the IW model: *innovation, information, and productivity.*

These three strategies can also be viewed in two additional dimensions: (1) internal (self) application or external (customer) application and (2) as a leader or a follower. This represents 12 (3 × 2 × 2) strategic planning options to the technology planner, as illustrated in Figure 4.4. A further discussion of these options follows.

Technology Innovation. Technological innovation is generally supported by a CSS. To support a product differentiation strategy, information managers need to work closely with product managers, marketers, and strategic planners to "invent" new or enhanced products and services that

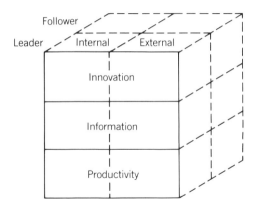

Figure 4.4. Information weapon model.

will provide the business with uniqueness in the marketplace. This could range from a major new competitive product that is difficult or impossible for competitors to match to a simple terminal located on a customer's premises offering access to unique information data bases. Innovation needs to be not only unique, it must also be responsive to the changing marketplace (fast development) and able to custom-tailor services to specific customer needs if it is to be effective in supporting a differentiation strategy.

Information Services. All businesses can be served by an information services strategy. Information services can be internal or external. Used internally, an MSS, for example, can provide financial and statistical data, decision support models, risk analyses, and other feedback that business managers need to make decisions, track business performance, or evaluate managers' results. External marketing information can help find niches through competitive analyses, marketing research, or customer demographics information to help augment the right customer niche. From a customer's perspective, information can be provided as part of a service offering (whether through printouts or online access) to enhance the value of the service to the customer as well.

Information services can also help in finding and/or enhancing niche products and services that offer a better service (efficiency), local specialization of systems (effectiveness), or both. Both the productivity and innovation strategies can also apply to niche product support.

Productivity. A OSS can increase productivity and thereby help a business to achieve a low-cost producer goal. Operational productivity can be achieved through automation of labor-intensive operations (reducing staff) or by increasing quality (reducing waste or error resolution) or units of work processed per employee (getting more done with the same people).

Data processing productivity can be achieved through better equipment scheduling and utilization, fine-tuning of systems to require less run time, and EOS processing. Managerial productivity can be helped through information centers, decision support systems, and personal computers. Thus a low-cost producer business strategy is matched with information technology strategies that focus on productivity gains.

Internal vs. External Focus

The second dimension of the IW model is to look for innovation, productivity, and information services opportunities in one's own firm first (internal focus) and then for customers (external focus). That is, how and when can these three strategies be used to lower your own costs, create unique products, or provide valuable information. Then, what are the customers' problems? Can we lower their costs, provide them with valuable management information, or help leverage competitive advantage with *their* suppliers or customers? In other words, if these three strategies are useful to our own firms, they can probably also be useful to our customers. With a little imagination, this double-vision perspective could double competitive advantage opportunities.

In Chapters 5–7, this internal/external dimension is explored further.

Leaders vs. Followers

The third dimension of our model is to view competitive advantage opportunities either as a leader or a follower. Risk is greatest when one is a leader, less when one is a follower. But both strategies can be used to gain competitive advantage. Porter suggests:

> Firms tend to view technological leadership primarily as a vehicle for achieving [product] differentiation, while acting as a follower is considered the approach to achieving low cost. If a technological leader is the first to adopt a new lower-cost process, however, the leader can become the low-cost producer. Or if a follower can learn from the leader's mistakes and alter product technology to meet the needs of buyers better, the follower can achieve differentiation (16).

As noted earlier, the Lotus 1–2–3 software product is a classic example of a successful follower strategy. Without question, Visicalc was a great breakthrough in terms of creating a new and innovative general business software product. The notion of using rows and columns to represent all sorts of financial, administrative, and management problems was brilliant. Overnight, Visicalc took the PC market out of the hobby stage and into a broadly used business office product. Visicalc was a leader. Then came Lotus, clearly a follower. But Lotus took the Visicalc idea and improved upon it. They put the commands at the top of the screen so the user wouldn't have to remember them (Visicalc was easy to learn, but even easier to forget.)

They integrated the spreadsheet with graphic representations and data management. In other words, they achieved product differentiation as a follower. In a short time, Lotus dominated the spreadsheet market and ultimately bought out the Visicalc inventors and retired the product, thereby eliminating the competition. (It is interesting to note, however, that they have had less success with follow-on products such as Symphony and Jazz.)

Leadership and followership can both produce cost advantage and product advantage (differentiation). As Porter points out, a leader can achieve cost advantage by pioneering lowest cost products, or by being first down the learning curve (getting costs down faster than the competition). A follower can achieve cost advantage through lowering his cost by learning from the leader, or by avoiding cost (research and development) altogether through imitation (17).

A leader can achieve product advantage by pioneering unique products or by innovatively extending the functionality of a product or service. A follower can achieve product advantage by adapting his product to the buyers' needs by learning from the leader. Whether to be a leader or a follower depends on whether one perceives a definite advantage to being first, and whether that advantage can be sustained. An advantage that can be met by the competition overnight is probably not worth the risk and cost of being first. If one can learn from the leader and be quick to respond with a better product or service, it may be even more successful than the leader. But if the follower is too late with too little, a "second strike" will not be effective against the "first strike" leader. Victor Janulaitis, President of Positive Support Review (Los Angeles), recently noted that only 5–8% of companies today are leaders in the competitive use of technology. These are mostly the small entrepreneurial risk-takers and the large corporate R&D departments. Everyone else is content to pursue a protective follower strategy, it seems, as exemplified by this quote from the CEO of a medium-sized office equipment supplier:

> We don't want to die on the cutting edge of technology. . . . We'll wait until new technologies are proven, then use our sales and services organization to get and hold market share. (18)

Even mighty IBM has been accused of following that philosophy from time to time.

Combined Strategies

Although each SBU may have a primary strategy, combinations are also possible. For instance, a SBU may seek to be a low-cost producer while at the same time providing some product differentiation to have a double-barreled marketing advantage. Similarly, both cost and product advantage may be used within a niche market, benefiting by all three business strategies.

The same is true of the three technology strategies. More than one can be used to create competitive advantage. In fact, one can often benefit by combining all three simultaneously. By considering them along the other two dimensions of the model (internal vs. external and leader vs. follower), the Competitive Advantage model expands the possible options in the search for IW. Sometimes, information technology (i.e., technological innovation) is used to create competitive advantage rather than information itself, since the information may have been previously available, but not in direct electronic form. An example would be putting a terminal in a customer's office to provide access to an internal database. Other times, the information itself (i.e., an information service) is strategic, either because it was previously not available or is being used in new ways. A company librarian accessing an online database to search for competitive data would be an example of a new information service. Finally, sometimes the technology and/or the information can enhance productivity, as in the case of a PC spreadsheet (the technology is innovative and the information leverages managerial productivity).

By combining the three IW strategies as shown in Figure 4.5, the 12 planning options of the IW model enlarge to 28 (7 $\times$ 2 $\times$ 2).

	Technological innovation	Information services	Productivity
1	X		
2		X	
3			X
4	X	X	
5	X		X
6		X	X
7	X	X	X

Figure 4.5. Possible information weapon combination.

New Alliances Needed

The building of IW systems requires new alliances. In the past, information systems planners allied themselves primarily with finance, operations, and other back-office types that were primarily concerned with the efficiency of internal operations. To build competitive systems requires a new alliance: merging information systems people with those who deal with the external environment—strategic planners, marketers, and product managers.

In the final analysis, it is the users, the business product managers, who will be the most fertile ground for new ideas on the use of technology for competitive advantage. They understand their business and their markets. By allying themselves with these customer-focused planners, CIOs and other IW planners can open up hundreds of new and competitive ways to put technology to work unimagined in the Computer Era. The management of information technology will be shared in the future through these new alliances. Information managers will no longer be an "island," distant from the competitive forces of the "mainland." They will be bridged to that mainland through new partnerships, new alliances in technological entrepreneurship. These new alliances are the key to creating the information weapons that will put the visionaries at the leading edge in *winning customers and markets with technology.*

IMPLEMENTING INFORMATION WEAPONS

Many senior managers do not need to be convinced of the value of information as a strategic weapon. There has been enough evidence of success and enough ballyhoo in the press about the new vision of competitive technology to convince even the skeptics. The problem is that business managers often do not know how to go about searching out information weapons.

Planning models are useful as frameworks for thinking about how to search out IW opportunities. Examples of competitive strategies and cases such as those discussed in Chapters 5–7 can also be very helpful. However, IW planners must recognize that there is no "cook-book" solution to the search for competitive technology. Nor can innovation and ideas be preengineered. Most of the time they are spontaneous and unplanned. Ideas are often the product of subconscious incubation that suddenly illuminates (the "Aha!" factor) through "stereo" thinking. By this I mean the integration of the left hemisphere of the brain (the analytic side) with the right hemisphere (the intuitive side). The stereo thinker assimilates facts, thoughts, and concepts and lets them incubate until the intuitive side has had a chance to mull them over and turn them into ideas.

Idea generation also comes from a mixture of hard and soft data and hunches with facts, brainstorming and more formal planning, computer analysis and personal intuition. It is not done once; it is continuous. This is not the fodder of long-range planning committees, it is an ongoing process by individuals. And it is also not likely to come from information managers, for it is the line managers who know the products, the customers, and the markets; therefore, most of the IW ideas are likely to come from line managers, not systems people.

A variety of techniques and strategies have been used by industry leaders in the search for information weapons. The following is a compilation of strategies used by a number of companies, which may help readers to start developing their own methods.

- *Foster Corporate Education.* The starting point for IW planning is often a series of "awareness" sessions prepared for top management and other senior business managers. This may be done by inside people or by outside consultants. The purpose is to promote a better understanding and sharing of the vision of information technology as a competitive force in the marketplace. Getting the senior management team on board is a critical prerequisite for success. Without it, the competitive systems notion will likely go nowhere.

- *Find a Champion.* In almost all cases where companies have been successful in carrying out this vision, a corporate champion (or champions) in the senior management ranks spearheaded the drive. A CIO cannot make this dream come true alone; a strong user champion is needed. In every organization, there will be at least one such champion waiting to be prodded. Indeed, in many cases, the champions provide the drive and the CIO only needs to be suitably responsive. So, find a champion who will get the ship off the launching pad, and success in one area is very likely to breed enthusiasm and interest in others.

- *Establish New Alliances.* Get the systems people allied with customer contact people. It's fairly obvious that to build customer systems, one needs to be connected with the people who serve customers. In the past, the focus was on building operating systems, so systems people were matched up with operating and financial folks. Now that the focus is moving to customer systems, systems people need to be directly connected to those who deal with customers—the product managers, the marketing people, the strategic planners. These are the people who will generate the new ideas; they only need the enlightened support of the technology wizards.

- *Conduct Market Research.* Marketing research studies and customer focus groups are needed to learn what customers need and want and why they buy given products and services. Armed with this data, IW planners can find ways to create new or substitute products, and/or enhance and differentiate existing products/services by adding value with technology. There is no substitute for learning customer needs directly from the customers themselves.

- *Collect Competitive Intelligence.* Find out what it is that competitors are doing right. Do a "WOTS-up" analysis (WOTS = weaknesses, opportunities, threats, strengths). Exploit competitive weaknesses, search for opportunities, head off threats, and attack competitive strengths with one better. Sometimes a good defense (follow the leader) is the best offense. In any event, knowing the competition is critical to competitive product planning.

- *Fund Corporate Research and Development.* Manufacturing has for years set aside funds for corporate research and development (R and D). Why not IW research and development? I know of at least one major financial services company that sets aside a sum of money that business managers can apply for who have a promising idea for a new technological product or service. If granted funds from the R and D pool, the manager is free to pursue the idea with corporate funds, without risk to his/her own budget. This encourages intrapreneurship while fostering riskless (to the SBU manager) information technology initiatives.

- *Establish an IW Group.* Form a stand-alone group whose sole purpose is to nurture and encourage IW ideas, before they get cut off at the pass. Anyone can suggest an idea to this group, and they will pursue it independently until it flies or dies. This is another form of corporate R and D, except here the funds go directly to the research group. Eastman Kodak has one called the Office of Innovation, and Citibank has a group called the Information Services division, which considers new ventures in the use of information services.

- *Promote Integrated Planning.* As discussed in Chapter 3, business and information planning should be an integrated process, with information systems people involved proactively with business planners during the planning process, not reactively after the business process is completed. If this is done, technological trends and directions can be considered up front, as well as technological options, feasibility, and cost. Hence, IW planning can then be made a deliberate part of that process.

- *Create a SWAT Team.* A small SWAT (Strategic Weapons Analysis Team) team can be put together that combines knowledge of company, products, marketing, and technology into a bilingual vision of potential IW weapons. This is akin to the "new alliances" strategy, except that a lean and mean SWAT team of diverse specialties can be a very effective means to carry out IW searches in selected business areas.

- *Conduct Brainstorming Sessions.* Another form of the SWAT team approach is to bring together groups within specific SBUs or product line responsibilities to "brainstorm" ideas for IW. The idea is to throw out as many ideas as possible, without comment or criticism, under the leadership of a "facilitator," for further consideration after the brainstorming session. A planning model, such as the IW model (Figure 4.4), can be used as a framework for generating ideas, running each product or service through the model's various strategies. The most worthy ideas can be ranked for further investigation. Repeating the brainstorming process with different groups can produce a plethora of IW ideas to pursue.

- *Set Productivity Targets.* Using the overhead value analysis (OVA) technique described in Chapter 7, establish "stretch" targets of 30 or 40% of expenses in high expense areas; that is, try to generate ideas for reducing expenses by eliminating, combining, or changing work activities such that reductions of 30–40% of expenses are achieved through productivity initiatives. Often this will lead either to new automation or to increased automation penetration.

- *Do Informal Planning.* One-on-one planning between a Product Manager and a CIO, for example, can also be a very effective IW search strategy. Informal discussions over lunch or cocktails often lead to a number of ideas worth pursuing. Although innovation is often unplanned, sometimes creating the right atmosphere and spark can kindle the imagination.

- *Practice Incrementalism.* Rome wasn't built in a day. Many of the most competitive systems evolved over time. Starting with an internal application system aimed at productivity, IW planners have often been able to later add new functionality in the form of new information services or product enhancements that have competitive value, for example, the American Airlines reservation system. Every house starts with a foundation and a plan, but unplanned additions are often what turn it into a truly outstanding showpiece.

- *Create "Trojan Horses."* In Greek mythology, the Greeks gave the city of Troy a wooden horse filled with warriors hidden inside. When the Trojans took the horse into their well-fortified city, the soldiers crept out at night, opened the city gates, and Troy was conquered. In a more beneficent fashion, the "Trojan Horse" strategy involves transferring systems people into user organizations to open the gates to IW planning. By seeding business units with technically trained people, over time there will be a stronger natural interest and inclination to promote technology initiatives, including IW planning. This longer range strategy has two benefits: it promotes career pathing at the same time as it promotes technology.

These are but some ideas used by leading companies to search out and exploit competitive uses of technology in the firm. Readers will undoubtedly develop others of their own, or find combinations of strategies that work best in their environment. The important thing to remember is that IW planning is not done in a vacuum. Nor is it done only once. It must be an ongoing collaborative effort that brings the bilingual vision of diverse groups to bear on the objective: the use of IT as a competitive weapon. Any planning strategy, method, or technique that helps to accomplish that goal is useful.

The IW model is one such planning model. To get a better understanding of how companies have gained competitive advantage through technology within the framework of the IW model, in the next three chapters we examine strategies and case examples that fall within each of its main IW strategy areas: *innovation, information,* and *productivity.*

References

1. *Computer Decisions,* 6/30/86, p. 48.
2. *American Banker,* 12/26/85, p. 1.
3. *American Banker,* 7/3; 8/21; 11/4/85.
4. *The New York Times,* 6/30/85, Sec. 3–1.
5. *Information Week,* 9/2/85, p. 40 and internal company sources.
6. Chas. Wiseman, *Strategy and Computers,* Dow-Jones-Irwin, Homewood, IL, 1985, p. 166.
7. *The New York Times,* 8/27/85, p. D1.
8. *Computerworld,* 12/10/85, p. 51.
9. Wiseman, p. 146
10. Gifford Pinchot III, *Intrapreneuring,* Harper & Row, New York, 1985.
11. *The New York Times,* 7/7/85, Sec. 6.
12. Abraham Zaleznik, "Management & Leaders: Are They Different?", *Harvard Business Review,* May–June 1977.
13. Peter F. Drucker, *Innovation & Entrepreneurship,* Harper & Row, New York, 1983.
14. Ibid.
15. *Stage by Stage,* Vol. 6, No. 1, a newsletter of Nolan Norton & Co., Jan.–Feb. 1986.
16. Michael E. Porter, *Competitive Advantage,* The Free Press, New York, 1985.
17. Ibid.
18. *Business Week,* 7/7/86, p. 78.

5

TECHNOLOGICAL INNOVATION

His genius he was quite content
In one brief sentence to define:
Of inspiration, one percent
Of perspiration, ninety-nine.

Thomas Alva Edison

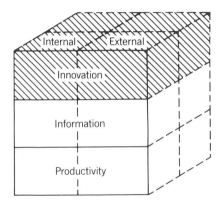

Figure 5.1. Information Weapon model.

Technological innovation should begin with an understanding of what your business really is. Both the businessman and the CIO must ask: What business am I in? The business of the CIO is certainly not data processing; that was the business of the Computer Era. The CIO of the Information Era is in the *information management* business. More specifically, Warren McFarlan of the Harvard Business School suggests that the information function is:

> . . . in the business of bringing a sustained stream of innovation in information services to change the company's internal operations . . . and external products. (1)

This is a good proactive, innovation-minded, and competition-driven definition that fits the Information Era well.

The importance of innovation as a competitive force was underscored by Peters and Austin in *A Passion for Excellence:*

> There are only two ways to create and sustain superior performance over the long haul. First, take exceptional care of your customers via superior quality. Second, constantly innovate. That's it! (2)

And, as Peter Drucker points out:

> Entrepreneurs innovate. Innovation is the specific instrument of entrepreneurship. (3)

As suggested earlier, for information technology planners to be innovative, they need to become more closely allied to the business product managers, marketers, and strategic planners. They need to focus on business and not technology, and these are the people who know the business and the customer's needs. These are the people who will generate most of the ideas. The IW planner, by working interactively with these people, can help define their needs, generate ideas for IW solutions, and develop those that are selected for implementation. The IW planner should help to create vision and be an imaginative idea generator, and an aggressive implementor. The true intrapreneur combines vision with action. Gifford Pinchot distinguishes between workers, inventors, and intrapreneurs as follows. Workers are action-oriented but are not inventors. Inventors are idea generators but may or may not be good implementors. Successful intrapreneurs are both; they dream up an idea and then put it to work (4). Thus, whereas idea generation may be invention, turning it to business success is innovative. Implementation is just as important as idea generation. Pinchot suggests a number of ways to go about generating ideas. Here are a few (5):

- *Brainstorming.* Assemble a bunch of people and have them throw out as many ideas as possible—with no prejudgment.
- *Cross-Fertilization.* Put systems people together with marketers, product managers, and strategic planners—to mix up ideas from different perspectives.
- *Development Projects.* Look to current development projects for ways to add new ideas for product or service improvement.
- *Market Research.* Understand customer needs, then try to fill those needs.
- *In-Place Technology.* Find new ways to use what you already have (e.g., sell excess capacity or put it to alternative uses).
- *Complementary Products.* Find ways to develop new products that add to the value of existing products (e.g., the scotch tape dispenser as a way to sell scotch tape).

- *Sell Internal Technology.* Turn something developed internally (data processing, information systems, networks) into new income sources.
- *Training.* Provide information on how to use products or services to better advantage (many users never use many of a product's features—teaching adds value).
- *New Technology Ventures.* Look for opportunities to join with other firms, such as the joint ventures discussed in Chapter 4, to create new product or services.

Customer needs can be identified through market research (understanding markets and customer wants and identifying trends in the marketplace). Existing products can be examined to see how well they serve the marketplace and customers' needs. Product enhancements may be possible to fill those needs with a minimum of investment. Or new products may be built, or bought, to satisfy unfilled needs. Using the IW model developed in Chapter 4, the IW planner can look for ways to fill needs through product innovation, new information services, and/or increased productivity that enables competitive pricing. The IW planner searches for ways to provide competitive advantages both internally (self) and externally (customers). And opportunities can be considered both from a leadership or a followership strategy. Idea generation for competitive support systems thus present a number of dimensions for the IW planner to explore.

INTERNAL INNOVATION

CUSTOMER SUPPORT SYSTEMS

The type of support systems that lend themselves best to technological innovation are Customer Support Systems (CSS). A CSS has an external focus aimed primarily at achieving competitive advantage through customer service rather than satisfying internal information needs or automating the back-office. In this chapter we examine a number of different types of customer support systems in the search for innovative information weapons. The categories of CSS that follow are certainly not meant to be all-inclusive, but are merely illustrative of ways technological innovation can be implemented.

A **New Products**

> **IW 16—NEW PRODUCTS**
> Constantly innovating with new competitive products and
> services.

Clifford and Cavanagh in *The Winning Performance* state:

> Winning companies innovate continuously. Among our survey participants
> [midsize high growth companies], 84% characterize themselves as frequent
> innovators. . . . On average, more than a quarter of their sales come from
> products that did not exist five years ago. (6)

With technology-based product life cycles becoming shorter and shorter,
it's vital to continuously innovate with new products. In the search for new
information technology products and services, IW planners can start with
market and product research. Market research identifies customer needs
that are not being satisfied so that products can be developed that fill those
needs better than the competition. Market research identifies "problems
looking for solutions." Product research helps to identify new products
and services of possible use in the firm. Product research thus searches for
"solutions looking for problems." Product research is both business and
technical. New business services, for example, might be new or better
ways to manufacture, deliver, market, or service a product. New technical
products are both hardware and software products, for example, new non-
stop computers that enable better customer service, new communications
offerings (such as the new T-1 carrier service now available for commercial
private networks), or new systems packages and turnkey systems aimed
at customers (such as a personal financial planning package).

Once needs are identified through research, the IW planner has the
choice of "buy or build" solutions to fill those needs. Buying an information system can save considerable time and money over developing it
yourself. The trick is to find a product that fills your needs without extensive modification or compromise. Vendors, trade shows, and media advertising are all good sources for new product research. Membership in research organizations (e.g., Diebold Research Group, The Conference
Board, International Data Corp., the Yankee Group) is another good way
to keep current on trends and products. Subscriptions to professional publications, such as the ICP Quarterly (a software directory) and Auerbach
or Datapro (vendor product descriptions) are also good sources. Trade organizations also publish product directories. For example, to help bankers
and merchants keep pace with the marketplace and assist in finding the
right products for their needs, the *Magazine of Bank Administration* publishes an annual "Point-of-Sale Terminals" directory that compares over 60
listings and includes product descriptions, addresses, and phone num-

bers. *Banking* magazine does the same with an annual run-down on ATM vendors and installations. Many other trade publications publish similar directories.

What you can't find, you can always build. Opportunities exist on mainframes, minicomputers, or microcomputers. Building it yourself may take more time and money but it may also afford the opportunity to develop a differentiated and unique product that is hard for competitors to duplicate. In fact, a technologically innovative system often involves a transformation from supporting a business to driving the business. (Sometimes, it *is* the business.) A new business, to be successful, needs a quality product, a leading edge system, good marketing, and (in some cases) scale operations. The information system builder can help provide at least two of these needs. However, building systems requires an investment in staff. Most companies spend more money maintaining existing systems than developing new ones (60:40 is the common ratio). To develop a competitive edge in technology, more CSSs will have to be built in the future. As new systems are developed, more people are needed to maintain them. Hence, if systems staffs are not increased, more and more will be devoted to maintenance, squeezing out development. Rather than being innovative with technology, this can put you out of business.

Whether the CSS is bought or built, Dr. Michael Hammer, a management consultant, suggests that new product development needs three things to be strategic. First, it should not be easily replicable, that is, your competitors can't easily copy it. Second, it must be supported financially to sustain its competitive advantage. Third, it should have the potential to enlarge the market, not just redistribute market share (7).

The creation of CSS products involves the following steps:

- Conduct marketing research to determine customer needs.
- Generate ideas for a product that fills the customer's needs. (Use the IW model, Figure 4.4, to help think through possibilities.)
- Identify risks (economic, technical, marketing).
- Get funding to develop the product.
- Put together the resources needed to develop the product.
- Develop a marketing program to promote and support the product.
- Begin development.

Extended Products

> **IW 17—EXTENDED PRODUCTS**
> Leveraging old products with new competitive extensions.

Don't overlook opportunities to find innovation by leveraging existing products. Old products can be made to look new by redesign or by adding new functionality. An existing product or service can often be enhanced or extended to create a competitive offering at little additional cost. An information service, for example, might be added to an existing product through the simple expedient of putting a terminal in the customer's office, giving him online access to his account information in your data base. Other times two or more services can be combined to produce a new service. This is what Merrill Lynch did when they introduced their highly successful Cash Management Account (combining banking, brokerage, and money market accounts). Adding functionality can sometimes revitalize an old product. For instance, Chase Manhattan Bank added MIS capabilities to an old undifferentiated product, coupon bond collections, which allowed correspondents to track and allocate their costs for the first time.

Old products can also be used in new markets (find new customers for old products). In the early 1970s, Cullinet developed an early version of a report writer called CULPRIT which was aimed at DP departments. Its sales were lackluster until it repackaged it for a new market, EDP auditors, (appropriately they renamed it "EDP Auditor"). The EDP auditor, an old product for a new market, became Cullinet's first commercial success (8).

Warrington Assoc., a Minnesota-based service bureau, and the largest doing investment accounting/trading processing, found a new market for their product in companies that wanted to do their own processing in-house. By licensing their programs to run in customer shops instead of only at their service bureau, they captured what would otherwise have been a lost market.

An enhanced service can also increase the cost of switching from one service to another and thus serve as a barrier to competition. By providing a valuable information service that makes switching to a competitor costly, switching costs become part of a product differentiation strategy. This is what American Hospital Supply did when they put order-entry terminals into customer hospitals. As the hospital used the service, they became more and more tied to it, making it less likely that they would turn to a competing service.

A useful strategy model for thinking about new and old products and their potential markets is shown in Figure 5.2. New products aimed at new customers require technological innovation; new products aimed at existing customers require differentiation of your product over your competitors; an old product aimed at new customers requires entering new markets (like the EDP Auditor example); and an old product aimed at existing customers requires adding new functionality to be attractive.

Whether product innovation is bought, built, or is an extension of an existing product, CSSs come in a variety of forms. These include new and better substitute products, unique differentiated products that beat out the competition, supersystems that are difficult for the competition to match, network services that take advantage of existing scale operations, marketing support opportunities, and new electronic product delivery systems.

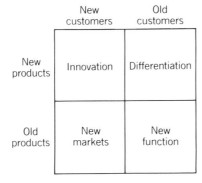

Figure 5.2. Customer–product matrix.

Substitute Products

> **IW 18—SUBSTITUTE PRODUCTS**
> Creating competitive discontinuities through substitution.

Substitution creates discontinuity. Discontinuity, in turn, usually results in competitive war between the attackers (substitute products) and the defenders (existing products). The attacker that offers better value to a customer will often gain competitive advantage, especially if the defender is asleep. Richard Foster in *Innovation* cites the case of NCR, which tried unsuccessfully to hang on to its electromechanical cash register business in the face of substitute electronic cash registers. By clinging to the past and refusing to see the potential of computerized cash registers, NCR lost 80% of the cash register market in just four short years (from 90% in 1972 to 10% in 1976). In the process, the company lost hundreds of millions of dollars, the chairman was ousted, most corporate officers were "furloughed," and 20,000 people lost their jobs (9).

A substitution strategy offers a new way of doing things, preferably providing greater value for less cost. Wood skis were replaced with metal skis which, in turn, were replaced by fiberglass skis, each time offering lighter weight for easier turning; that is, greater value. The pen was replaced by the typewriter, which is now being replaced by the word processor. Analog telephones are being replaced by digital telephones, offering the potential of voice and data integration. Swiss movement watches have largely been replaced by more accurate and cheaper digital watches (practically eliminating the Swiss watch industry in the process). The automobile replaced the horse and carriage, and airplanes all but replaced long-distance railroad travel.

An example of substitute technological innovation is the movement toward electronic banking noted earlier. Electronic banking substitutes for traditional banking offices. Tellers and bank branches are being replaced (substituted) by automatic teller machines and POS terminals in banks, stores, and plants. Credit cards substitute for cash; debit cards substitute for checks; and electronic funds transfers substitute for paper payment settlements between corporations.

"Dumb" terminals are being replaced today by PCs to provide greater functionality at a workstation. Indeed, the substitution of Wang PCs for Wang word processing stations may be key to Wang Laboratories survival in the business office. From the mid-1970s to the mid-1980s Wang enjoyed considerable growth as its office word processing systems won favor in thousands of companies. But, by the mid-1980s, the office word processing market was largely saturated. The secretary-terminal ratio was close to 1:1 in many companies. Installations continued but not at the pace of the previous decade. Growth in the office, in fact, has swung to PCs for professional and managerial people rather than secretaries. Wang began to promote their PC as a substitute for their word processing terminal to capture both markets and capitalize on their installed base. Their very survival in the office may depend upon how well they can carry off this substitution strategy.

Although not often thought of in this way, substitution occurs all the time in information systems organizations. The first time an operation is automated, that's substitution—of capital (technology) for labor. When an old system is replaced, that's substitution—for a better product. When a computer is upgraded or replaced, that's substitution. Computers, systems, and networks are all substitutions for something else. Substitution is such a powerful innovation strategy that it was identified by Porter as one of five basic competitive forces that drive industry competition [the other four are the bargaining power of suppliers, the bargaining power of buyers, the threat of new entrants (competitors), and the rivalry among existing competitors] (10).

Substitution begins with a new product that does something better. The change stage follows, during which the product will either be accepted or rejected. If the change is accepted, the product will move up the product life cycle curve until the technology has been fully transferred. If rejected, it will fade away. Examples of this process are shown in Figure 5.3. Home banking as a substitute for brick and mortar banking is in the embryonic stages. It is too early to tell whether it will be accepted widely or rejected by the public. Personal computers, however, have been accepted and are rising up the curve. However, acceptance has been different with various groups. Middle management and professionals have embraced it much more heavily than top executives. The telephone is clearly a transferred technology. It's pervasive and cheap.

Some of the factors that determine acceptance versus rejection include value over price (value must be perceived to be greater than the price, or

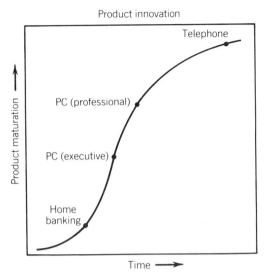

Product innovation

Figure 5.3. Product innovation

the competitor's price), the cost to switch (e.g., converting from one DP service bureau to another would be costly and difficult), the customer's propensity to switch (you probably won't change 10 banking relationships because of one better service elsewhere), and your competitors' response (whether they match or better your product immediately).

Differentiated Products

> **IW 19—DIFFERENTIATED PRODUCTS**
> Gaining advantage through unique products or added value.

Product differentiation is a very powerful business strategy. It generally is thought of as providing a unique service to a specific market segment, often for a premium price. Differentiation can be achieved in a variety of ways: product uniqueness, product delivery, product marketing, or product support. Whatever is perceived by buyers as having *value* can be the target of a differentiation strategy.

Arthur Anderson and Co. suggests three ways to be successful with a product differentiation strategy (11):

1. Respond to buyer values. That is, conduct market research to get hard information on the three or four key factors that influence the cus-

tomer's decision to use one product or service over another, for example, quality, service, or function.

2. Respond uniquely. Your product must be perceived as being uniquely better than the competition. This is especially important in a followership strategy (e.g., Lotus as a follow-up to Visicalc, a leap-frogging in technology).

3. Command premium prices. Added value generally results in added costs. Some customers want quality and are willing to pay a premium for it (e.g., premium automobiles (Rolls Royce, Mercedes Benz), wines, perfumes, etc.).

A perfect example of product differentiation is the automobile industry. Every year, manufacturers introduce new models that attempt to differentiate themselves from their competitors (note that cars that are already unique don't need to do that, e.g., the Volkswagon "Bug" never changed its styling).

Wiseman (12) suggests that product differentiation is a matter of "marketing mix." Marketing mix covers variations of marketing elements such as product quality, price, promotion, and distribution (delivery system). Technology responses to marketing mix objectives might be as follows: Product differentiation can be served through new technology-driven products and services. Price differentiation can be supported through lower costs leading to lower prices (productivity). Promotion differentiation can be supported, for example, by providing product information in warehouses (information services). Distribution differentiation might be aided by an order-entry inventory system in the distribution outlets.

Differentiation can be achieved through improved processes as well as new products. Product innovation satisfies unmet customer needs. Process innovation improves the efficiency or effectiveness of a process associated with a product. Product innovation can be a brand new idea (like Apple's microcomputer in 1976), or it could be a substitution product that improves on the original (like word processing terminals replacing typewriters). Process innovation is like American Hospital Supply's placement of terminals in hospitals as a way of improving order entry and inventorying, a ploy since copied by many companies because of its competitive innovativeness. Azco Coatings, the paint division of the Dutch chemical, paint, and pharmaceuticals company, introduced process innovation for their auto body-shop customers. Azco created a system that gives auto body repair shops access, via a PC, to spare parts listings, repair procedures, and labor-hour guidelines for some 2000 car models maintained on Azco's computers. Employees punch in a description of the car and the parts and repair work needed and the system prints out a parts–labor calculation (13). By providing this differentiated service, Azco strengthens customer loyalty over its competitors.

Bergen Brunswig, a health products distributor, changed the process of inventorying drug stores from manual to automated. In the past, the wholesaler's representative called on the pharmacist, wrote down orders for hundreds of items, carried the list back to the warehouse, pulled the items from the shelves, and delivered them to the drug store. The new method linked the wholesaler to the retailer (and locked out the competition) with a newly designed hand-held computer terminal "scanner" that enabled pharmacies to order merchandise with great speed and accuracy and at a quarter of the labor time of the old systems. Since labor and inventory constitute the major costs of running a drug store, its customers began to rely on Bergen as their primary source of supply, thus locking out the competition (14).

Another way to achieve differentiation is through integrated systems. However, these are often costly and difficult to put together. Merrill Lynch's Cash Management Account is a classic example. Many banks had a hard time instituting such accounts because their systems were not integrated. Few banks have been inclined to undertake the investment needed to do that. As a result, some vendors have stepped into the breach to provide integrated banking relationship systems, for example, Hogan Systems, UCCEL (University Computing Corp.), and Cullinet (Cullinet Banking System). These offer only partially complete packages, however, so that at this writing, less than 1% of U.S. banks have integrated relationship systems.

Super Systems

IW 20—SUPER SYSTEMS
Erecting competitive barriers through major systems developments that cannot easily be duplicated.

Super Systems are major systems that automate large segments of a business that are difficult, if not impossible, for competitors to match, thereby giving the Super-System owner a long-term competitive advantage. Super Systems are often avoided because they are costly and take a long time to build. Yet, properly conceived and developed, Super Systems can be a very effective entry barrier to competition. Even the largest mainframe systems of many companies today have only automated a narrow slice of a business, generally the labor-intensive transaction processing functions. When such systems are rewritten, they generally go deeper into the organization, automating functions and processes that were not touched the first time around. This is because in the early days of computing we did not have the experience to build such sophisticated systems. The emergence of Super Systems means we have learned how to build good systems that work, and we are ready to dig deeper. Proof that such systems work was given by Robert Crandall, of American Airlines, when referring to its Super System, the Airline Reservation System:

> . . . the data processing business is going to make a substantial contribution to the corporation's profits, on the order of $100 million in 1986—pretax. (15)

Many Supersystems are EOS systems aimed at dominating a niche market, the corporate trust services offered by banks, for example. Corporate trust includes stock transfer operations, custody (or safekeeping) of securities, and management of institutional employee benefit plans. In 1983, the top five banks (J. P. Morgan, Manufacturers Hanover, Bradford Trust, Bank of Boston, and Harris Bank) dominated with 54% of the market share. J. P. Morgan offers a full range of shareholder services, serving over 500 corporations and 8 million shareholders. Their stock transfer business is a stand-alone profit center with its own dedicated systems and data processing support, all done online in realtime using a state of the art Super System. Corporate customers use terminals to access shareholder information relative to securities, dividend and interest payments, tax information, stock, voting data, and so on (16). Economy of scale is so important in this business that many banks have dropped out, unable to make a profit. In addition, many large corporations have developed their own in-house stock transfer systems, depleting the market still further.

A similar situation exists in the commercial finance business. Commercial finance is asset-based financing (financing accounts receivable and inventories). The first time Bank of Boston automated this function the cost was $1.5 million and the process took 20 months. It focused almost exclusively on transaction processing because commercial finance is a very intensive transaction-heavy business. Ten years later, the system was completely rewritten, penetrating several layers deeper, automating credit functions (including automatic credit approval) not touched the first time around. This time the process cost $10 million and required 5 years of development. Once again, many banks and factoring companies have dropped out of the commercial finance business because they couldn't make a go of it. Bank of Boston, with its new online realtime system has, therefore, been able to capture a good share of the market, achieving EOS and high return from this Super System.

Another example of a Super System that aims at dominating a niche market is mutual funds accounting. Mutual funds processing combines some of the most unappealing aspects of manufacturing and office bureaucracy, processing millions of pieces of paper, endlessly repeated without producing a single product. As a result, this niche market is filled by fewer than a dozen companies nationwide. The largest is Boston Financial Data Services, a company run under a joint venture by State Street Bank in Boston. Some 50% of the profit of State Street Bank comes from fee income from the custody of securities falling out of their mutual funds accounting system. While ranked 80th in asset size among U.S. banks, it ranks 54th in profitability—all due to this one Super System (17).

We now have the technology, the tools, and the experience to build Super Systems, and companies that are doing so are capturing impressive market share over competitors.

⌐ Micro Systems

```
IW 21—MICRO SYSTEMS
Leveraging microcomputers for external management and
external customers.
```

At the opposite end of the spectrum from Super Systems are Micro Systems. In addition to competing with big systems, you can also compete with small systems, products that run on PCs. There are literally thousands of products to choose from. Although the bulk of these are aimed at leveraging personal productivity (word processing, spreadsheets, data base managers, etc.), quite a number of new and innovative packages are also on the market aimed at customer service opportunities. Examples include information data bases that are accessed by PCs to retrieve competitive data, sales support packages that assist salesmen in tracking sales calls and status information on customers, and PCs placed in customers' offices that provide a wide variety of services.

To learn how micros were being used, especially innovatively, at Bank of Boston, the author and his staff conducted a survey in mid-1985 of the applications being run on some 614 micros in the bank's head office in Boston. The results were compiled and classified into nine categories which were patterned after a model developed by Index Systems and Hammer and Co. of Cambridge, Massachusetts.[1] As shown in Figure 5.4, of 315 different reported uses, the vast majority (73%) were in the task-automation and increase-quality areas, which are considered the personal productivity side of PC usage; that is, leveraging managerial/professional productivity. Department applications, which might otherwise have been on a mainframe or departmental minicomputer, were classed under process-automation and high-performance uses (20%). The remaining boxes represent the more innovative side of PC usage. While the numbers there are not large, they did show that once up the learning curve, users were beginning to think of micro technology in competitive terms. In summary, the upper left side of the matrix represents *productivity;* it's what

---

[1]For a description of this model, the reader is referred to the July 1985 issue of *Indications,* a newsletter published by Index Systems, Inc., Cambridge, Massachusetts.

Task automation 171	Process automation 21	Extend market 7
Increase quality 58	Higher performance 42	Enhance service 7
Expand role 6	Define new role 2	Product innovation 1

Figure 5.4. Bank of Boston PC applications portfolio, based on 315 reported uses.

justifies the investment in PCs. The lower and right side of the matrix represents *innovation*, the targets of opportunity that leverage the investment in PCs and provide competitive advantage. Here are a few examples of PC uses that fit these innovation boxes:

- *Expand role* is the leveraging of expertise. A senior loan specialist with in-depth experience in financing the energy industry prepared a template spreadsheet that analyzes energy companies' financial statements and compares a company to industry norms, flagging potential problem areas so that credit analysts, with less experience with energy companies, will know where to focus their attention. An expert in Industrial Revenue Bond (IRB) financing created a program to assist others in structuring IRB financing deals. A multinational corporation specialist created a marketing data base for calling officers as a sales support tool. The data base contained information about the country, industry data, economic reports, contact names (prospects and customers), current status of business dealings, and so on.
- *Define new role* represents new functional capabilities and responsibilities resulting from technical underpinnings. The transformation of the librarian from a keeper of books within the four walls of the library to an information researcher, accessing hundreds of outside online data bases, is a case in point. Another is the automation of an internal training program by creating a PC lab to facilitate the number-crunching process, giving credit trainees more time to do financial analysis.
- *External market* seeks to develop competitive support systems that extend market share, such as putting terminals in customer spaces. For example, PCs that allow customers to initiate their own letters of credit applications is an example of a product innovation aimed at capturing share of market with importers and exporters of trade goods.

- *Enhance service* provides lock-in/lock-out product features. Adding a customer terminal (PC) to an *existing* service, for example, allows customers access to their information on your data base; touch screens in customer areas can provide information on products and services, prices and terms, and so on.
- *Product innovation* involves development of new technology-based value-added products and services. An example is an innovative international multilateral netting system. The PC-based program, placed in a multinational corporation, is used by the customer to track transactions between the company's overseas offices, effecting a single monthly settlement between those offices, which minimizes foreign exchange costs for the company. Previously, offices settled with each other as goods were shipped, resulting in costly foreign exchange losses. This is innovative because it is new—it has never been done before.

EXTERNAL INNOVATION

CUSTOMER TERMINALS

> **IW 22—CUSTOMER TERMINALS**
> Putting terminals in customer spaces (lock out the competition).

Many of the innovations discussed so far have one thing in common: they involve putting terminals in customer spaces. This is a relatively new competitive force. In the 1970s, the focus was on putting terminals into employee spaces. Instead of the work coming to the computer (as in the Computer Era's punch-card days), the computer was brought to the work site. Centralized data entry gave way to decentralized online transaction processing with terminals spread around the firm. In the 1980s, the focus began to shift toward moving the terminals to the customers. This shift from internal to external processing has resulted in lower costs by moving backshop operations to the customer while, at the same time, giving the customer greater control over his own transactions, records, and information.

Customer terminals offer new and innovative service opportunities. Customers get better service while enjoying direct control of their activities. Customer terminals offer competitive advantage opportunities in all three information technology strategies: innovation, information services, and productivity. For example, companies can lower costs by moving some of their back-shop operations into the customer's space (letting them enter their own transactions). Or the customer terminal could provide direct access to your proprietary information data bases. By being the first to get a terminal in the customer's space, you might effectively lock out the competition because of switching costs and because the customer will not want more than one terminal on his/her desk.

Customer terminals can be dumb or smart terminals (i.e., PCs). They can be transaction processing systems or simply information access systems. They can be given to customers, suppliers, and even competitors (like airline reservation systems in competitive airline offices). Customer terminals are a fast-growing technology innovation strategy being used by wholesalers, retailers, manufacturers, and financial servicors. The strategy fits just about any industry. It can be a small innovation that offers powerful "value-added" service. Keeping innovation small can, in fact, be a key strategy of entrepreneurship. Just as it is not always the large firms that produce the ideas (a 1981 study by the U.S. National Science Foundation found that small firms produced 24 times as many innovations per research and development dollar as big firms), it is not always the big systems that produce innovation. The lion's share of new ideas still come from individual users and Product Managers seeking new ways to serve their markets. Here are some early examples of the customer terminal strategy.

Wholesaling. The movement to customer terminals is not really new. It actually began in the mid-1970s. The overused American Hospital Supply case was one of the earliest examples of putting terminals in customer spaces (18). Back in 1978 its market share soared after it began installing thousands of terminals in hospitals, allowing the hospitals to order supplies directly over the terminals. The value added to the hospitals was that by doing their own order entry, they could lower inventory carrying costs (known as "just-in-time" inventorying). American Hospital Supply thus gained productivity by moving its back-office operations to the customer. Its salesmen were also more productive because they could concentrate on selling new products rather than on taking reorders. Information services came from sales analysis data captured by the system which was then fed back to the manufacturers to assist them in production scheduling. Competitive innovation was gained by locking out the competition. The more the hospital uses the system, the more they get locked in to American Hospital Supply—a barrier to entry to other suppliers. In fact, in the fall of 1979, American Hospital Supply was sued by four local distributors claiming that the system created unfair advantage.

At about the same time, McKesson Corp. (formerly Foremost McKesson) also began installing customer terminals in pharmacies (19). The terminals there were used to capture not only order-entry information, but prescription data as well. The value added to the pharmacist was to cut inventory costs and to get rid of the nuisance of preparing insurance forms for prescriptions. McKesson uses the prescription data to automatically prepare the forms for the pharmacist. Productivity (as in the AHS case) comes from lower back-office costs and more productive salesmen. Information advantage stems from using sales analysis data to prepare insurance forms, to advise pharmacists on optimum floor-plan layouts to increase sales, and to provide manufacturers with sales data (free marketing research) to better plan production. Competitive advantage is again through competitive lock-out.

In both of the cases described above, it was the middle man, the wholesale distributor, who used customer terminals to advantage. In at least one instance that I am aware of, a medical manufacturer is in the process of putting terminals in customer offices directly, bypassing the middle man, and thereby threatening to cut him out of the equation altogether. (Is it possible that customer terminals in the future might actually be used to eliminate participants entirely in the delivery system?)

Banking. In the banking industry, ATMs, a form of customer terminal, were also introduced in the mid-1970s but took a decade to develop to their present ubiquity. Today, there are about 60,000 ATMs installed throughout the United States. Not only are ATMs now on almost every street corner, but banks have joined forces to share their machines with each other to cut costs even further. (An ATM transaction costs one-fourth of a paper check transaction.) The three largest joint ATM networks according to INPUT (a leading research and planning services firm) are: the PLUS system with 1000 banking installations and 3000 ATMs across the country; CIRRUS, with 900 installations and 5000 ATMs; and NATIONET, with 3500 installations and 6000 ATMs. The big attraction of ATMs to banks, of course, is that it enables them to bring the bank to the customer electronically rather than through expensive brick and mortar branches. As interstate banking legislation allows nationwide banking in the next several years, electronic banking will be the enabler, not bank branches. A typical branch office costs about $500,000 per year to operate compared to an ATM's approximate $15,000 per year. Branches were affordable when deposits were free. Now that all deposits draw interest, branches are too expensive a way to gather deposits compared to customer terminals. As a result, banks are closing branches (Bankers Trust sold 80 branches recently to a Canadian bank; Bank of America has announced the closing of over 100 branches) and installing ATMs. In the future, ATM customer terminals will be so dominant that banks without them will doubtless lose market share.

To match their consumer customer terminal strategy, banks have also begun putting terminals in corporate offices, tying them in to information data bases for a variety of applications. Among the most popular are the cash management services (also known as treasury management systems) offered by many of the larger banks. According to a recent survey, more than half of large U.S. companies either have an automated cash management system already or plan to buy one in the near future.

Cash management involves electronic delivery and movement of money. Customer terminals in their offices allow corporate Treasurer's to contact their bank to determine consolidated balances from all their banks, to transfer funds, and to do cash-flow forecasting and debt management. Because of the investment required, only the larger banks offer cash management services. Cost is a barrier to smaller banks. One of the leaders is Irving Trust (New York), which introduced a Cash Management service called CA$H-Register in 1978. The IBM PCs in customer offices connect to the bank's Cash Management systems. More than 175 users in 27 countries reportedly use the system for funds transfer, letters of credit, reimbursements, and broker/dealer clearance applications (20). Manufacturers Hanover's Interplex Cash Management system runs on a PC linked to the bank's computer and it provides company treasurers with their cash position based on account balances, investments, day's receipts, and checks presented for payment, and information about when and how to invest their funds. Barnett Banks in Florida offers a Cash Management system called Antrics which is targeted for smaller companies.

Other mainframe-based customer terminal systems aimed at the corporate market include such applications as letters of credit creation, mortgage origination, investment portfolio management, shareholder services, and commercial finance systems. An example of the latter is the client interface modules of Bank of Boston's commercial finance systems (CFS is asset-based financing). There are three automated interfaces to clients of that system: direct invoice processing is used to transmit account assignments and invoices; direct order processing allows direct input of orders and adds an up-to-date confirmation of orders for client inquiry; and client networking, which gives clients direct access to the bank's online data base via terminals in their offices, thereby vastly reducing the need for telephone inquiries.

Retailing. An offshoot of the customer terminal strategy is the growth of point-of-sale (POS) terminals, which are beginning to appear in retail operations almost everywhere. Many retail stores use POS terminals connected to banks or their own credit operations to allow customers to charge merchandise to company or national credit cards (e.g., Visa, Mastercard, and American Express). American Express travelers checks machines in airport terminals dispense travelers checks and even handle refunds for lost checks. Lift-ticketing machines at ski areas such as at Vail, Colorado allow skiers to purchase their day ticket from a credit card machine without even removing their skis. Machines in gas stations allow customers to charge gas directly to their credit cards, without a service attendant. First Texas Savings Association's Money Maker EFT Services, for example, features a customer-activated Diebold terminal located at the pump island which lets customers buy gas with credit cards, debit cards, or cash. Banks in general are going to POS terminals as part of their revolutionary electronic funds transfer systems (EFTS). These terminals are likely to be the successor to ATMs because, located in retail outlets, they are much less expensive than ATMs ($3000–$4000 vs. $18,000–$25,000). Although POS is still largely experimental in supermarkets, gas stations, and retail stores, as a customer terminal strategy it is rapidly gaining converts and should spread rapidly by the 1990s.

ELECTRONIC DELIVERY SYSTEMS

> IW 23—ELECTRONIC DELIVERY SYSTEMS
> EDS as a substitute for paper transactions and global expansion.

Going beyond the customer terminal strategy are electronic delivery systems (EDS) that combine terminals, networks, and computer systems to create new and innovative substitutes for traditional business operations. Electronic delivery systems offer great promise for competitive advantage. They have the potential for lower costs and elimination of geographic boundaries (even opening up worldwide markets), and customer service is improved by bringing the service closer to the customer. Three industry examples of electronic delivery systems are the airline reservation systems (ARS), the emergence of electronic data interchange (EDI), networks in various industries and the development of electronic funds transfer systems (EFTS) by banks.

Airline Reservations

One of the early and successful electronic delivery systems was the ARS of American and United Airlines. The Sabre and Apollo systems developed in the 1970s have been highly publicized success stories. These classify as customer terminal systems not because they are used by customers (passengers) but because they are used by competitive airlines and travel agents who found the capital barrier to entry (the systems cost over $250 million each) too great to develop their own system. As a result, American and United have 80% of the ARS market to themselves (21). It is well known that both Sabre and Apollo gain competitive advantage by giving priority listing to their own flights when travel agents request flight information over their terminals.[2] However, a more subtle competitive advantage comes from the marketing information gathered by the ARS from all travel data entered. Only American and United have total flight data. From it, they can set more competitive flight schedules, prices, and "specials" to beat out the competition. In fact, a new service offering, Frequent Flyer programs, were an outgrowth of this, utilizing ARS data to increase traffic at little or no cost using projected excess capacity. American and United used all three IW strategies in their EDSs. They gained productivity by selling their system to competitors (revenues to offset costs), they got information services through built-in marketing research data, and they gained competitive advantage through an innovative nationwide EDS. Other ARS leaders include Pan Am, Eastern, and TWA.

Electronic Data Interchange

Electronic data interchange (EDI) deals with intercompany communications. Most commercial companies handle numerous intercompany contracts, purchase orders, and invoices, which are the heart of EDI. Some large companies have installed their own private EDI networks, but most simply buy time on time-sharing networks to avoid the huge outlays of capital needed to install a private network. Thus third-party EDI networks have become attractive to such vendors as IBM, AT&T, Control Data, General Electric, SCM Corp., McDonnell-Douglas and Informatics General Corp. All have developed EDI network clearinghouse services to cash in on what experts predict will be a billion dollar business by 1990. The automobile manufacturers have also shown a strong commitment to EDI. All four major U.S. automakers (General Motors, Ford, American Motors, and Chrysler) have given notice to suppliers of their plans to fully implement EDI. This system had its beginnings in the transportation industry in the early 1970s, but has since extended to manufacturing, groceries, warehousing, brokerage, and government. Time-sharing vendors now market their data networks as intercompany purchasing links, processing purchase orders, shipping notices, invoices, and even payments wired from supplier to manufacturer to distributor to customer and back again, reducing processing time by several days. However, for EDI to enjoy the growth projected for it, more standards work needs to be done. The first standard was developed in 1975 by the Transportation Data Coordinating Committee (TDCC), an association formed by transportation companies to coordinate the move from paper documents to EDI. These standards were implemented in the railroad, shipping, and trucking industries. Later standards were developed for the grocery industry [the bar codes known as

---

[2]When the Justice department began investigating "bias" in the system, that is, favoring their own flight schedules on the "primary" screen, a bypass to a second screen (still favoring their own schedules) was put in the system.

Industries Served	EDI Network
Grocery, transportation, electronic, automotive, warehousing	McDonnell Douglas EDINet
Office products, auto, grocery	GE Information Services (GEISCO)
Transportation	Transettlements (Atlanta, GA)
Grocery, drugs, auto, medical, service merchandise	Information General Corp. (Los Angeles, CA)
Industrial supply distribution	Control Data (Greenwich, CT)
Steel, auto, electronics	AT&T Information Services Net1000

Figure 5.5. Data compiled from Computer Decisions, July, 1985

the Uniform Commercial Standard (UCS) and a warehouse information network standard (WINS)] (22). However, more work still needs to be done to establish cross-industry standards and avoid incompatible EDI networks between industries; otherwise, crossing from one network to another could still be a major problem.[3]

Nevertheless, EDI represents an innovative electronic delivery service that is being used by more and more companies seeking to speed up business transactions between suppliers, manufacturers, distributors, and customers. Some EDI nets currently in place are shown in Figure 5.5.

Electronic Funds Transfer

Electronic funds transfer systems (EFTS) in banking also go back to the late 1960s when there was much talk in the industry of the "checkless" society. In those days, businesses were preaching the demise of the use of checks in favor of totally electronic banking. As the unlikelihood of this prophesy emerged, talk shifted to a "less checks" society. Even this didn't happen, as check usage continued to grow. In 1984, over 40 billion checks were written by 88% of all Americans who have checking accounts. Nonetheless, automation of check processing did take place with the introduction of magnetic ink character recognition (MICR) in the late 1960s which at least permitted the electronic processing of these billions of checks by electronic sorting machines that could read the MICR information off the checks and into mainframe computers for automatic processing. Despite the number of checks written, however, some 90% of all dollar movements in the United States take place electronically through electronic funds transfers between banks. These domestic transfers go either via the Federal Reserve System or directly between banks over the Bank Wire system (a consortium of several hundred major banks who are members of Bank Wire). In the 1970s, many major banks began to automate their wire

[3]The American National Standards Institute (ANSI) and others have developed one such standard, known as ANSI X.12, but more work is needed.

(money) transfer operations, primarily on minicomputer-based systems that automatically interfaced with the Federal and Bank Wire systems, the TWX and telex networks, and SWIFT (the International funds transfer network).

In the early 1980s, EFTS was extended by adding customer terminals in corporate offices to allow corporate treasurers direct access to bank balance information and to arrange to transfer funds to other financial institutions or to invest funds temporarily in liquid (but earning) money market investments. Banks rushed to get into cash management services, adding functionality to create product differentiation that would wed the customer to their services and not the competitors'. On the consumer side, electronic delivery took the form of teller and administrative terminals in bank branches, ATMs, POS terminals, and home banking terminals outside branches, extending EFTS to people where they work, shop, and live. In some cases, consortiums have been formed to provide stronger network services. An example is the more than 440 financial institutions (banks, savings and loan associations, and credit unions) in Wisconsin and Michigan that banded together to provide a statewide financial network called TYME (Take Your Money Everywhere) that supports ATMs for deposits and cash withdrawals and POS terminals used to buy merchandise. Members compete to place machines in stores or other locations. The member who succeeds in winning a store placement is paid a fee by other TYME members for each transaction that goes over his terminal. To date, terminals have been installed in auto dealerships, stereo shops, clothing stores, supermarkets, bowling alleys, and oil companies (23).

Another consortium is the New York Cash Exchange (NYCE), a network of financial institutions originally formed by eight New York City banks to allow one another's debit card holders to have access to any member bank's machines. NYCE has not only broadened the ATM market for their customer base, but has proven to be a powerful tool in reducing Citibank's competitive advantage in electronic banking. At this writing, the network was up to 74 member institutions with 1450 machines and 5.3 million cardholders in 7 states. Member banks say that the primary benefit has been to offer customers broad access to ATMs that would not be possible if they operated independently (24).

Home banking is another EDS which is still trying to get out of the starting block, despite a number of pilot tests conducted around the country. Home banking provides a customer with account information, automatic bill payment, investment profiles, and other banking services through PCs or special-purpose terminals linked to a bank. According to one source, about 50,000 U.S. households are now using home banking services. Citicorp and Chemical Bank, for example, have launched large-scale home banking sales campaigns. Dozens of other bank have pilot programs in operation. But customers have been slow to respond. Home banking is a chicken-and-egg problem. Customers will not subscribe to video banking until costs come down, and banks will not offer low-cost services until a mass market is there to support them. In this author's opinion, a mass market is not likely to be there until a nationwide videotex service is available (IBM, CBS, and Sears have announced a joint venture to install such a network.) Home banking by itself will probably not fly, but as a part of a bigger service like videotex, it just could take off.

As barriers to nationwide banking drop in the years ahead, EFTSs will enable interstate banking to succeed, not brick and mortar banking. Terminals, networks, and electronic money (debit and credit cards) will blanket the country, permitting low-cost self-service banking to be offered by the nation's major banks on a countrywide scale.

MARKETING SUPPORT

Earlier it was suggested that new alliances are needed to promote competitive support systems; alliances of IW planners with the marketing side of the house. Such alliances can not only result in customer support systems, they also promote the development of marketing support systems. These are internal systems that help with product planning, marketing analysis, customer analysis, competitive intelligence, sales call planning, research and development, production scheduling, distribution support—any and all areas dealing with marketing and sales activities. Here are some examples in the areas of sales support, customer services, and distribution systems.

Computer-Aided Sales

> **IW 24—COMPUTER-AIDED SALES**
> Systems that provide computer support to marketing and sales.

Manufacturing has CIM (computer-integrated manufacturing), engineers use CAE (computer-aided engineering), and sales people have CAS (computer-aided sales). Three forms of CAS for sales support are telemarketing, transactional terminals, and computer video screens.

Telemarketing. Telemarketing, or "Electronic" marketing, permits potential customers to view merchandise on a video screen, do comparison shopping, and order merchandise directly from the home. Retailers can put up their "electronic" mail-order catalogs on the home TV and allow customers to shop from home. Real estate agencies can show homes for sale, complete with interior layouts, and arrange home showings from customer selections. Ticket agencies can preview shows and plays (with critic reviews) and display the theatre seating layout, showing seats available, which the customer can order and charge to his credit card. Herewith are some examples of telemarketing services:

- Comp-U-Card International, Inc. provides CITI$HOPPER, which it claims is the nation's largest electronic shopping service. Its 1 million members choose from a data base of some 60,000 brand-name products. Members call in and get price quotes and can order merchandise, if desired. Because of the volume it generates, CITI$HOPPER gets vendor discounts which it passes on to members (after an appropriate commission). They own no inventory, carry no overhead, and have no salespeople. All they have is an information data base to bring buyers and sellers together.
- The Source Telecomputing Corp. (McLean, Virginia) offers a broad range of teleshopping services through its COMP-U-STORE service, which boasts 60,000 products available to electronic shoppers.
- Electronicstore Services, Inc. (Chicago, Illinois) has ELECTRONI-STORE for companies to show products on a telemarketing system. ELECTRONISTORE uses a free-standing or build-in kiosk with a video screen for product display and demos; a color monitor touch screen is used to display product information. The "shopper" can move through product categories and access product displays by touching control points on the screen. The shopper can place an order, obtain the shipping date, and get a printed receipt—all without a salesperson (25).
- An electronic grocery service in California allows shoppers to order groceries by phone from a computer listing. A terminal operator enters the order in the computer, arranges delivery, and electronically charges the customer's account.
- Montgomery Ward has moved away from its walk-in catalog selling to telemarketing, replacing personnel in retail outlets with telephone operators, online data bases, and communications to deliver catalog information to customers.

Transactional Terminals. Another computer-aided sales support strategy is the use of "Transactional" terminals. A recent *Newsweek* article described how transactional terminals (computer screens that help close a sale) are allowing mass retailers to plug in to technology to sell everything from shoes to cars (26). Here are examples: *Automobiles, Paint, Book.*

- *Automobiles.* General Motor's Buick division put PCs in dealer showrooms to assist salesmen with sales. Through a system called EPIC (Electronic Public Information Center), salesmen can get answers to customer questions on automobile models, colors, options, prices, and financing terms. They can also access (through communications modems) a car locator system to find the nearest dealership that has the particular model the customer wants. And, by accessing Compuserve, can get comparison prices on competing makes and models of cars (e.g., compare Buick to Chrysler for price, fuel economy, features, etc.).

- *Paint*. Benjamin Moore uses a computer to measure the light frequencies of a color sample and concocts a formula for the dealer to mix to match it exactly. Another system called the Visual Color System (VCS) lets a customer punch in various combinations of color mixes and shows what the resulting shade would look like by spinning a "color wheel" that simulates the color combinations the customer punched in. This allows an endless variety of colors, including some never before seen by man.

- *Books*. "The Bookseller's Assistant" is a touch-screen system developed by the Delmar Group (San Diego). Placed in bookstores, the system asks customers which authors, movies, or TV shows they like, correlates that information with a data base of more than 10,000 book titles and prints out a list of recommended books. Delmar is working on similar systems for video and record stores, car dealers, and general merchandisers (27).

By one estimate, there could be 50,000 transactional terminals in the retail marketplace by 1990 selling just about anything: cars, clothes, paint, shoes, eyeglasses, cosmetics—anything that speeds up creative selection from a large number of options.

Computer Video Systems. A unique computer-aided sales tool is the ingenious union of computers and video technology known as "computer video systems," which enable clients and customers to see how they will look in new clothes, restyled cosmetics, a reshaped nose, or a new head of hair—before they plunk their money down. Some examples include:

- *Clothing*. L. S. Ayers department stores use something called the "Magic Mirror." A customer trying on clothes sees a reflection of her face in a full length Magic Mirror. The rest of her body is projected onto the mirror by a computer that shapes a figure similar to her own on which are projected outfits that the customer would like to see "on herself." Only when the customer finds something she really likes does she actually try it on, dramatically speeding up the selection process. Ayres put an entire spring collection on the system at three stores and reported a 700% sales increase in 1 week (28).

- *Cosmetic Surgery*. Using the same technique, doctors can show a patient how they would look with a reshaped nose or eyes, or sans wrinkles, to help the patient decide if they want to undergo cosmetic surgery. One such doctor is Dr. Barry Weintraub of Beverly Hills who uses the computer video system to "talk to his patients through pictures" (29).

- *Hairpieces.* Candidates for hairpieces make use of a similar computer video system. The hair stylist electronically fills in bald spots on the video image of the client's head while the customer decides how he would like his hair parted or where his hairline should begin.

PC-Based Sales Support. Personal computers are also used in other ways to support sales efforts. First Boston Corp.'s Shelternet places PCs in realtor's offices which are tied to a data base of mortgage financing terms and conditions offered by a number of subscribing banks. With the prospective home buyer in the realtor's office, the broker brings up on the terminal a list of mortgage rates and terms and a prequalification program shows the buyer what he/she can afford. If the buyer is ready to proceed, why not take the mortgage application right on the broker's terminal? Shelternet not only helps the broker close the sale, but turnaround time in getting a mortgage becomes days instead of weeks.

Coopers & Lybrand has developed an expert system that "sells" insurance policies. The system acts as an underwriter—designing, authorizing, and issuing personalized policies to corporate insurance clients like a vending machine (31). Expert Systems are another major technological entrepreneurial activity that should grow 10-fold in the next decade.

Computerized sales support can sometimes be aided by focusing on only a small facet of competitive advantage. In a recent issue of *MIS Quarterly,* authors Breath and Ives cited no less than 17 examples of just one subset of marketing support, product pricing. The cases cited ranged from Delta's use of data obtained from the Air Traffic Publishing company to monitor fares so as to be able to respond quickly to competitor actions; to Arco's use of Western Union's Easylink to quickly communicate price changes to thousands of destinations; to a PC-based program used by the Red River Construction company in Texas to develop last-minute bids (to increase the chance of being the lowest bidder) (32).

Laptap computers are also growing as a sales tool. Because of their portability and low price, salesmen can easily carry them around on sales calls. Allegheny Beverage, for example, provides their salesmen with Hewlett Packard portable computers so that instant answers to questions on customer account status, inventory, and pricing can be obtained right in the customer's office through direct connection to Allegheny's central processor over a private data network. When a customer decides on an order, the sales representative can reserve the item, file and transmit the order, and promise delivery within days (something their competitors can't yet match) (33).

New PC applications for marketing support are sprouting every day, as systems professionals, working with marketing and sales people, find new ways to support them indirectly (sales-call tracking, project lists, cross-selling), and directly [through computer-aided sales (CAS) tools].

Customer Services

One of the most potent competitive weapons any company has is good customer service and information is often the key to good service. Here are some examples of technology-aided customer service ideas. The Customer Service Center, trained computer operations online to company data bases, has been adopted by hundreds of companies as an improved technology-aided method of serving customer inquiries and problems. These online terminals give the customer a single "hot-line" telephone number to call to resolve problems. At Bank of Boston, it was found that 87% of customer calls were simple inquiries that could be handled by a single operator with online access to a half-dozen consumer application data files. Another 10% were problems that required research and callback (still the same contact person, however), and only 3% were complaints or problems that had to be referred elsewhere for resolution.

Lechmere in Woburn, Massachusetts installed an IBM Series/1 in its catalog showroom stores to reduce paperwork and speed customer checkout. The system, called Laser, consists of 32 sales stations that enable store clerks to tell customers whether the items desired are in stock, sends a pick order to the storeroom, and processes orders so that they arrive at the pickup counter before the customer gets there (34). Bloomingdale's in New York speeds checkout times using IBM PC XTs with touch screens at the checkout counter. The clerk goes through a series of screens, touching the appropriate items indicating class of goods sold, vendor, and so on. The system reduced the number of keystrokes needed to make a sale from 89 to 12, speeding up customer checkout time from 6 to 1 minute (35).

Another form of in-house customer service terminal is the use of PCs to open accounts, perform account maintenance (such as name and address changes), or process applications. Several leading banks, for instance, now advertise 15-minute credit approval of consumer loan applications by phone. This is made possible by customers entering application information by phone on a PC with a built-in credit-scoring algorithm which automatically approves (or rejects) 90% of the loan applications on the basis of the data supplied, plus an online connection to a local credit bureau.

Another example is an IBM PC-based service offered by Infoware Corp. (Nashville, Tennessee). The customer and the representative sit at the terminal and select from options that include information on financing a child's college education, installment loan alternatives, available loan amortization schedules, and a variety of financial calculations such as CD early withdrawal penalties, IRA growth analysis, and investment analyses (36).

Externally, interactive video systems that provide information about products or respond to customer questions are another customer service aid. The Fidelity Group, a mutual fund company in Boston, for instance, provides touch screen terminals in their offices and at Logan airport, which give information on alternative financial programs to customers and prospects. Banks like Bank of America and Banc One (Columbus, Ohio) have interactive video terminals installed in local branch offices to provide information on interest rates, office hours, and branch locations.

Distribution Systems

Getting the product to market better and faster than the competition through technology is another marketing support strategy; consider these examples. The grinding wheels division of Norton Co. (Worcester, Massachusetts), strengthened its competitive position by giving its distributors terminals so that they could enter orders electronically and get instant responses to inquiries about the status of orders, pricing, and catalog items. As a result, when customers call, distributors are able to promise a delivery date over the phone, a process that formerly took days (37). It is not coincidental that Richard B. Kennedy, the man in charge, is a former IBMer who understands technology's competitive value.

Dr. Michael Hammer, management consultant, offers another example. Consider production scheduling, which is often based on out-of-date market research data and other misinformation. Compare this to a system that is based on data from POS terminals in retail outlets and from satellites indicating the location of trucks and freight cars in transit. With such a system, a company could optimize decisions on realtime consumption patterns and direct online control of production and realtime management of distribution based on store-level stocks and the location of delivery trucks on any given day (38).

Federal Express's overnight delivery service utilizes a data base system called COSMOS to track all letters and parcels in its system. Using barcode scanners and 3270 terminals, Fedex employees check the air-bills of packages against COSMOS several times during their travels, thus allowing the employees to know exactly where a package is at all times. Delivery vans, equipped with mobile data terminal radios for sending and receiving data, can be detoured to make pickups while on the road, as orders come in, thus generating a 99% overnight delivery rate (39).

A unique example of electronic distribution is the distribution and use of *debit* cards as a substitute for money. Debit cards serve as substitutes for checks or cash. The same card that works in an ATM can be used to buy merchandise in stores through POS terminals. In a debit-card transaction, the salesperson rings up the sale and inserts the customer's debit card in a POS terminal, the customer punches in his/her PIN (personal identification number) onto a keypad, and the funds are immediately transferred from the customer's account to the store's account at the participating bank. A growing number of banks have debit card programs. Florida's Honor System, as an example, is a debit card system owned by nine major Florida banks. The system has 9.2 million card holders and handles over a million transactions a year over 2100 ATMs and 1770 debit terminals in retail outlets throughout the state (40).

But debit cards are not limited to banks. Vons Grocery, one of California's leading supermarket chains, signed up virtually every financial institution in Bakersfield, California to participate in a POS test conducted by the store. Vons issues its own debit cards and also accepts debit cards for any bank in town (41).

Sears Roebuck has one of the largest debit card systems in the country, the Sears Discover card. Introduced in mid-1985 in test markets, Sears unleashed a nationwide campaign to gain acceptance of its debit/credit card early in January 1986 by direct mailing 25 million cards to its Sears retail credit card holders. They also signed up national companies like American Airlines, Holiday Inns, Budget Rent-A-Car, and Hospital Corp. of America to extend to Discover cardholders discounts of 20–50% (42). Sears issues the card through the Sears-owned Greenwood Trust Co. of Delaware. Because it is a bank-issued card, the retailer is in a position to negotiate access to automated tellers across the country—all without having to install a single ATM of its own. Sears has made it clear that it intends its Discover card to win out over all other credit cards in customers' hands. In fact, the company claims that the card will do so much that consumers will have little need for credit cards issued by banks.

Because debit cards are expected to become a major substitute for credit cards, checks, and cash in the future, the nation's top credit card firms, Mastercard and Visa, have shown interest in acquiring the nation's two prominent debit card networks. Cirrus and Plus (43). Such a linkage would enable debit cardholders to use their cards to buy merchandise all over the country, which would be the equivalent of having a nationwide bank handling your checking account.

A variation on electronic money is the "smart card." Originally introduced in France, the smart card is slowly finding its way into the United States. The smart card looks like a debit or credit card, but is embedded with a microchip that can store monetary value in the card. Both Mastercard and Visa have introduced smart-card tests in various states in the first significant application of smart-card use in the United States. Unlike a debit card, which has to electronically access a bank to transfer funds, the smart card needs no such access. The purchase is simply deducted from the credit line imbedded in the card. Smart-card costs are high, however, so it will probably be some time before real inroads are made for this new and innovative EDS.

Leading Information Age companies are aiming their IW at external targets—the competition—rather than on internal operations, and they are discovering that the payoff can be enormous. Whether it is through customer support systems, customer terminals, electronic delivery, marketing support, or any other of dozens of competitive strategies, today's IW planners are pulling technology out of the back shop and unleashing it as a competitive force. They are winning with technology. Companies with the cutting edge of information technology often have the competitive edge as well.

References

1. F. Warren McFarlan and James L. McKenney, *Corporate Information Systems Management: The Issues Facing Senior Executives*, Richard D. Irwin, Homewood, IL, 1983.
2. Tom Peters and Nancy Austin, *A Passion for Excellence*, Random House, New York, 1985.
3. Peter F. Drucker, *Innovation and Entrepreneurship: Practice & Principles*, Harper & Row, New York, 1985.
4. Gifford Pinchot, III, *Intrapreneuring*, Harper & Row, New York, 1985 p. 43.
5. Ibid., p. 101.
6. Donald K. Clifford, Jr. and Richard Cavanagh, *The Winning Performance: How America's High-Growth Midsize Companies Succeed*, Bantam Books, New York, 1986, p. 42.
7. "A Conversation with Dr. Michael Hammer," *SPECTRUM*, Vol. 2, No. 6—A publication of the Society for Information Management, Dec. 1985.
8. Clifford and Cavanagh, p. 52.
9. Richard Foster, *Innovation*, Summit Books, New York, 1986, p. 140.
10. Michael E. Porter, *Competive Strategy*, The Free Press, New York, 1980, p. 4.
11. Joel P. Friedman, "Information Technology, The Path to Competitive Advantage," *The Magazine of Bank Administration*, Jan. 1986.
12. Charles Wiseman, *Strategy & Computers: Information Systems as Competitive Weapons*, Dow Jones–Irwin, Homewood, IL, 1985, Ch. 3.
13. *Business Week*, 10/14/85, p. 111.
14. Clifford and Cavanagh, p. 48.
15. *Technology in Banking: Path to Competitive Advantage*, Salomon Bros., New York 1985, p. 20.
16. *The Boston Globe*, 10/29/85.
17. Drucker, *Innovation & Entrepreneurship*, 1985.
18. *Fortune*, 7/26/82, pp. 56–61.
19. *Business Week*, 12/7/81, pp. 116–120.
20. *Nation's Business*, Sept. 1985, p. 48.
21. *American Banker*, 9/18/85, p. 18.
22. *Technology in Banking*, Salomon Bros., 1985.
23. *Nation's Business*, Sept. 1985, p. 48.
24. *American Banker*, 10/30/85, p. 10.
25. Wiseman, p. 6.
26. *MIS Week*, 12/18/85, p. 29.
27. Idem.
28. *The New York Times*, 10/1/85.
29. *American Banker*, 2/19/86, p. 8.

30. *Nation's Business*, Sept. 1985, p. 50.
31. *Infosources 1986*, Annual directory of the IIA, Washington, D.C., 1986.
32. John Diebold, "Taking Stock of the Information Age," *Management Review*, Sept. 1985, p. 20.
33. *Newsweek*, 9/23/85, p. 46.
34. *Nation's Business*, Mar. 1986, p. 61.
35. *Newsweek*, 9/23/85, p. 46.
36. *Nation's Business*, Mar. 1986, p. 62.
37. *Time*, 2/10/86, p. 76.
38. Idem.
39. *Nation's Business*, Mar. 1986, p. 62.
40. Cynthia Mathis Breath and Blake Ives, "Computer Information Systems in Support of Pricing," *MIS Quarterly*, Mar. 1986, p. 85.
41. *Nation's Business*, July 1986, p. 67.
42. *Computerworld*, 1/20/86, p. 14.
43. *Idem*.
44. As reported in *Bank Automation Newsletter*, Warren Gorham & Lamont, Boston, Aug. 1985.
45. *Business Week*, 10/14/85, p. 114.
46. "A Conversation with Dr. Michael Hammer," *SPECTRUM*, Dec. 1985.
47. *Information Week*, 5/26/86, p. 48.
48. *The New York Times*, 10/1/85.
49. *American Banker*, 1/8/86, p. 1.
50. *American Banker*, 2/5/86, p. 9.
51. *American Banker*, 1/10/86.

6

INFORMATION SERVICES

Knowledge is power:
Information is knowledge:
Hence, information is power.

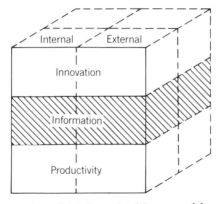

Figure 6.1. Information Weapon model.

In the Information Era, those who possess "information power" may well hold the ultimate information weapon. Throughout the evolution of man, the amount of information available has grown exponentially. Strassmann (1) observed how the information medium has changed over time. He noted that the Hunting Society used speech as the means of communication. The Agricultural Society moved to writing as a way to record information (such as land ownership). The Industrial Society graduated to printing to reach more people and to mass-market products (e.g., advertising). And now, the Information Society uses "electronic" communications to reach vast markets with a staggering amount of information.

Electronic communications makes information and information services instantly available everywhere. The telegraph moved text messages across the country; the telephone followed with voice; electronic workstations that combine voice and data now do both.

The competitive potential of electronic information is unlimited. The availability of fast, cheap, broadband transmission anywhere is opening up worldwide markets for information services never before possible, while at the same time customizing information on a mass scale; that is, individuals can access vast databases of information and selectively pull together only the information needed to provide a customized response on a person-to-person basis. The Information Era has, in fact, spawned many new businesses whose business *is* information (e.g., information brokers). To others, electronics has dramatically impacted the way they do business (e.g., electronic publishing). And even companies that are not in the information business per se can benefit from the revolution. For example, they can add information to products and services to make them easier to use or to enhance their usability. In other words, they can use information to make what they have better (innovation through information), or they can use process information to improve quality control (productivity through information). Thus information can support both a product differentiation and a cost leadership strategy.

In this chapter we examine opportunities for competitive advantage through new information services. The focus here is on the provision of *information* itself rather than on the systems or technology that underlie it.

INTERNAL INFORMATION SERVICES

MANAGEMENT SUPPORT SYSTEMS

> IW 25—MANAGEMENT SUPPORT SYSTEMS
> Three classes of MSS leverage managerial
> decisionmaking.

The customer support systems (CSS) discussed in Chapter 5 used technological innovation as a competitive strategy. Management support systems (MSS) focus on information services for competitive advantage. Information services can be both internal and external. Internally, information is provided to management (and others). Externally, information is provided to customers. In both cases, the aim is to assist managers in planning (such as new competitive offerings), decisionmaking (implementing strategic decisions), and control (running the business efficiently). Let's first consider internal MSSs.

The focus of management support systems is the opposite of operating support systems, as shown in Figure 6.2. An OSS collects a great deal of detailed information covering a short period of time (e.g., a list of trans-

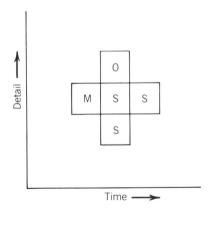

OSS Characteristics	MSS Characteristics
Efficiency	Effectiveness
Record-keeping	Management information
Standard reports	Flexible reports
File-based	Data-based
Technical domain	User involvement
Centralized	Decentralized

Figure 6.2. OSS versus MSS.

actions on a given date). An MSS tracks selected data over a long period of time (historically, e.g., monthly sales volumes over the past 5 years). An MSS is interested in trend information, exception reporting, warning indicators—in other words, information, not just data. The differences can be seen by reviewing the systems characteristics of each as listed in Figure 6.2.

It is important to understand these differences because an MSS is built in a much different manner than an OSS—by people trained in a different discipline. Whereas an OSS is designed and developed over a long period of time, an MSS is built without traditional systems specifications in a very short period of time. An OSS is built with third-generation languages (e.g., COBOL); an MSS uses fourth-generation languages (4GL). The MSSs are reportless systems; that is, the focus is on building a flexible data base, not reports. The user generates his/her own reports as needed. They are developed as "prototype" systems, with several iterations likely. They are inquiry/analysis systems, not transaction systems. They use data-base technology, not files. They take the form of Information Centers, are graphics-oriented, and employ PCs.

These prototype systems have the virtue of fast development (weeks, not years), which managers like, they are flexible and can be changed easily, and they fit the less structured environment of the management world. In *A Passion for Excellence,* Peters and Austin suggest two alternate paths of innovation:

Path One, the "home run" approach, typically involves lots of people, time and money. Often the product gets to market only after more agile outfits have come out with competing wares. Path Two is the "Wee Willie Keeler" approach, named after a Hall of Fame baseball player who hit few home runs but plenty of singles. On Path Two, small teams work within modest budgets and narrow time frames. Taking Path Two can cut the time it takes to complete the development cycle by 50% or more.(2)

The Super System strategy discussed in Chapter 5 is representative of the "home run" approach, whereas a Prototyping strategy is the "Wee Willie Keeler" approach. Small, rather than large, scale can be achieved with a small group building prototype systems. Prototypes on PCs can often be an even faster prototyping strategy.

When is a prototype MSS appropriate? Whenever traditional development will take too long; when a management system can be built independently of an operating system; when working in an unstructured environment; when a flexible reporting system is needed; or when use is expected to be infrequent. A prototype MSS is best built by one builder for one user using a 4GL and data-base technology. Fourth-generation languages include query languages (QBE, EZ-Trieve), report writers (Focus, Ramis), graphics generators (Sas-graph, Tell-a-graph), applications generators (Focus, Mark V, Adds On-Line), and decision support models (Express, Strategem, Lotus 1-2-3).

The MSS is also a specialized information center (IC) built for a specific individual or individuals. It can be accessed by dumb terminal or personal computer, or downloaded to a local minicomputer operated by trained IC specialists responding to specific management requests for information.

Types of Management Support Systems

I classify management support systems into three types: executive information systems (EIS), management information systems (MIS), and decision support systems (DSS). My definitions are as follows:

- An EIS is a system that is custom-built for an individual manager (or small group of managers). The data elements are carefully preselected to fit a specific manager's information needs and responsibilities. It often contains historical data patterns over time.
- One CIO asked his boss: "What are the 10 things you would want to see first when you get back from a 3-week Caribbean vacation?" The CIO took his boss's list and gave him a terminal with a menu of these 10 choices. By pushing a single button, the executive could get a summary of the information needed. Each menu could be blown out with further detail, if desired. Eventually, the system grew to 150 screens

of information as the executive was slowly weaned on the value of his EIS.

- An MIS is a general-purpose information system meant to be accessed by a large number of people. An MIS generally takes the form of an IC, residing on a mainframe host or departmental mini. It is an inquiry and analysis system. Selected data are sometimes extracted from a number of "feeder" systems and consolidated to create a customized MIS but, more often, files are simply dumped (or copied) to a non-production data base and users access the data using a 4GL to format, consolidate, and massage the data into reports as desired. One way MISs are used is to provide profitability data on individual SBUs so that resources can be properly allocated to the high contribution SBUs. The First National Bank of Atlanta, for example, spent $10 million to develop a state-of-the-art MIS that produces income statements and balance sheets for its SBUs that fully allocate capital overhead to SBUs for profitability analysis and performance tracking. Relatively few companies have the edge of knowing their true profitability so that they can shift competitively as needed.

  Customer relationship systems (CRS) are another example of MISs. Companies that have good CRSs have global information on markets and customers that gives them a competitive edge over those who do not (a case of an MSS providing competitive advantage). Citicorp, for instance, carries global data on customers, allowing officers to not only access customer relationship data, but also to track customer needs. An overseas Citicorp officer, for example, can access the system to find a customer looking for a particular foreign exchange transaction that he is trying to sell. Pru-Bache installed an MIS minicomputer in each branch hooked to PCs at each broker's desk. Brokers can access quotation services, client information, and company data bases. They also have two financial planning systems to help brokers in developing specific investment plans and financial strategies for clients. New information services being added include E-mail, a portfolio valuator, tax analysis, "what if" analysis, and calendering (3).

- A DSS is a special-purpose system developed to accomplish a specific task. It is often a statistical, or analytic, modeling system designed to aid managers in analyzing alternate decision possibilities. In the past, these were usually mainframe or minicomputer-based systems such as Express, Strategem, and System W. Today, PC-based DSS packages are appearing. An example is "Rules of Thumb" from Technology Strategy, Inc. (Cambridge, Massachusetts). This PC package draws on the experience and judgment of users to establish parameters relative to a problem to be solved and then uses Monte Carlo simulation to determine the probability of results. It supplies many of the attributes of a linear program, but with a fraction of the effort.

All three systems (EIS, MIS, DSS) fit under the general umbrella of management support systems. Sometimes an MSS actually incorporates all three: customized, general, and decision support information. Such a system is the Asset and Liability management system in place at Bankers Trust in New York. Bankers Trust's trading room integrates security trading (funding and managing the bank's liquidity position) and foreign exchange sales and purchases, aided by financial data bases that hook up their trades to global money market conditions. Salomon Bros., the investment banking firm, estimates that, in a good year, up to 30% of Banker's Trust income before taxes comes from trading, funding, and asset and liability management supported by this MSS (4).

Finally, the three types of management support systems described can reside on a corporate mainframe, a departmental minicomputer, or a personal microcomputer:

- *Mainframe MSS.* Many companies have off-loaded production data bases to a dedicated mainframe IC, which can be accessed by terminals using high-level report extractor languages. Managers often (usually?) do not access these directly, but go through a specially trained group of IC specialists to get the information needed. A number of companies are now merging outside and inside data bases to combine general competitive data (obtained from outside sources or your own sales force) with internal customer information.
- *Mini MSS.* These could be departmental IC that function much like the previous example, or decision support models customized to solve specific management problems. One company, for example, built itself a strategic model that creates financial data on all of their SBUs and their products and services to enable continuing product profitability and unit performance analysis.
- *Micro MSS.* The ubiquitous "spreadsheet" is probably the best and widest used example of a MSS on a micro. Most MSSs today, in fact, run on minis or micros. The big mainframe computers are used more to hold large data bases, which are downloaded to minis and micros. Information services on micros range from information on how to use a micro product or service ("help" screens), to software that facilitates information retrieval (such as "key word" searchers), to "touch" screens for browsing information data bases without having to use a keyboard. Fidelity Investments in Boston, for example, carries information about their products, retirement funds, and rates on touch terminals in their offices and at Logan airport for passing customers.

As the matrix in Figure 6.3 illustrates, the planner thus has nine different options for developing internal MSS information services.

Management information takes many forms: soft (verbal) and hard data,

Type	Function	Mainframe	Mini	Micro
EIS	Management aid	Performance reporting	Ad hoc reports	Personal files
MIS	Inquiry and analysis	Corporate Information center	Departmental information center	Access Corporate DB
DSS	Decision support	Strategic planning	Analytic modeling	Spreadsheets

Figure 6.3. MSS information services

manual data, and internal and external data. Thus far I have focused only on developing information services from internal data. External data are also an important source of management information. External data deal with industry and competitive information and market, economic, and political information that is usually not available in-house. Internal data deal with performance and control; external data are strategic, dealing with competition and survival in the marketplace. Both are needed to make sound decisions.

The traditional way executives get external data is through topical reading and listening. They sort through the mountain of newsletters, reports, newspapers, and magazines that they receive. They listen to news broadcasts. And they talk to people. There is an overload of information available, and the executive has to spend a great deal of time sorting and sifting through it all to find what is really needed and important to business decisions. It is said that "all good things come to he who waits." In the Information Era, the competitive edge often depends on having the most up-to-the-minute information first (e.g., foreign exchange or commodity trading). An information service that helps managers get outside information in a timely and condensed form is information brokering.

INFORMATION BROKERING /. 2

> **IW 26—INFORMATION BROKERING**
> Tapping into external databases to expand the information resource.

Information brokers are people who gather information for others as a professional business. They sort out information available on a mass scale and deliver it on a personalized basis. They do this by accessing information databases to selectively provide information on specific subjects of interest to a specific person or persons. In effect, they take electronic "junk" mail and convert it into abstracted and customized information of value to the recipient, saving hours, even days of valuable executive time.

There are two types of information brokers: in-house and professional.

In-House Brokers

In-house information brokers often spring from library automation. By putting corporate libraries online to outside database services, the walls of the library open to a window on the world. According to one source, there are over 10,000 commercially available online information databases in the United States today and there are many comprehensive *database directories* to help find them. Here are three popular examples from *Information Sources 1986* (5):

- The *Directory of Online Databases,* produced by Cuadra Assoc., Inc. (Santa Monica, California), is available on the Westlaw online information service, among others. The directory describes more than 2700 databases of all types that are available through one or more of the hundreds of online services located in both the United States and abroad.

- The *Database of Databases,* available on the Dialog information service contains records on 2500 publicly available databases.

- *Knowledge Industry Publications Database* (produced jointly with the American Society for Information Science) on BRS (Bibliographic Retrieval Services) contains over 2000 records describing online databases available in North America.

Of the hundreds of *online services,* some provide access to only a single database, whereas others access hundreds. One of the best known, *Dialog,* from Dialog Info Services, Palo Alto, California, a subsidiary of Lockheed Corp., operates the world's largest information retrieval service, providing access to over 225 databases that collectively cover over 100,000 publications in all major subjects. Typical uses are for research, new product development, planning, and competitive analysis.

Information brokers also have a variety of tools to help them perform their function. Here are some examples:

- *Information Sources 1986* is an annual directory of the Information Industry Association (Washington, D. C.), a trade group. This comprehensive reference work lists over 400 ITA members who are all information creators or providers of one kind or another. The directory alphabetically lists all members and their services, products, publications, and resources and contains a subject and geographic index. Fig-

Subject	Coverage
Awareness services	DB Publishing, information brokerage and retailing, newsletters, looseleaf services
Business information	Acquisitions, finance, industry, international, management, investments
Computer industry	Equipment, industry data
Corporate information	Business data, corporate planning
Corporate planning	Consulting, corporate and management information, strategic planning
DB Distributors	Companies supplying DBs, their own or those prepared by others
DB Information	Companies with products that provide information about DBs
DB Producers	Companies creating DBs, for themselves or under contract to DB distributors
Demographic information	Demographic data, market research, statistics
Direct mail	Mailing lists, advertising, marketing
Document delivery services	Companies that specialize in information brokerage or information search and retrieval reporting
Electronic publishing	DB Publishing, electronic news services
Forecasting services	Financial, economic
Government information	Legislative, regulatory, procurement, statistics, international
Index publishing	Indexes, DB publishing, electronic publishing
Information brokerage	Information brokers, awareness services, document delivery, research, search and retrieval
Information industry	DB Directory services
Information management	Information DBs, industry information, consulting
Information retailing	Information sellers, awareness, document delivery, search and retrieval
International	Country services data, import–export, industry
Management information	Management data, business, finance, education
Marketing research	Marketing, advertising, demographics, research services
Marketing	Sales, advertising, mail, market research, public relations, telemarketing
Micropublishing	Micrographic services
New venture planning	Competitive planning, product development, venture capital
Product development	New ventures, venture capital
Publishing	Databases, directories, indexes, news services (printed and electronic), subscription services
Research	Market research, information brokers, search and retrieval services
Search and retrieval services	Information brokers, document retrieval, information retailing, research services
Telemarketing	Teleshopping, advertising, marketing
Time-sharing services	Private files, computer hardware, software
Videotex	Electronic communications media, including video, cable, videotex, satellite services

Figure 6.4. Partial subject index of information services; from Information Sources 1986, IIA.

ure 6.4 is a partial subject index created from *Information Sources 1986* to illustrate the breadth of coverage provided.

- Pro-Search, a product of Menlo Corp. (Santa Clara, Calif.) is a database access program that uses the Dialog online database service. With Pro-Search, it is not necessary to learn the complicated Dialog command language; Pro-Search does it for you. You simply select the database you want searched, enter a search request (keywords), and retrieve the records desired.

- Faxon Nationwide Services (Westwood, Massachusetts) offers online and distributed systems for serials management to libraries through their LINX network, a global network that links libraries and publishers together.

- Inmagic, Inc. (Cambridge, Massachusetts) is a text management software package for information brokers to organize and retrieve business information. It is used to create in-house databases to serve business managers, and could also be extended to customers as an information brokerage service.

- A number of information providers now offer information databases on optical disks that attach to a standard PC. Known as CD-ROM (compact disk, read-only memory) devices, these can save up to 200,000 pages of text on a 4.7-in. platter and, therefore, represent an impressive alternative to "connect time" fees for librarians to access remote databases, especially static or infrequently updated databases.

Another excellent source of information (almost information overload) is the U.S. government. Almost 2500 databases from governmental sources are commercially available online. However, most people are unaware of their existence or of how to find them. The U. S. Department of Commerce, for example, produces NTIS (National Technical Information Services), which consists of a series of abstract newsletters covering different industries. Their *Business and Economic Newsletter,* for example, covers domestic and international commerce, marketing and economics, consumer affairs, minority enterprises, banking and finance, and foreign industry development and economics (and that's only *one* of their newsletters). The NTIS newsletters cover abstracts of books, articles, research reports, and other publications for reference purposes.

And for those just getting started in information brokerage there are conferences such as the Seventh Annual National Online meeting, which was held in New York during May 1986. Sessions covered all aspects of business information gathering in the online world, hardware/software services, perspectives on online searching, and a wide variety of product presentations. (A number of sessions dealt with how to get started in information brokering.)

Professional Brokers

For companies not large enough to have in-house "information broker" librarians, there are professional information brokers. These companies perform information search services for clients for fees. These are the information industry retailers. Many are ex-librarians who discovered that the lucrative world of information brokerage paid more than their old jobs. Some act as searchers only, others add research services, awareness and alerting services, document (report) delivery, and competitive intelligence gathering. Companies that produce and/or distribute online databases also often provide professional information brokerage services. A sampling of professional information brokers from *Information Sources 1986* follows (6):

- BRAIN (Business Research and Intelligence Network) is an Alpha Systems Resource (Shelbyville, Indiana) company. It has direct access to nearly every major database in the world. BRAIN is Alpha's information brokerage arm.
- Find/SVP (New York City) is an information broker that does over 10,000 computer database searches a year on more than 400 databases for clients, half of which are *Fortune* 100 companies. Their service is available on a retainer basis or on a per search basis.
- Information on Demand, Inc. (Berkeley, California) offers three kinds of information brokerage services: research, document delivery, and NTIS report delivery. They regularly access over 350 databases to research customized client information needs, will provide copy or originals of any published literature, and offer a fast, easy, and reliable source for NTIS reports.
- Infosource, Inc. (Pittsburgh, Pennsylvania) is a specialized research firm providing market research information searches for business clients. Customers use the information to develop market strategies, monitor competitors, analyze existing and emerging markets, sell products, and search for candidates for mergers, divestitures, and joint ventures.

How does one go about finding the right professional information broker? Try looking in the *Information Industry Marketplace,* a directory published by R. R. Bowker (New York), or contact the main trade association for professional Information Brokers, the American Society for Information Science (Washington, D. C.).

Whereas MSSs supply business managers with internal information on performance for control purposes, information brokers provides business managers with a window to the external information vital to competitive decisions. These two information services techniques are part of the IW planner's tools for bringing information services to internal managers.

Now let's turn our attention to ways to bring information services to external customers.

EXTERNAL INFORMATION SERVICES

ONLINE INFORMATION SERVICES

IW 27—ONLINE INFORMATION SERVICES
Selling proprietary information to customers.

The IW model (Figure 4.4) suggested that information planners should look for ways to apply information technology strategies both internally and externally (self and customers). In the previous examples I suggested ways that MSS can be used to bring internal information to management. Information brokering was suggested as a strategy for bringing external information to management. Next we examine how both internal and external information can be delivered to *customers*.

Proprietary Databases

The customer terminal strategy cases discussed in Chapter 5 all involved putting the customer online to an in-house proprietary database, either to process transactions or just to get information. Retailers, wholesalers, and bank cash management services, all give customers access to internal proprietary databases as an integral part of an online transaction processing service. Many internal operating systems can be turned into customer systems by the simple expedient of providing the customer with online information access to an existing system.

Recognizing the value of information developed internally, some companies have created new information services as a by-product of internal databases. For example, there is a growing trend among high-technology banks to sell financial information to corporations, information that is not directly related to any underlying transactions:

- Security Pacific National Bank, for instance, provides late-breaking financial news, economic reports, and interest and commodity rates to corporate cash managers.
- The First National Bank of Chicago acquired a database from Rand McNally and Co. that contains current freight rates for a wide variety of goods. Companies shipping goods can access the database via a

computer terminal to find the most inexpensive trucking company, saving on average 10% of shipping costs.

- Aetna Life now gives customers access to its Aecclaims system, which processes group insurance claims. Using Aetna's database, the customer can perform some analysis of his own, such as examining the effectiveness of his own cost-containment efforts.

- TRW Information Services created a by-product database service from the 120 million consumer credit files it maintains as one of the nation's biggest credit businesses. The service, called Credentials, tracks consumer's financial affairs and is marketed to credit grantors, such as banks and retailers, as a faster and more efficient way for them to process loan applications. Consumers fill out a financial profile form for TRW, providing information on assets, debts, bank accounts, employment data, monthly payment obligations, and personal references. They are given a membership number. When they apply for a loan, they give their Credentials number to the credit grantor, who uses it to get the credit and financial information from TRW, thus speeding up the loan approval process. The new information service enables TRW to leverage its existing credit databases to target new markets of opportunity.

Dun & Bradstreet has always been in the information business, but recently it has begun to use its vast information databases to generate new revenue-producing business, such as a variety of online services (Duns-Dial, DunsVoice, DunsNet, DunsPrint), and a number of financial report services (DunsQuest, Duns Financial Profiles, Duns Million Dollar List), which are available to subscribers for a fee. Electronic information delivery now accounts for 70% of their credit reports business (7).

Not all databases, of course, are salable. Most should stay in-house because they have little appeal to outsiders. According to one expert, some factors to consider in determining the potential value of a proprietary database include its time-sensitivity (is timely access critical?), how frequently it is updated (the more frequent, the more valuable), its value to outsiders (is it of general interest?), and the ease with which it can be accessed (8).

Commercial Databases

Rather than simply using existing internal databases to create by-product information services, some companies have actually developed databases for the sole purpose of creating a new information service:

- Chase Manhattan Bank formed Interactive Data Corp. (Waltham, Massachusetts) to be a leading supplier of financial information services serving banks, brokerage firms, insurance companies, and corporations with securities, economic, and financial markets information.

- Lockheed Corp. formed Dialog Information Services, Inc. as an online information service provider that is now the world's largest information retrieval service.

However, few corporations outside the information industry have gone into the information industry business. Most companies producing commercially available information databases are in the information business itself, not just providing information as a by-product of another business. The imaginative IW planner can use such databases to provide information services to customers by having his/her company serve as an information broker to its own customers, combining both internal data and outside databases to create new information value.

Citibank has done just that. They formed the Global Electronic Markets (GEM) Group to provide corporate customers with information services to facilitate decisionmaking. The GEM group calls upon Citibank's international infrastructure to develop value-added information services focusing on information components critical to both cross-border and domestic financial decisionmaking. In effect, GEM acts as an information broker for bank customers, packaging proprietary data with data available from external data suppliers to create an "information package" to fit corporate customer information needs.

These "customer" information brokers can be corporate librarians or some other specially trained group established to perform search and retrieval services for both management and customers. In either case, the information broker will require an understanding of the world of commercial online databases.

Let's take a look at the two types of online database providers: database producers and database distributors.

Database producers are companies that create the databases themselves. They may be publishers, researchers, consultants, government agencies, or others who do work in the area covered by the databases they produce. Some collect data prepared by others, primarily the federal government, and package the data into specialty databases, sometimes adding data of their own. Database producers are sometimes also database distributors, but more often than not they license their databases to distributors.

Database distributors provide the *online services* that access commercial databases. They provide the computers, software, and communications needed for remote users to gain access to the databases. These are essentially time-sharing services. They sometimes produce their own databases, but most license the use of the databases covered by their online services from database producers.

Database Producers

There are a wide variety of database producers creating commercially available online databases which can be accessed by corporate information brokers to deliver information services to customers. Some are industry-specific (e.g., airline industry, government agencies, health care, real estate); others are subject databases (e.g., econometric data, marketing, engineering, law); some cover geographic regions (e.g., Europe, Brazil, Japan); and still others are simply broad databases covering a wide variety of subject areas. To give the reader a flavor for the breadth and depth of online database producers, the following is a representative sampling taken from *Information Sources 1986*(9):

- *Agriculture.* Agriculture Network's (Milwaukee, Wisconsin) *Agriscan* provides agricultural, business, finance, marketing, price, and weather information for farmers.
- *Airlines. The Official Airline Guide* (Oak Brook, Illinois) is a Dun & Bradstreet database of domestic and international airline schedules, fares, and rates.
- *Business. ABI/Inform*, a product of Data Courier, Inc. (Louisville, Kentucky), was the first online database for business and management. Available worldwide, it contains article summaries from 660 journals. *Vu/text* Info Services., Inc. (Philadelphia, Pennsylvania), a Knight Ridder Co., provides online access to newspaper, newswire, and general business information, including market quotes. Data Resources, Inc., a McGraw-Hill subsidiary, supplies the world's largest commercially available economic and business information database on a time-sharing basis.
- *Economics.* The Conference Board (New York) and Chase Econometrics (Waltham, Massachusetts) both have extensive economic data bases.
- *Engineering.* Inacom, International (Denver, Colorado) has a series of six online engineering databases.
- *Finance. Innerline*, produced by American Banker, Inc. (New York), is a financial services database for financial executives. Information is provided by the American Banker newspaper, Bank Administration Institute, and the Bank Marketing Association. *FINIS*, from Financial Industry Info Service (Chicago, Illinois), is a product of the Bank Marketing Association. It is a database devoted exclusively to financial services marketing topics.
- *General Information.* Alpha Systems Resources (Shelbyville, Indiana) produces the business research and intelligence network (*BRAIN*), which directly accesses nearly every major database in the world. BRS Info Technologies (Latham, New York) offers a full range of scientific, medical, social science, and business bibliographic retrieval services. The *Directory of Online Databases*, Cuadra Associates (Santa Monica, California) describes thousands of online databases of all types available through hundreds of online services worldwide. Dialog Info Services, Inc. (Palo Alto, California) accesses 225 databases covering

100,000 publications on all major subjects. *Database Directory Services* (White Plains, New York) is a comprehensive directory of online databases. Find/SVP (New York) is the largest information clearinghouse in the field. Info Sources 1986, Information Industry Association (Washington, D.C.), publishes an annual directory of information industry suppliers and publishers.

- *Government.* Congressional Information Services, Inc. (Bethesda, Maryland) provides a wealth of government and state legislative and statistical information. Lambert Publications, Inc. (Washington, D. C.) is the world's leading publisher of databases and directories of international government officials. Derwent, Inc. (MCLEAN, Virginia) provides American and worldwide patent information which is available on the Dialog, Questel, and Orbit information services. Legi-Slate, Inc. (Washington, D. C.) is *The Washington Post's* online service covering bills filed in Congress and announcements in the Federal Register.

- *Hi-Tech.* Dataquest (San Jose, California) produces offline research on semiconductors, peripherals, design and manufacturing automation, and information systems. EIC/Intelligence (New York) produces online databases on the hi-tech industry, including robotics, artificial intelligence, energy, biotechnology, CAD/CAM, and telecommunications. Harris Information Services (Twinsburg, Ohio) produces online electronics purchasing directories containing profiles of over 10,000 U. S. electronics firms.

- *Human Resources.* Executive Telecom Systems, Inc. (Indianapolis, Indiana) maintains nine networks on human resource management subject areas.

- *Investments.* Knight-Ridder Business Information Services (Leawood, Kansas), offers online commodity quotation services. Quotron Systems, Inc. (Los Angeles) has financial information and quotation services. Telerate Systems, Inc. (New York) is a leader in electronic coverage of international financial markets.

- *Law.* Lexis and Westlaw, from Mead Data Central (Dayton, Ohio) and West Publishing (St. Paul, Minnesota), respectively, are the two leading computer-assisted full-text legal research services.

- *Marketing.* CACIs Market Analysis Service (Fort Lauderdale, Florida) provides demographic databases for market research. Disclosure Information Group (Bethesda, Maryland) has a database of financial and textual information on 10,000 public companies obtained from SEC filings. Donnelly Marketing Info Services (Stamford, Connecticut) lists demographic data from the 1970 and 1980 censuses. *National Demographics and Lifestyles* (Denver, Colorado), is a comprehensive database of U. S. consumer information. Diems Marketing Services (Parsippanny, New Jersey) has a database of over 5.5 million U. S. companies for sales and marketing support.

- *International.* Dataline Dados Internacionais Ltda. (Sao Paulo, Brazil) is a Brazilian data bank serving worldwide clients. Datasolve, Ltd. (Middlesex, England) is a full-text European computing services database. Kyodo News International, Inc. (Japan) has a summarized news service from Japan.

- *Publishing.* Data Courier, Inc. (Louisville, Kentucky) offers electronic publishing of business and computer-related information. Dow Jones News/Retrieval Service (Princeton, New Jersey) is probably the leading provider of a broad range of online business and financial information. Information is provided on business, stock, news, sports, and weather from sources such as *The Wall Street Journal, Barrons*, and various wire services. Grolier Electronic Publishing, Inc. (New York) provides electronic publishing in a broad range of information products, including the online *Academic American Encyclopedia*. Nexis, Mead Data Central (Dayton, Ohio), has full-text business news from newspapers such as *The New York Times*, and various magazines, wire services, and newsletters.

Database Distributors

The corporate information broker is probably more interested in database distributors than producers, because access to online databases is through distributors, who are the online service providers. One of the best sources for locating database distributors is the *Directory of Online Databases* (Cuadra/Elsevier, New York). The 1986 directory contains some 2900 databases from 1379 database producers offered by 454 online services. The directory covers two types: reference and source databases. Reference databases alert the user to the existence of an information source and refer the user to that source for detailed information. Source databases contain original data, full-text copy, or information prepared especially for electronic distribution. The following are among the larger providers (each provide access to 50 or more databases): BRS (Bibliographic Research Services); Chase Econometrics; Compuserve; Data Resources, Inc.; Data-Star; Dialog Info Services; ESA-IRS; GE Information Services (GEISCO); I.P. Sharp Associates, Interactive Marketing Systems; Mead Data Control (Lexis/Nexis); Newsnet, Inc.; QL Systems Ltd.; SDS Info Services; The Source; Telesystems-Questel; and Vu/text Info Services.

INFORMATION BUSINESSES

> **IW 28—INFORMATION BUSINESSES**
> Information as a business in and of itself.

Information as a business is sprouting everywhere. Information is an asset that can be bought and sold; consequently, selling information has become big business. Credit agencies sell credit information to banks. Banks sell economic and political risk data to importers and exporters. Quotation services sell market data worldwide. The Information Era has particular meaning for those who are in the information business. This includes many of the service businesses, such as banking, insurance, brokerage, education, government, and the professions (e.g., lawyers, accountants, and doctors).

There is also an information industry comprised of a multitude of businesses devoted to the delivery of information itself. Some companies normally involved in the delivery of products and services have found opportunities to enter into these information businesses, sometimes as by-products of other activities or information gathering. Earlier I discussed the notion of information *conduit* (the information delivery system) vs. information content (the information itself). The information industry can be divided similarly. Information conduit businesses include broadcast services (radio and TV), communications channels (telephone, cable TV, satellites), document delivery (Post Office, facsimile, microforms, electronic delivery, printing), and facilitating services (EDI, EFTS, time sharing, and software systems). Information *content* businesses include the packaging of information itself: newspapers, magazines, and books; films, records, tapes and video disks; micropublishing, report preparation, and directories; news services, newsletters, libraries, videotex, and data bases of all kinds.

Everyone participates in the information industry, as either a user or a provider. For example, as noted earlier, a company can act as an information broker to gather external competitive information or to do product research. It could also package inside information with outside databases and become an information broker for customers. It could become a database producer/distributor as a by-product business from information originally developed for internal use. Some companies produce monthly newsletters, even "electronic" newsletters, for customers on their areas of expertise. Every company is in the information business as a user. Why not look for opportunities to turn internal information assets into value-added products that enhance company image or an existing product or service, or create new revenue sources? Here are a few examples of companies that have branched out into information businesses.

Electronic Publishing

Electronic Data Systems (EDS), Ross Perot's data processing services corporation, was awarded a $1 billion contract, the largest electronic publishing contract ever, by the U. S. Government Printing Office. The contract was to automate all U. S. Army publications, a project involving capturing millions of pages of text into a central database. The system would digitize, electronically compose, return, and edit all existing Army publications. It was EDS's first electronic publishing project. It was also an interesting case of joint venturing in that the bidding team, headed by EDS, also included Interleaf (software) and IBM (hardware). This one contract alone would put EDS firmly into the electronic publishing market with 5–7% of market share. In fact, it represented so powerful a competitive advantage that the competition immediately protested the contract. The Printing Industry of America, an industry trade group, also objected, claiming that the entire contract would create a monopoly over the Army's printing business and would, therefore, be destructive to the printing industry. Because of the protests, the government decided to rescind the contract and start all over again (10).

Time, Inc. moved into cable TV and home teletext services through its video division. That division soon took in more profits than Time's print publishing business, overshadowing magazines such as *Time, Fortune,* and *Life* and becoming the company's largest source of operating income (11).

Database Production/Distribution

Lockheed Corp. owns Dialog Information Services, Inc., the world's largest information retrieval service. Typical applications include research, engineering, new product development planning, and competitive analysis.

Security Pacific Bank (Los Angeles) uses data originally developed for internal consumption and planning purposes by its International and Regional Economics Dept. to provide access to the largest available computer database of economic data for California cities, towns, and the state itself. Called the "California Database," data are made available at various time intervals (e.g. monthly, quarterly, or annually) on 10 subject categories: population, employment, finance, income levels, consumer prices, trade, real estate activity, transportation, agriculture, and miscellaneous. The California Database is an information service that provides analysts, businessmen, economists, planners, and researchers with online access to demographic, economic, financial, and industrial data on the California marketplace (12). Chase Manhattan Bank's subsidiary, Interactive Data Corp., is one of the leading time-share suppliers of financial information services to bankers, financial analysts, brokers, portfolio managers, economists, and individual investors who use IDC's databases for investment research, portfolio management, and pricing operations.

Joint-Venture Information Services

In a move designed to step up the business of selling nontransactional financial data to corporations, Citibank's GEM Group formed a joint venture information business with McGraw Hill, Inc. The new company, called Gemco (Global Electronics Markets Co.), is a partnership that provides an electronic network that combines information access, trading, and settlement capability in the commodities markets. The partnership took over a round-the-clock commodity information and trading service formerly operated by McGraw Hill and added such services as the ability for customers to issue settlement instructions to their banks, arrange letters of credit, obtain financing, transfer funds to pay for trades, arrange spot or future foreign exchange transactions, and monitor bank balances, cash, debt, and foreign currency positions (13). In this case, Citibank moved into the information business by selling financial information that was not directly related to underlying transactions.[1]

The Citicorp/Nynex/RCA joint venture mentioned in Chapter 4 is a marketing research-based information service. This joint venture is studying the potential of home banking, home shopping, electronic newspapers, and entertainment services. In this case, the venture does not intend to market products or services, but will engage in market research activities to learn what customers want and how the three giants can mutually pool their strength in consumer banking, telecommunications expertise, and consumer electronic products.

Investment Information Services

The importance of information in the investment world has been recognized for centuries. Peter Benton, in a summary presentation at a Nolan Norton and Co. symposium, said:

> In 1815 the Rothschild family had a carrier pigeon service operating from just off the field at Waterloo. The information that flew back to London enabled the Rothschilds to make a killing. In that era advanced information could offer an individual firm the opportunity to grow rich . . . Today, on the other hand, information becomes universally available in an instant, and it is not possible to survive unless you take advantage of it. Your competitors certainly will. (14)

From a humble beginning providing stock and bond quotations on dumb terminals, the investment trading information business has grown to be a flood of worldwide realtime information that has revolutionized investment markets. The three leaders in this information business, Reuters Holdings (London), Telerate (New York), and Quotron Systems (Los Angeles), combined have over 160,000 terminals installed worldwide in banks, brokerage offices, portfolio management firms, and other investing organizations. Reuters provides news and data about currency and commodity markets, stock quotes, and money market information. Telerate provides financial news and market information as well as data on debt instruments, precious metals, and currencies. Quotron provides stock

---

[1]As this book went to press, the joint venture was scrapped due to failure to achieve market scale (the risk of innovation).

quotes from U. S. and foreign stock exchanges, as well as news retrieval and historical financial data (15). British-based Reuters dominates the international information business while Telerate is the leader in the United States in providing quotations on domestic money markets and fixed-income securities. Quotron leads in providing stock quotations. Both Telerate and Quotron are now expanding rapidly abroad. They are also all moving beyond the simple provision of information to provide transaction processing as well. According to *The New York Times:*

> Soon it will be possible to buy a cargo of oil and arrange payment, insurance, and inspection all on the computer keyboard. (16)

In securities trading, often those with the latest and best information win. Recognizing the importance of information services, Citicorp was, at this writing, attempting a takeover of Quotron as the centerpiece of its own push into the information business.

The examples described above represent only a few of the many new information businesses that leading companies are branching out to enter. Why are so many companies getting into information service businesses? Because it's highly profitable. One study reported on by Harvey Poppell of Broadview Associates showed that electronic information services businesses, on average, earned a 20% return on equity and sold for 4 times book value per share, which is far and away better than most businesses and is indicative of the high value put on information services businesses by investors (17).

MICRO INFORMATION SERVICES

> **IW 29—MICRO INFORMATION SERVICES**
> The extensive possibilities of internal and external micro-based information services.

Microcomputers offer unique information service opportunities of their own. By focusing on personal computers as the electronic delivery vehicle, IW planners can create a wide variety of internal information support services and customer service offerings.

PC Software

There are literally thousands of PC packages on the market from which to choose. For example, while looking for a micro package that does credit analysis recently, I developed a listing of 14 packages that fit in one database search alone. There are so many choices that a valuable information service in itself is to establish an internal PC group that can sift through and select packages that have potential value in the organization, either internally or externally. This PC "product research" group can save managers the hundreds of hours spent searching out solutions to fit their problems, and can do the same for product managers looking for new customer service offerings.

There are many manuals and directories to assist in locating these products. *The Microcomputer Index*, for example, a publication of Database Services, Inc. (Mountain View, California), is a bimonthly abstract publication covering the most widely read publications in the microcomputer industry. (It is also available through Dialog online services). A companion product, *Microcomputer Product Announcements*, covers new hardware and software products, both in print and online (18). *Software Digest*, a rating newsletter, provides a thorough rundown on new PC packages, by industry and product classification, including ratings of competitive products. International Computer Programs (ICP) publishes the *ICP Microcomputer Directory*, listing software packages by industry and application. There are even industry-specific directories, such as the *Microbanker Software Directory*, available from Microbanker (York, Pennsylvania), which lists 800 PC software programs aimed at the banking industry.

Competitive Analysis

Competitive information services, using PCs for analysis, represent another fast growing area of opportunity. The building of competitive databases (markets, competitors, pricing data) and the accessing of outside databases (A. C. Nielson, A. D. Little, Duns Marketing Services) are an exciting recent new information service development. Competitive information research involves (1) general competitor information (financial, share of market, capacity, markets entering or leaving, cost structures, pricing, product information); (2) competitive situation analysis (in-depth analysis of a competitor's strengths and weaknesses, problems faced, opportunities awaiting); and (3) competitive audits (periodic or special situations such as acquisitions under consideration or decisions to enter or leave a business). Such marketing information services tend to be "signaling" information systems that flag difficulties, opportunities, and indisciplines (symptoms of erosion) for market planners.

Marketing Support

The PC systems that support marketing and sales activities are becoming increasingly popular. Here are but three examples taken from The Source's Microsearch database:

- "The Sales Manager" from High Caliber Systems, Inc. is a sales analysis package which can be used to prepare sales reports, sales and expense forecasts, activity reports, quota/commission summaries, and performance reports (actual vs. planned).

- "Business Extended Sales Analysis" from Bristol Information Services is a statistical software package for sales analysis. Product sales analysis can be done by territory, salesperson, or customer. Customer sales analysis can be done by territory, salesperson, or product.
- "The Prospect Organizer" from Dow Jones & Co. is a software package that allows the user to manage customer prospect files. The effectiveness of a given sales promotion can be analyzed and prospect status reports are generated.

One company uses a PC-based system as a sales support information system, collecting data in the field for consolidation and analysis at headquarters. This "Territory Management System" generates sales and marketing reports, studies sales cycles, organizes sales plans, coordinates, sales and follow-ups, manages a prospect pipeline, critiques sales representatives' performances, and allows the development of prospective customer profiles.

Applications Support

Applications support on PCs is another form of internal information service. Applications support includes financial, investment database management, and other packages that aid managers in planning and managing the business applications under their control. The use of micros for investment analysis, for example, is a growing trend. A 1985 survey conducted by Computerized Investing of 20,000 subscribers found that roughly 55% use micros for applications support—in this case, investment analysis (19). The applications used were primarily spreadsheet programs for investment analysis and market quote services. However, a growing number use financial information services such as the Dow Jones News/Retrieval service. CompuServe, and The Source. (Only 5%, however, were found to be actually trading securities online.) The major investment-related uses of the micro were for portfolio management, financial planning, and technical analysis. "Managing Your Money," an integrated financial planning program, was the most popular commercial program, followed by the "Dow Jones Market Manager."

"The Commercial Lending Guide" from Dun & Bradstreet is another example of an application support system. This interactive micro software package links financial statement analysis with industry-wide assessments. Simply put, the model objectively quantifies a company's riskiness over time. By drawing on its extensive database of company and industry information, Dun & Bradstreet created a new database of industry norms and industry outlook data (i.e., general riskiness of industries relative to one another). By matching a specific company's data against the database, the potential investor/lendor can quickly obtain a risk assessment of the company, its industry, and the company's financial status relative to its industry. This is another example of creating a micro information service as a by-product of an existing proprietary database.

Customer Terminals

Personal computers hold considerable promise as customer support tools. The customer terminal strategy discussed in Chapter 5 is primarily based on the use of micros; that is, all customer terminal opportunities are also micro information service opportunities. For the most part, services are offered that will run on a PC in the customer's office (the PC itself can be provided by the service provider or the customer). A large southeastern bank placed PCs in investment advisory firms that provided access to personal trust custody account information on their clients. The advisory firm's money manger dials in to the bank and gets direct access to his client's custody account information and other details of investments made for his customers. Here is a case of a micro information service that helps the bank's customers serve *their* customers better.

Sales Tools

A number of micro services that support the sales organization were covered earlier. For instance, the use of touch-screen systems in customer lobbies or public areas such as hotels and airports are offered by investment companies and banks to advertise services, rates, and office locations. The auto dealership system supplied by Buick to support its regional sales forces is another example.

Another way to support sales is to advertise through an online information utility service aimed at PC users. Two such services are The Source and CompuServe. The Source is a service mark of Source Technology Corp. (McLean, Virginia), a subsidiary of Readers Digest. Compuserve, Inc. (Columbus, Ohio) is owned by H&R Block. Both provide a broad range of information services to subscribers. Although primarily personal in nature, these utilities offer an opportunity for corporate information service providers. For example, their teleshopping service could be used to advertise products and services (an electronic throw-back to mail order catalogs). Their publishing service could be used to publish catalogs of services, issue newsletters, or provide advisory services to subscribing members. Since there are 190,000 Compuserve and 64,000 Source members, this is a reasonable market for an information service, particularly since 60% of the Source members (less for Compuserve) are reportedly business users (20).

Template Packages

A variety of applications that involve putting micros in customer offices have already been discussed. But one more applications support strategy needs to be mentioned because it is one of the fastest-growing commodities in the software industry today, that is, the use of *template packages.* Templates package the flexibility of spreadsheets into customized applications support tools. Such templates can be made to fit any number of specialized applications: accounting, real estate management, investment analysis, project management—just about any situation you can devise. They are fast, simple to use, flexible, and cheap (usually $50–$550 each). At this writing, there are reportedly over 1500 template programs on the market.

One company that is capitalizing on this strategy as a way of extending its services into applications support is a small New York accounting firm, Salibello and Broder, which has written some two dozen Lotus 1-2-3 templates to help their customers computerize their financial records in formats their banks can use. They do not sell the templates, but customize them for clients as part of their accounting service. By working closely with major banks, Salibello and Broder tailors its templates so that its clients can fill in financial statements and supporting spreadsheets and deliver a diskette to their bank when they apply for a new loan or renew an old one. The bank can read it on its own micros or load it into its mainframe computers. Lotus templates developed to date by Salibello and Broder include cash-flow management, cash projection, line-of-credit trader, loan amortization calculator, lease vs. debt evaluator, and ratio analyzer (21).

Desktop Publishing

A new technology that goes by the name of "desktop" publishing (DTP) is gaining customers daily. It enables customers to prepare complex documentation, reports, newsletters, and so on, using multiple typefaces, charts, graphics, and drawings to product slick finished products on an ordinary PC.

Until recently, electronic publishing was too expensive for smaller operations. But now, desktop publishers can go into business for themselves with as little as $10,000 to cover the cost of a PC, software, and a printer. At that price, everybody can afford to produce documents in volume. According to *Nation's Business,* three developments have combined to make DTP attractive: the low cost of PCs, the low cost of laser printers, and available software to translate a computer page to the printer. The magazine points out that because there are at least as many writers in the business world as financial analysts, DTP could eventually have as far-reaching an impact on the office as Lotus 1-2-3 (22). But the real impetus for DTP will, once again, likely come from IBM, which recently established a "Publishing Systems Business" unit aimed at selling its DTP products to the corporate marketplace. IBM's entry not only makes DTP official, but will likely be the catalyst for moving large corporations to this new technology. IBM's DTP system is based on its newest small computer, the RT, which is sold with publishing software from Interleaf (Cambridge, Massachusetts), and a variety of IBM electronic printers (23).

PC Centers

> **IW 30—THE PC CENTER**
> In-house computer stores as a way to promote the intelligent use of business microcomputers.

The internal PC center has become a popular strategy to introduce, and intelligently lead, the proliferation of PCs in organizations. In the last few years, many companies have formed in-house PC centers, which act as a store, laboratory, and training center to introduce PCs into the organization. By training managers and professionals in the use of micro hardware and software, PC Centers have provided a valuable micro information service. Today, PC Centers represent the most popular strategy to simultaneously lead and control PCs in the corporate arena. In fact, the American Management Association reported that at the end of 1985 roughly 40% of all businesses, and 80% of all billion-dollar companies, had PC centers in place (24).

At Bank of Boston, a PC center (PCC) was established, with top management support (a must), initially to serve as an in-house computer store and laboratory. The PCC served as a micro service and support organization for the intelligent and controlled growth of PCs in the company. Managers and professionals could come to the PCC to be introduced to PC hardware and software and get advice and counsel on potential uses as well as specific ways to solve business problems. Users were welcome to use the PCs at any time, could borrow them to take to their office or home for a "test drive," or could purchase one. The center sold, installed, trained, and supported PC usage. This was the introductory, hardware-oriented Phase 1 of the PC evolution.

As the number of PCs grew, the need for the center subsided. Users had their own machines and had acquired some computer literacy. Phase 2, advanced end-user computing, focused not on hardware but on software; that is, how to leverage the investment by finding more and better ways to use PCs in the organization. A small group of high-powered strategic consultants conducted research on new software offerings so as to better advise and lead users to the best solutions to their problems and needs.

This turned out to be a valuable user service. A preferred list of vendor packages covering the most popular applications was developed to assist the user in finding the best software package to do the job without having to sift through a bewildering array of offerings. Preparing such a preferred list is not as difficult a job as one might at first imagine. The bulk of the PC market is, in fact, actually covered by only a dozen or so companies. In 1985, the top 15 companies in PC software accounted for 72% of sales. The top three independents—Lotus, Ashton-Tate, and Microsoft—accounted for half of that amount. There are also PC software rating services that can help narrow the search. *The Software Digest* (Wynnewood, Pennsylvania), for instance, produces a monthly *Ratings Newsletter* of PC programs that have been independently tested by their researchers. Applications rated included program categories such as spreadsheets, word processing, data management, graphics, and integrated programs (e.g., Dunsplus, Framework, and Symphony).

Bank of Boston's PCC, as it has for so many companies, proved to be a valuable and welcome service to introduce micro usage into the organization. It remains as a most useful strategy to provide the PC leadership needed by any company that hopes to use micro services as a management productivity and customer services tool.

References

1. Paul A. Strassmann, *Information Payoff,* The Free Press, New York, 1985, Ch. 12.
2. Peters and Austin, *A Passion for Excellence*, Random House, N.Y. 1985.
3. Diane Crawford, "New Automation Strategies Dynamize Pru-Bache," *Wall St. Computer Review,* May 1985.
4. *Technology in Banking: Path to Competitive Advantage,* Salomon Bros., May 1985, p. 51.
5. *Information Sources 1986,* Annual Directory of the IIA, Washington, D. C., 1986.
6. Ibid.
7. *Information Week,* 5/26/86, p. 46.
8. Walt Rowinsky, "Sell Yourself First on Merits of Online Service," *PC Week,* 2/11/86, p. 141.
9. *Information Sources 1986.*
10. *The Boston Globe,* 6/21/86, p. 34.
11. *MIS Week,* 1/20/86, p. 1.
12. *Information Sources, 1986.*
13. *American Banker,* 9/1/85, p. 1.
14. Peter Benton, "Transforming Business," a summary Presentation at a Nolan-Norton and Co. Symposium, Tarpon Springs, FL, 1/16/86.
15. *The New York Times,* 10/7/85, p. D1.
16. Ibid.
17. Harvey Poppell, in a speech before the Boston Chapter, SIM, 4/17/86.
18. *Information Sources 1986,* p. 62.
19. *American Banker,* 12/31/85, p. 9.

20. Craig Millow, "Life is Discovered at the Source," *Across the Board*, July–Aug. 1985, p. 50.
21. *American Banker*, 9/25/85, p. 7.
22. *Nation's Business*, March 1986, pp. 56–59.
23. *The Boston Globe*, 7/5/86, p. 26.
24. *The 1985 AMA Report on Information Centers*, American Management Association, New York, 1985.

7

PRODUCTIVITY

Cost advantage is one of the two types of competitive advantage a
firm may possess.

MICHAEL PORTER (1)

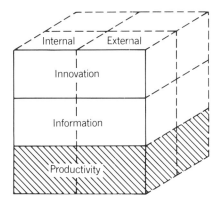

Figure 7.1. Information Weapon model.

"Productivity through people" was one of the eight attributes identified
by Peters and Waterman in their celebrated book *In Search of Excellence* as
the marks of distinction of excellent companies. Productivity promotes
cost leadership, the second major strategy for achieving competitive advantage (the other being product differentiation). In this chapter, we examine productivity options for achieving competitive advantage through
cost leadership.

The cost leader has a significant advantage because he can sustain lower
prices longer than competitors and can match or better price offerings of
competitors while still retaining a profit margin. In a recent report on technology in banking, Salomon Bros., the investment banking firm, said:

. . . we continue to believe that the most successful banking organizations in the future will be those capable of delivering products and services at the lowest effective cost. (2)

This applies broadly to most companies in all industries. Having the lowest cost enables the lowest price which can, and often does, lead to increased share of market. Information weapons that increase productivity, therefore, can and do provide a competitive edge.

In the Computer Era, productivity was the primary goal of most automation efforts. Automation equals productivity in labor-intensive areas. That is why the early automation targets were activities that offered the greatest potential for eliminating jobs or leveraging labor through computerization. This is still a goal, of course, but the fact is that most of these areas have now been largely automated in most companies. Therefore, we need to look for productivity in areas that have previously not been automated and that can benefit from new technological developments, and in customer-service arenas.

Once again, we should not limit ourselves to introspection. We need to look at productivity opportunities both within and without the company—internal and external.

INTERNAL PRODUCTIVITY

CORPORATE PRODUCTIVITY

The common definition of productivity is output divided by input. In an IT vernacular, this translates to *information products and services divided by the investment in technology,* or "Are you getting a bang for your buck?" Productivity to the IW planner is many things. It is cost reduction, manpower control, increased quality, increased output per manhour, substitution of technology for labor, efficiency, optimum use of resources, and new applications of technology. Let's examine some of these opportunities both from a business impact perspective and an information resource perspective.

The Enterprise's Investment in Technology

IW 31—THE TECHNOLOGY INVESTMENT
The level of investment in technology is the real measure of management's commitment.

Why should a company invest in technology? To achieve the strategic systems advantages brought out by the IW model: technological innovation to gain a competitive edge; information services to improve communications internally and externally; and productivity to streamline internal operations. Here we examine the last strategy—*productivity.*

To save money, one often needs to spend money. The investment in technology in the Computer Era was 1–2% of sales.[1] The leaders in the use of technology in the Information Era are already spending several times that amount—on the order of 5% of sales and more. These leaders have discovered the power of the information weapon. To fail to invest appropriately in automation is to risk falling seriously behind the competition. Automation can often achieve broad gains in productivity and competitive advantage. Some examples of various enterprises that realized this potential are described below.

Airlines. When the airlines were first deregulated, they tried to gain competitive advantage by route positioning, fare reductions, and mergers. Much of this strategy failed to pay off. By the end of 1980, airline industry profits had fallen from a 1978 record level of $1.4 billion profit to a $225 million loss. In desperation, airline managements turned to cost reduction, or productivity improvement, to solve their problems. American Airlines, for example, drastically reduced its work force from 41,000 to 35,800 between 1979 and 1983. It also moved to invest aggressively in technology. Building on its well-known SABRE reservation system, it extended computerization into flight planning, flight control, crew and aircraft scheduling, maintenance scheduling and records, fuel usage, fuel price monitoring and purchasing, and meal planning, and payrolls. Today, just about every function of American Airlines has been automated to one degree or another (3).

Financial Services. Prudential-Bache also spends heavily on automation. Their rate of spending on technology increased by 321% between 1979 and 1984. According to Harold A. Rich, SVP and Director of Computer Systems and Communications:

> Seven years ago, we were below last place in terms of technology . . . we had obsolete hardware and software systems that were written in the early 1960s. (4)

Since then, Pru-Bache developed and completed a 5-year automation plan which called for a totally automated worldwide network of operations by the end of the decade, designed to reap huge revenues and keep the com-

---

[1]In banking, which has no sales per se, the investment average has been 10–15% of noninterest expenses.

petition at bay. Their entire operating environment has been revamped from order processing to trading operations, cash management, communications, distribution, broker workstations, and nationwide networking. Every department was touched by the automation effort. The investment in technology, according to Rich, is expected to yield tremendous savings in operating costs and result in vast reductions in errors and a dramatic increase in daily business and trading volume.

Brokerage. The Chicago Board Options Exchange (CBOE) is a company that relies on up-to-the-minute information for its very existence. The speed with which the latest trading data from the world's financial markets can be gathered, processed, and flashed to the booths and pits of the exchange floor can make or break CBOE. Since the exchange collects a fee for every transaction, speed also means volume. The more volume that can be pushed through, the more revenue. To ensure technological superiority, CBOE invests fully 25% of its annual budget in its information processing and communications network facilities (5).

These cases illustrate not only a commitment to technology investment but also a productivity strategy of automation penetration. By undertaking a study of the degree of automation penetration in each of its business units, companies can determine where greater automation would be beneficial. The first time an activity or function is automated, productivity gains are usually realized. The second time around (i.e., replacing old systems with new and modern technology) functions are often automated that were previously untouched, thereby achieving additional productivity gains. Like peeling an onion, each automation iteration can penetrate deeper into the organization, realizing even greater productivity opportunities.

HARVEST businesses are particular targets for productivity gains, since their aim is to "milk" as much cash as possible out of the business as it reaches maturity. As a product reaches the end of its life cycle, cost reduction becomes a strategic goal. As sales decline and profits go down, every effort is made to cut costs (and/or raise prices) to keep the profit margin up as long as possible. Systems changes are held to a minimum, staff is reduced, the application may be moved to less expensive hardware, and so on. Therefore, a productivity strategy is appropriate for every mature product and HARVEST business.

It should be noted that quality and cost leadership generally do not go together. Quality increases cost; hence cost leaders may have a good product, but seldom will it be a top-of-the-line product. Cost leaders focus on EOS as a competitive strategy, not on quality. Because technology often requires high fixed costs, the cost leader looks to EOS in business (high growth markets, large market share, wide domination) as well as in technology (mainframe data processing, communications networks, large transaction systems), which could mean having to sacrifice something in quality.

Management Productivity

> IW 32—MANAGEMENT PRODUCTIVITY
> Applying computing power directly to managerial work leverages management.

The internal management support systems (MSS) discussed in Chapter 6 not only provide information services to managers but, in doing so, leverage managerial productivity. Opportunities abound to use new technology tools to leverage management productivity.

Information Centers. The growing use of ICs as managerial productivity tools not only allow managers and end users to more quickly extract the information they need directly, but by offloading report generation to users, programmers can reduce their maintenance tasks, allowing more time for important development work. Thus ICs not only increase managerial productivity, they can also double the productivity of programmers. In a recent survey of 1000 U.S. companies, increased job productivity was seen as the largest single benefit of ICs by 86% of the companies in the survey. IBM's semiconductor facility near Burlington, Vermont established an IC for use by both managers and end users. Aided by a major promotional and educational campaign, the IC reportedly has resulted in savings of several millions of dollars for IBM.

Computer Graphics. Computer graphics systems are another new tool to support managerial productivity. These range from simple PC presentation graphics applications (such as that produced by Lotus 1-2-3), to more sophisticated analytic graphics (produced by minicomputer decision models), to expensive mainframe systems used for control and performance monitoring purposes. The following examples of large-scale and successful management graphics systems were taken from the files of AVI Data Graphics/ISSCO (6):

- *McDonalds.* Following the month-end closings, every company-owned McDonald's store receives a set of graphics charts comparing the stores performance against its goals. Each chart is unique for each store. The charts have been reportedly so successful in helping managers reach higher productivity goals that they are now being extended to all 8000 company-owned and franchised stores. (Mc-

Donald's uses a Xerox 9700 laser printer and Disspla and Tell-A-Graf software to produce the charts.)

- *Electronic Data Systems.* EDS has three online computer graphics management systems: one monitors data center performance, another monitors income and expenses, and the third is an early warning system for clients, alerting them to budget overruns. EDS claims the system has helped them avoid buying a 3033, has cut overhead growth significantly, and has increased customer satisfaction. (The system runs on an IBM 3287 and ISSCO slide service with Tell-A-Graf, Disspla, and Tellaplan software.)
- *New England Telephone.* NET created a centralized graphics department that is accessible from every terminal in their computer system. Because of its speed and quality output it has enjoyed high-volume operations. Each user feels he/she has his own color laser printer, even though they all share the same one. The savings in manpower and in the cost of alternative graphics services enabled NET to recover its investment in less than three months. (This system utilizes a Xerox 6500 laser printer and Tell-A-Graf software.)

Personal Computers. The PCs, of course, represent the most phenomenal productivity potential to managers yet invented. Thus far, middle management and professionals have been the largest users, though the number of senior managers directly using PCs is growing. (Many use "executive chauffeurs," or assistants, to get the information for them rather than use the machines directly.) Experts predict that 80–90% of all managers will be using some kind of PC or workstation by 1990. That's phenomenal growth from its humble beginnings in the late 1970s; but consider it's role. The predominant use of PCs in business offices today is task automation (e.g., word processing, spreadsheets, database management). Although this increases productivity, the opportunity to further leverage PC productivity is great. Consider, for example, that a manager with a $5000 PC and a $500 spreadsheet program can double the value of the PC by simply buying a second program, such as a database manager or a sales support package, or hundreds of other possibilities. The investment in hardware versus software is greater than 10:1 in most companies. Therefore, extended software use is an opportunity to further leverage managerial productivity through PCs.

Expert Systems. Expert systems may well turn out to be one of the greatest aids to management by the 1990s. It has taken a long time to get there, but the practical use of artificial intelligence (AI) in the commercial marketplace has made rapid advances in the last few years. Artificial intelligence spans four key areas: natural language processing, expert systems, robotics, and reasoning. Of these, the first two are of interest in terms of increasing managerial productivity. Natural-language computers are easier to use because they understand ordinary language commands, a user-friendliness of particular value to executives. Expert systems are programs that diagnose problems by having users answer a series of questions that lead to a logical and deduced conclusion. They are built from information extracted from human experts. Thus they can be particularly valuable in increasing the productivity of novices to a field, be it medical diagnosis, oil exploration, or personal financial planning. Armed with an expert system, the novice can perform at a much higher level of expertise than would otherwise be possible.

These examples are merely illustrative of the possibilities for leveraging management work through these new technologies. The opportunities are plentiful and the potential for management productivity is enormous to the IW planner.

Span of Control. One of the greatest opportunities for productivity in management is, in fact, to eliminate or reduce layers of management in the organization. Many companies have as many as 10 or 12 levels of management, whereas experts in the field suggest that most can get by with only 5 or 6. Span-of-control management leads to flatter organizational structures, which can result in impressive productivity gains. As more top managers use computers directly to get their own information, fewer middle managers will be needed to manage the data for them. Also, as work is pushed down in the organization, the quality of work increases. Paul Strassmann, in *Information Payoff*, suggested that the productivity impact on jobs through technology will continue to raise the overall quality of work. According to Strassmann, top executives will change from financial investors to strategic planners, focusing on being innovators, entrepreneurs, and visionaries and on passing financial management down to middle management. Middle managers in turn will move from a coordinator's role into financial and human resource management. The information middleman will be eliminated and information management will be passed down. The professional/technical staff will no longer be specialists, but generalists managing information delivery, especially customer service. Finally, clerks will expand from simple support roles to specialists (e.g., systems development and market research), a higher-level job, because the mundane clerical tasks will have been automated (7).

Efficient information processing can not only reduce the number of managers but can increase the level of responsibility of those that remain. Collapsing the organizational pyramid has been a goal extolled in many best-selling books devoted to corporate excellence, because it has been found that in many organizations, managers are either under-spanned (manage too few people—sometimes only *one*) or do not perform management tasks (technicians given management titles). Recent illustrations of the trend to reduce white-collar and manager levels include the following (8):

- AT&T decided to reduce its staff by 24,000 employees; 30% of which were management positions.
- Ford Motor Company's North American automative operations decided to eliminate 9600 white-collar jobs over a 5-year period.
- Union Carbide Corp. decided on a massive restructuring involving the elimination of 4000 jobs, about 15% of its managerial work force.

Management support systems growth is one of the enabling forces allowing these contractions. Managers make better decisions with better information don't need as much support.

Computers are even used to help identify excess personnel and management layers. General Electric, for example, used a program called "Introspect" to determine that it had 25–40% too many managers and too many layers of management (9). The GE program based its analysis and findings on two documents: (1) an organizational memo that displays each manager's reporting relationships (immediate superior and direct reports) and (2) a "work activity distribution" form that breaks down the work activities (and percent of total) performed by each manager and his group. (Work activities come from a dictionary previously prepared by the project team.) Computer-generated graphics display organizational units in terms of "houses" (e.g., a finance house, a marketing house, etc.). The floors of each "house" represent the various layers of management. Salary data, number of people reporting directly to a manager, and percent of time spent on management activities are all displayed. From an analysis of this model, decisions can be made to eliminate layers of management whose span of control is too narrow, to broaden others by adding more direct reports, to combine functions under the same management, and to eliminate redundancies.

Many companies, including General Motors, Ford, Chrysler, Xerox, Weyerhauser, and Bank of Boston, have undertaken span-of-control programs and many more are likely to do so as the pressure to reduce managerial layers continues to be aided by more direct management—machine interactions.

Operations Productivity

> IW 33—OPERATIONS PRODUCTIVITY
> Methods and techniques for increasing operational
> effectiveness for less cost.

When it comes to increasing the productivity of internal operations, one normally does not think in terms of entrepreneurial activity. Entrepreneurship is, after all, usually seen as the highly aggressive (and risky) style of the bold product manager, trying out new products in new markets against stiff competitive rivalry. These often employ "skunkworks," research groups that are provided with funding to "create," knowing that only 1 in 100 ideas may pan out—but that *one* could be fantastically successful. Such people focus on product differentiation as their entrepreneurship strategy.

But there is another type of entrepreneur, one who works from within to produce quality products, efficient operations, and better customer service. These entrepreneurs focus on helping the business to be the low-cost producer. According to Jim Mayers of Mayers and Mayers, a consulting firm, this type of entrepreneur stems from a different corporate life cycle. During the *initiation* and *maturing* stages of the business life cycle, strategists have no external focus. They are prepared to accept high risks and the trial-and-error approach of the highly entrepreneurial "skunks." However, in the later stages, *degeneration* and *expiring*, there is a shift from momentum to inertia and less tolerance for "skunkworks." Attention is redirected internally, to what Mayer calls "the quiet and slow marsupial approach of the 'possum.'" In his view, possums work at sustaining sales levels and market share in declining markets, in extracting more from less resources. Whereas skunks are effectiveness-minded, possums are efficiency-oriented. All organizations have their share of both. It mainly depends on where the business is in its life cycle and whether the competitive strategy is product differentiation or low-cost producer. In the former, skunks abound and there are few possums. In the latter, there are hardly any skunks but there are loads of possums (10).

It is the possum type of entrepreneuring that comes to play in operations productivity planning activities such as those described below.

Operations Analysis. Several new techniques that have emerged in recent years aimed at improving operational productivity are worth noting. These include overhead value analysis (OVA), productivity evaluation programs (PEP), and quality circles (QC).

- *OVA.* Overhead value analysis involves a general review of work activities with the aim of understanding the functions, outputs, and services performed. These are studied to determine if they are really needed, whether any can be eliminated, combined, shrunk, changed, or improved. The aim is to reduce the labor ingredient to a minimum through management changes, work changes, automation, productivity control measures, and so on. The OVA methodology amounts to a fundamental redesign of the organization being studied, through an evaluation of each overhead activity that is performed, an assessment of the value received versus the cost of the activity, and a factual analysis to determine if redesign or restructuring could result in the reduction or elimination of activities (and thus jobs and costs). OVA is a six-step process:

1. Project preparation—areas to be covered, establishment of a steering committee, the working task force, and so on.
2. Develop a database on the current use of resources—the purpose of activities, outputs, and costs.
3. Generate and evaluate ideas for cost reduction—change, combine, and eliminate activities and processes.
4. Make decisions—select worthy ideas after consultation with affected parties and consideration of the risks involved.
5. Develop implementation plans—organizational restructuring, reassignments, and eliminations.
6. Implement—assignments, schedules, and follow-up (post mortems).

- *PEP.* A modern form of work measurement, PEP is applied to white-collar workers instead of the traditional blue-collar workers. It identifies incremental tasks, structures work into controllable tasks, does unit-volume recording to measure departmental performance by task, and uses time-unit standards to compare productivity among various units of work. Indexes prepared from the statistical recordings are used to prepare management reports on performance. A. T. Kearney Co. (Chicago), a management consulting firm, is marketing a PEP program. A company that has used a PEP program to advantage is Canada's Hudson Bay Co. Consultants working with company management and employees analyzed the tasks performed in Hudson's credit operations consisting of 2 million active credit accounts. After task descriptions and time standards were set, workers recorded the tasks they performed on forms which were collected daily, compiled, and used to prepare reports for supervisors. Hudson Bay reported experiencing a 36% productivity improvement in its credit operations as a result of the PEP program (11).

- *QCs.* Introduced in the 1970s, the QC approach has attracted considerable interest among U. S. firms. Quality Circles are small groups (5–10) of employees from similar or the same work area who meet regularly in a collaborative effort to identify, analyze, and solve various work problems. The purpose is to promote company-wide improvement and productivity by optimizing worker capabilities through greater work satisfaction stemming from participative management. Not all QCs are effective however; 25% of manufacturing firms using QCs have experienced failure (12). Usually this is not due to the QC concept itself, but to poor implementation (i.e., lack of planning, false expectation of easy rewards, weak management support). Lack of management commitment is cited by many as the main problem.

Quality circles have been more successful in Japan than in the United States[2] because they are founded on the notion that group performance is better than individual performance, that workers want to participate, and that participation improves productivity. Group consensus playing is something the Japanese believe in more than Americans. Thus Japan's QCs are based on *group* performance and reward, whereas America's QCs are generally based on *individual* performance and reward. For any productivity improvement effort to work, it must be a managed process. It will not happen by itself. Moreover, it must hold benefits for both the employer (productivity and quality production) and the employee (reward and quality of work life).

One company that has benefited from QCs is the JFK Medical Center in Edison, New Jersey. Hospital employees began a pioneering project to increase productivity and quality of services. In 1983, a QC program was started and in 1984 the IMPROSHARE system was installed. The two programs complement each other, combining the economic motivation of IMPROSHARE with the group-solving techniques of quality circles. Workers share in the actual cost savings realized by the hospital. The program helped to reduce the cost of patient care by realizing a cost savings of $2 million in its first year of operation (13).

Automation Penetration. The best productivity tool to ever hit company operations was the computer. Automation is perhaps the most obvious productivity strategy when it comes to manual and high labor-content operations. Automating the labor out always leads to productivity gains and lower costs. That is why automating the "back shop" has been the chief focus of DP for the past 25 years. Operating support systems (OSS) represented the early beginnings of automation. The primary goal of an OSS was operational productivity. Automation started by computerizing internal labor-intensive operations. This is still a good place to look for productivity opportunities in the application of support systems, data processing, and telecommunications. But because efforts have been concentrated on this area for some 25 years or more, further productivity will need to come from systems that penetrate deeper into the organization, bringing automation to functions previously untouched, or by employing new technologies that can bring renewed cost/performance gains to the firm.

The manufacturing sector's computer-integrated manufacturing (CIM) developments are an excellent example of automation penetration in the factory ranging from computer-aided design, manufacturing, and engineering (CAD/CAM/CAE), to materials requirements planning and man-

---

[2]Some 19 million Japanese, nearly two-thirds of the office work force, are involved in QCs, compared to only 1 million, or 2%, in the United States.

ufacturing resources planning (MRP and MRPII), and to manufacturing automation protocol (MAP) standards. Because CIM penetrates to all facets of manufacturing (inventorying, production, and delivery), it is being implemented widely throughout the manufacturing sector.

In the services industries, the Super Systems discussed in Chapter 5 are examples of systems that go deeper into the organization the second time around, automating processes that were untouched in the first automation effort. Robert McDermott, the new President of the USSA Group, for example, initiated a Super System effort on taking over the reins of the life insurance company and discovering the amount of paperwork involved in its policy and claims-processing operations. A 10-year systems program was undertaken to automate all of the paper handling operations into a more streamlined, efficient environment. As a result, claims adjusters now do about 75% of their work on line, without referring to paper files, thereby speeding up the process and giving them a competitive edge (14).

Deep automation penetration can also reduce dependence on labor to the point where business interruption through union "strikes" becomes far less disruptive. The air controller's strike in 1981 illustrated this well. The reason the President was able to fire the striking controllers without completely disrupting air traffic in the United States was the heavy penetration of automation that kept the bulk of air traffic moving in spite of the short supply of controllers. A telephone strike a few years ago had the same effect. Because of the heavy automation of the telephone system, a small cache of supervisors kept the system going while the strikers were out, minimizing the impact on the public.

One way to determine the degree of automation penetration in the organization is to perform an automation penetration audit, or survey, of the company's information systems portfolio. A useful methodology for this purpose is one suggested by Richard Nolan of Nolan Norton Co. (15). Start by taking inventory of all applications systems. For each application, conduct interviews (or send questionnaires) to both the responsible systems staff and the system users to determine how they view the system. The systems people are questioned about the system's technical efficiency (design, maintainability, operating efficiency). Users are solicited for their view of the system's functional effectiveness (quality, reliability, satisfaction of information needs). By ranking subjective responses on a scale of 1–10, each system is ranked as Good, Marginal, or Poor. Correlation of the two views, as shown in Figure 7.2 provides a "report card" on the general health of in-place systems. Those ranked Poor (lower left) by both parties are candidates for replacement; those ranked Marginal should be enhanced; those considered Good are left alone.

Second, all systems should be classified according to whether they are internal (OSS), information (MSS), or external (CSS) and matched against the missions of each business (see Chapter 4). GROW businesses should have a healthy share of CSSs in their mix to provide competition and differential products and services; HARVEST businesses should be heavily

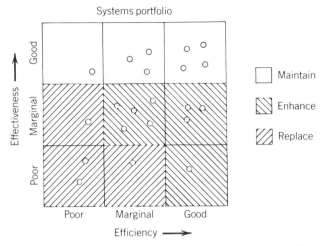

Figure 7.2. Systems portfolio, © Nolan Norton & Co., 1984 (15). Used with permission.

automated with OSSs, providing productivity in support of low-cost operations. Needless to say, any labor-intensive areas not automated are candidates for at least a packaged system solution, if not an in-house development effort.

Finally, analyze systems as to whether they are batch, online, or database. This reveals the age and status of the portfolio versus the state of the art. Today's information company should have little batch processing left, mostly online systems, and a good representation of not only online but database systems as well.

The Office

> IW 34—OFFICE PRODUCTIVITY
> Office automation initiatives aimed at white-collar
> workers at all levels of the organization.

For two decades, as automation was applied ever more broadly to the back-office operations, the office was largely neglected. Aside from typewriters and electronic calculators, investments in office automation were low. Whereas the United States spent $50,000 in technology to support the farmer and $25,000 in support of a factory worker, only $2500 was spent on the average office worker. Then, in the mid-1970s, word processing was introduced as a substitute for the typewriter, aimed at increasing secretarial productivity. In just 10 years the office has been saturated with a terminal:secretary ratio now approaching 1:1. Still, white-collar productivity has not shown as much improvement as it should, despite increased capital investments. Part of the reason for this, in some people's opinion, is that we have been applying new tools to doing the same things the same way. The real payoff generally comes in doing work entirely differently. Another reason is the "down-escalator" factor; that is, although computing may be increasing white-collar productivity, other countervailing influences are simultaneously pulling it down. Hence without office automation, we may very well have seen a sharp *drop* in office productivity in the last decade.

The personal computer, although introduced as a hobby kit by Apple in 1976, didn't go anywhere until Visicalc came along in 1979. Visicalc represented a major breakthrough, the introduction of a generalized program that could be used broadly for many business applications. Since 1980, the PC has catapulted through the business office world as well. Experts now predict that by 1990 the terminal:user ratio in the office will also be nearing 1:1. After 25 years, the confluence of management and machine is finally becoming a reality.

The Personal Computer as a Productivity Tool. Whereas word processing focused on better paper handling, the PC's productivity focus is on information management. Word processing was aimed at secretarial productivity; the PC aims at the high-priced professional/managerial market where the highest potential payoff in office productivity lies. If indeed we reach a terminal to user ratio of 1:1 by 1990, this means that it will have taken the PC just 10 years to dominate the office. It took the telephone nearly 50 years to do the same.

Productivity from PCs comes in two forms: "small" EOS productivity, and people productivity through task automation. Economy of scale on micros comes about because, for the first time in the history of computers in business, the best price/performance rates are on small systems. The cost of processing power and storage in micros is a fraction of that for mainframe computers today. William Zachmann, corporate Research Director for International Data Corp., points out the cost per MIPS of mainframe computer power is now $160,000–$175,000 compared to under $5000 for micros; and the cost of mainframe storage is $6000–$7500 per megabyte compared to $350–$1000 for micros (16). This opens up productivity options for micro users over traditional mainframe systems that enable leveraging the investment in micros many times over. Professional and managerial productivity from the use of micros can also pay for the machines several times over. Consider this. A typical corporate PC with software might run $6000. Considering a 3-year life, the after-tax cost per year is $1000. A typical office worker earning $30,000 per year needs to increase his/her productivity by 6.7% to return $1000 after-tax savings to the company. The productivity breakeven point of a $50,000/year manager is just 4%.

The justification for PCs is managerial productivity. But the potential for leveraging the investment in PCs is considerable. A survey by Newton-Evans Research Co. (Endicott, Maryland) of over 100 *Fortune*-ranked firms showed that, on average, most PCs are used between 2 and 4 hours daily (17). This leaves a lot of unused time. Considering a hardware to software investment ratio of 10:1, investment in another $500 software package can double the utility of a $6000 computer. By helping users find several additional uses for their PCs, IW planners can help a company realize considerable further productivity leverage from their initial investment.

As noted in Chapter 5 (see figure 5.3), a PC survey at Bank of Boston disclosed that 73% of PC uses were productivity-oriented, automating managerial tasks. Most users were primarily using their PCs for spreadsheet analysis. Very few had other applications running. By concentrating on introducing users to other possible uses (database management, graphics, accessing external databases, etc.), we were able to exert considerable leverage on the use and investment of the bank's PC base. We did it through the use of the Information Center strategy.

Information Centers. The information center (IC), as IBM originally conceived it, consisted of copying files to a mainframe accessible to users using fourth-generation languages (4GL) to access data directly; in effect, migrating the inquiry and reporting functions to the users. (Sometimes the data is downloaded to a departmental minicomputer-based IC instead of a mainframe.) Since some two-thirds of programming time is spent on maintenance activities such as defining, programming, and generating reports, users with 4GLs working off copy files not only increases user productivity (fast turnaround), but programmer productivity (offloading maintenance) as well. In this sense, the IC is an answer to the systems "backlog" problem. But ICs have evolved a second role in many companies—the promotion and support of PCs, or end-user computing, to leverage managerial productivity. These "PC centers," as described in Chapter 6 (IW-30), have been a key strategy for the promulgation of intelligent PC usage in thousands of companies across the United States. In fact, the number of companies using this strategy as a way to leverage the productivity potential of PCs in the organization has grown remarkably since 1982 when the concept was first introduced. As noted earlier, as many as 80% of the nation's large companies now have such PC centers.

Today, the major focus has shifted to connectivity. *There is no such thing as a personal computer in a business office.* There are only small, cheap, business computers using business data to solve business problems. Information center managers, therefore, are finding ways to include PCs in overall computer architecture planning, to facilitate information management at the user level while promoting appropriate control and data integration across the organization. Connectivity is being addressed at the individual level through integrated workstations, at the department level by local area networks (LAN), and at the corporate level through micro–mainframe connectivity. In the 1990s, it is likely that LANs will eventually overtake and replace both the corporate and departmental IC as we know it today. Information will be downloaded to LAN servers from inside and outside databases serving clusters of workstations interconnected to other LANs, forming one totally integrated communicating network throughout the corporation.

Electronic Mail. Despite all the talk about electronic mail, it has not flourished as many had expected. The reason is simple. It is still cumbersome to use for most people. To be efficient, it requires a critical mass, both senders and receivers need terminals, and both must use the same E-mail service. A number of large companies have installed major E-mail networks (Citicorp, Digital Equipment, General Motors), but most small companies have not. Nonetheless, the number of companies using E-Mail is growing, and more vendors are offering such services (e.g., MCI Communications, Western Union, and Federal Express). In addition, we may be seeing a trendsetting move in the linking up of different E-Mail services, such as GTE Telenet Communications with Telecom Canada's electronic messaging service and Compuserve with MCI Communications E-Mail services.

Electronic mail can help productivity by making communications more efficient, by eliminating the "telephone tag" that goes on in most offices as people try and fail to connect with each other. There are different kinds of E-mail: terminal users use computer keyboards to type messages to one another's "electronic" mailboxes; telephone users use voice mail to leave a telephone message in someone's mailbox; and voice-annotated systems use a combination of both. Each aims at different users: voice mail is generally favored by salesmen on the road and executives who are used to using telephones but not terminals; E-Mail is favored by engineers, professionals and scientists, people who are used to working with terminals; voice-annotated systems are used by information systems professionals and others who want both (i.e., voice in, annotated typed message out). It is almost a certainty that E-mail will come into its own in the next few years as the terminal/people ratio continues to increase and new standards come into place, such as CCITT's X.400, which promises to connect E-Mail users around the world without regard to what they are connected to; in effect, a universal electronic envelope. Tomorrow's electronic workstations will likely incorporate both a computer and a telephone. Several such products, for example, Northern Telecom's Displayphone and GTE's Omniaction telephone terminal, have already hit the marketplace.

Telecommuting. Yet another technique for increasing operational productivity is telecommuting, getting work done away from the office. Telecommuting can be done through working at home, at an alternate work location, or while on the road. Examples include self-employed secretaries working out of their home, establishing a data-entry office in a distant city to tap an otherwise unavailable supply of workers, and giving salespeople portable computers to enter orders or receive and send messages while on the road. Telecommuting involves the movement of information instead of people. In this sense, the telephone is a form of telecommuting; so is teleconferencing and electronic mail. Some companies that benefit from telecommuting are the following:

- Cummins Engine links up half of their 18,000 employees worldwide in an electronic office system called TOSS (Total Office Support System). Their employees can be virtually anywhere in the world and still tap into their electronic desk. The company originally targeted to produce company-wide productivity gains of 17.3% from TOSS. In addition, they report that with the system fewer middle managers are needed and many clerical positions are beginning to resemble administrative assistants (18).
- Homequity, Inc.'s telecommuting program is aimed at increasing the productivity of geographically widespread customer service personnel working with real estate clients (19).
- The California State Government's pilot with 100 state employees telecommuting from home and 100 more from satellite offices projected a payback in productivity gains in as little as 5 months (20).
- F International, a computer consulting firm, has over 1000 employees located in the United Kingdom, the Netherlands, and Denmark linked together *only* by computer terminals in their homes. They have no headquarters, no branches, and no offices anywhere (21).
- The Diebold Group's assistant to the Chairman, Catherine Marenghi, has begun each work day for the past several years without leaving her home in Boston, even though her employer is located in Manhattan. With a PC, modem, and telephone she keeps in daily touch with her colleagues as if she were working in an office down the hall from them. Ms. Marenghi reports that Diebold Group research has found an average productivity increase of 100% among home workers (22).

Telecommuting benefits both the organization and the individual. According to one expert, organizational benefits include improved productivity (on average, 20%), recruitment (tapping otherwise unavailable markets), employee retention (keeping scarce skills otherwise lost to maternity leave, retirement, or reluctance to relocate), and space savings (shared desks or no desks). Individual benefits are flexible scheduling, more control over work, fewer work interruptions, better coordination of home and work schedules, and savings on food, clothing, and transportation (23).

INFORMATION RESOURCES PRODUCTIVITY

Data Processing Resources

IW 35—DATA PROCESSING RESOURCES
Productivity from economy-of-scale computing.

The early application of business computers was to the back office, the labor-intensive areas of a company that offered high productivity potential. The fantastic advances in the cost/performance gains of computers continues unabated. The hardware contribution to productivity is well understood. But the potential contribution of software to productivity still has much untapped potential. To understand where the opportunities lie in the data processing arena, we need to focus on the three main functions of modern data centers: the production center, the development center, and the information center.

In large organizations, these three functions are segmented on different and multiple machines, even different geographic locations. In smaller shops, they may all be on a single machine; yet they are all there. Each performs a different function and services different users.

- *The Production Center.* This is the "factory" function, serving operations (clerical personnel, the DP users). It is concerned with processing large transaction systems, maintaining large databases, and serving the computer support needs of the corporation and its business.
- *The Development Center.* This function provides online support to the programming staff who are developing and implementing new applications systems. Serving as a program development tool, not a production facility, its purpose is to reduce development time and thus cost—which is especially important to the LEAD and NICHE businesses that get most of the development resources.
- *The Information Center.* As a repository of corporate databases, the Information Center serves the information needs of end-users. Databases are accessed using fourth-generation languages (4GL) by users directly, thereby allowing programmers to devote more time to development, rather than maintenance work, while facilitating direct information access for faster and better management decisions. Information Centers may be mainframe, mini-, or micro-based—or combinations of all three.

Each of these "processing" centers delivers productivity to its respective users. Each, in turn, has a variety of software product options to help achieve that productivity. We consider the production center possibilities here; development center productivity aids are discussed in the section on Software Resources; information center products were previously reviewed under Office Automation.

Production center productivity results from EOs operations. Economy of scale is aided by continuing advances in the cost/performance gains of computers. The larger the machine, the greater the gain as the cost per million of instructions per second (MIPS), the standard measure of computer power, declines with size. The same is true of internal memory and external storage. However, to take advantage of that power and size, one needs volume. A giant data center, a nationwide communications network, a massive Super System—these all represent EOSs that only the largest competitors can match. Full and imaginative utilization of EOS resources result in competitive advantage as the low-cost producer.

- When Mellon Bank in Pittsburgh bought out Girard Trust in Philadelphia the two banks' data centers were immediately merged to increase EOS in DP operations.
- The Texaco/Getty merger in 1985 also offered significant data processing EOS. Even before the lawyers got the legal problems of their mega-merger unwound, Texaco and Getty started working on the merger of their respective DP facilities. Prior to the merger, Getty had operated two corporate DP centers in Houston and Tulsa, as well as a development center in Los Angeles. Texaco had four data centers and a development center in three Houston area facilities. Following the merger, these were consolidated into two production centers and one development center. The former Getty DP operations in Tulsa were expanded to become the production and development center for the corporate and international users, and Texaco's Bellaire center in Houston became the production center for merged companies' domestic operations. In the process, old technology (IBM 3080 and 3033 processors) was phased out in favor of larger EOS technology (IBM 3090s) (24).
- Bank of America is moving 3500 people into a new office complex 25 miles from downtown San Francisco to cut costs by consolidating facilities and getting synergy and leverage through creation of a critical mass of systems people working together in a single campus. Bank of America counted on this EOS move to help turn around an abysmal earnings situation (a $338 million loss in the second quarter of 1985), the second largest quarterly loss in U. S. banking history (25).

Production center efficiency also results in DP productivity. Efficiency of operations requires good management, quality trained personnel, continued fine-tuning, and automated production aids. The DP manager can exert a great deal of efficiency leverage by investing in software productivity aids, which represents a small percentage of the DP budget but can add immense value. Support products include operating systems, compilers, teleprocessing monitors, database software, storage management, resource management, optimizers, job schedulers, performance monitors, and capacity planning tools. Many of these are vendor-supplied, but third parties also provide excellent products (e.g., Intercomm. IDMS, Datacom, SAS, ISPF, CMS, Focus, Ramis, and Easytrieve). New productivity support products appear almost daily. We are now even seeing Expert Systems appearing on the data processing scene. Here are two examples:

- An Expert System "Sysgen" generator called R1 has been developed by Digital Equipment Corp. for configuring VAX computers. Sysgen (system generation) refers to the need to do a system reconfiguration process every time hardware charges are introduced into a system. This takes many hours of scarce systems programmer's time, and is often done on weekends because the system usually must be taken down to make the changes. DEC's expert sysgener relieves systems programmers from tedious work, reduces human error, and optimizes system performance.
- Another Expert System productivity aid is IBM's YES/MVS for mainframe computer operations. YES/MVS automates many of the functions of computer operators such as Job Entry System (JES) queue space management, network communication between computers, response to hardware problems to prevent system crashes, monitoring software subsystems, monitoring system performance, and scheduling large batch jobs off prime site.

Another way to reduce DP operations costs is through remote operations. Firms with multiple computer sites can eliminate much of the need for on-site operations by monitoring operations from remote consoles. Access security can be controlled with card-coded access systems, printers can be eliminated either through remote printing or online reporting (e.g., IBM's RMDS facility), tape handling can be eliminated by designing disk-based systems, online systems eliminate batch processing, and job scheduling can be done from a remote console. Many small sites can be made to function without on-site operations, with a remote computer operator managing several sites, at greatly reduced operating costs.

In the future, much of the production center work will be eliminated as operating systems are moved (microcoded) into the hardware, and more automatic interfaces are provided by job schedulers, compilers, database management systems, and extract languages and products. Database software, teleprocessing monitors, and JES (IBM's scheduling system for MVS) will move into hardware as well, in the form of specialized processors that are easier to use and utilize automatic error detection and recovery. Meanwhile, DP managers need to be alert to, and use, the myriad software support aids available that can increase production center productivity. From a competitive viewpoint, DP productivity can expand market scope owing to EOS advantages, can achieve differentiation because it results in a superior service (quality product), and can provide product niches as a result of a strong and supportive DP function.

Systems Resources

IW 36—SYSTEMS RESOURCES
Attacking the software development bottleneck.

Productivity of systems resources results in faster development which, in turn, results in bringing products to the marketplace sooner. Therefore, anything that can be done to increase systems productivity potentially represents competitive gain.

Ironically, the biggest barrier to systems development today is programming! Demand for automation far outstrips the supply of programmers. The more exposure the world has to the value and potential of technology in the Information Age, the greater the demand for automation becomes. In most large organizations, the systems backlog is 2–3 years or longer. And this is only the known backlog. Behind that is an "invisible" backlog of needs that users do not even express because they feel the likelihood of getting them satisfied is low or nil. As the systems manager begins to make inroads on the known backlog, the invisible backlog immediately surfaces to fill the gap. The demand and the backlog are thus much greater than one thinks. Here are four solutions aimed at solving this dilemma:

- *Use Packaged Software.* Most small organizations use nothing but package programs. Even the *Fortune* 1000 is rapidly getting to the point where in-house development is a luxury that is no longer affordable. Packages should be used as much as possible for internal (OSS) applications. Development should be reserved for the building of customized management support systems (MSS) and external customer support systems (CSS) that provide competitive advantage.
- *Increase Programmer Productivity.* Online programming, structured techniques, and program development tools all offer opportunities to increase the productivity of this scarce resource. As valuable as these are, however, they generally offer productivity gains of 10, 20, and 50% when, in fact, gains of 500 and 1000% are needed. Breakthroughs are coming, however, especially in the development of computer-aided design and programming (CAD/CAP), which is discussed in the section about Workbench tools.

- *Put Software Into "Firmware."* Much of today's systems software—operating systems, teleprocessing monitors, database management systems—will ultimately be built into hardware, putting the system interface at a much higher level and reducing much of the need for systems programmers. We may eventually also see much generalized reusable applications code become microcode. It is in the vendor's interest to do this because more hardware is being produced than can be used. If the computer manufacturers want to continue to sell hardware, more firmware will be a necessity.

- *Move the Mountain to Muhammed.* Probably the most promising solution to the programming problem is to eliminate it altogether—by moving it to the end-users. End-user computing, microcomputers, natural languages, information centers, and fifth-generation languages (5GL) in the 1990s will turn the programming organization of the 1970s into an historical anachronism. Programming as we know it today will no longer exist. Systems designers will enter specifications on their machine and design diagrams and code will be automatically generated. End-users will be directly connected to information databases eliminating much of what is now maintenance programming. The first two of these solutions are directly controllable by the CIO, so we discuss these further here. The last two will continue to be pressed by the vendors and users, respectively; the CIO can facilitate these changes and take advantage of opportunities, but cannot control them.

Package Programs. In any systems effort, the first question to ask is: Buy it or build it? If the right package solution can be found, considerable time and money can be saved. Avoiding development altogether is a great productivity booster. In most small organizations, package software is not just an option, it's a necessity, since development staffs are small. But even in larger organizations, the benefits of packages are moving more and more companies to seek package solutions as a first alternative, particularly for internal (OSS) systems that have no competitive advantage. Software packages, for the most part, can provide high value at relatively low cost. They can create the added value either by lowering cost or improving performance (quality). And they represent a relatively small percentage of DP budgets.

In general, the pros of building are the cons of buying, and vice versa, as shown in Figure 7.3 (26). Package programs are available from a wide variety of sources, including software vendors and brokers, the federal government, the academic world, computer vendors, common-bond groups (user groups and trade associations), and individual companies. Software brokers, (middlemen between buyers and sellers) also produce software directories of available packages. A few of the more widely know are the ICP Software Review, Datapro Research, Auerbach, and the Dun &

Pros	Cons
Build	*Buy*
Get custom-tailored product	Modifications often extensive
Get state of the art system	System may not be state of the art
Integration with other systems possible	Integration with other systems is more difficult
Familiarity with system makes maintenance easier	Foreign systems are most difficult to maintain
Buy	*Build*
Lower cost	Higher cost
Less development time	Longer development time
Frees scarce resources for other work	Hard to get needed resources
System proven and tested	More debugging needed

Figure 7.3. Buy vs. build; source: Synnot and Gruber (26).

Bradstreet directories. Two indicators of leading packages are the ICP Million Dollar Awards (vendors who have sold over $1 million of their product) and the Datapro Software Survey (survey results of user software ratings).

Programmer Productivity. If a system is to be built for competitive or other reasons, the *development center* concept comes into play. The development center, as noted earlier, supports systems and programming personnel in the development of databases and applications systems. The productivity aim of the development center is to speed up the development process by leveraging these scarce resources. One of the best ways to do this is by putting program development *online.* Online program development increases programmer productivity significantly. As a result, in many leading companies today, the ratio of programmers to terminals is 1:1. The hardware resource is cheap compared to labor. Therefore, using the hardware resource to leverage scarce and expensive labor makes eminent sense. Structured design and programming techniques (Yourdan, Michael Jackson) can also yield productivity over conventional development techniques.

A variety of development tools have also been developed for the marketplace by vendors intent on capturing the market for the "automation of automation." Unfortunately, there is no single product solution to the application development problem. There yet exists a huge gap between the productivity of software versus hardware. Hardware has far outstripped software in productivity gains. A quantum leap in software automation is needed, but this development appears to be in the future. Meantime, information managers need to sort through the tools available today aimed at the various phases of the development life cycle. These tools range from specifications, design, coding, and maintenance aids. New products appear almost daily, promising to automate the old-fashioned way of doing things. Yet, in most organizations, software development continues to be largely manual. Information managers cannot wait for the "total" solution. The shortage of people and the demand for further automation continues to build the backlog. Some of the tools and techniques that have surfaced in recent years to increase the productivity of the systems development process include *application development tools* for systems specification and design, database design, and code generation; *fourth-generation languages,* or 4GLs, for systems development and/or information retrieval; *software maintenance tools* such as test data generators, debuggers, formatters, and software release control; and *conversion aids,* that is, batch to online, language convertors, operating system upgrades, and database upgrades.

Some applications development tools not only make programming productive, but actually enable the by-passing of programmers, putting computer power in the hands of systems designers and even end-users. In fact, in the future we could see all traditional development replaced by automated systems design and programming, eliminating programmers as we know them today.

Yet, with all this futuristic promise, third-generation languages (3GL) such as Cobol, Fortran, and PL1, still dominate, with three-quarters of all code in use still in these languages. There is a big market for such Cobol tools as structured compilers (IBM's Cobol SF), generators (DEC's VAX Cobol generator), and application generator products (Transform Logic Corp's TRANSFORM Cobol program generator).

Fourth-Generation Languages. A major shift is occurring today to fourth-generation languages as users discover that 4GLs produce a 5:1 productivity advantage in program development. They allow designers to quickly build prototype systems, using throw-away code. After several iterations to develop the correct code, it can then be recoded in a traditional 3GL for better machine efficiency, if desired. The purpose of 4GLs is to improve productivity by avoiding work, simplifying it, or speeding it up. James Martin says the world is spending $170 billion a year on systems development (analysts, programmers, and their managers). That's a big playground for productivity.

There are various types of 4GLs, including query and report languages (Focus, Ramis, Mark IV, Inquire, Easytrieve), application generators (Ideal, Adds-On, Mantis), program generators (IP3, SQL), and simulation modeling languages (Express, Strategem, System W). In all, there are over 900 4GL products on the market today. These can or should be used in combination—for example, build a prototype system using a 4GL; use automated design tools for the front end, a code generator for the back end, and a 4GL for retrieval.

Prototyping. One of the ways 4GLs are used is in *prototyping,* which, according to one survey, can improve programmer/analyst productivity by 1000–2000% (27); 10X is a lot different than 10%! Prototyping is a test version of an information system. As in traditional systems development, it starts with a thorough analysis of user needs. Unlike traditional systems, lengthy specifications are not prepared. Instead, interactive design begins immediately to produce a "quick and dirty" working prototype. The user critiques the system and revisions are made iteratively until the user is satisfied. It can then either be put into production as is, or be converted to Cobol (or other 3GL) as a standard institutionalized system. The key is the interaction between builder and user. Prototyping works best when there is one user and one builder. In addition to programmer productivity, the user benefits from heavier involvement in the system's creation, fast development, and earlier productivity of his/her own staff. When is prototyping appropriate? When a traditional systems approach will take too long to satisfy an immediate need, when a management information system can be built independently of the transaction system that feeds it, when working in an unstructured and amorphous environment (as in management systems), when a system is to be a reporting system only, or when use of the system is expected to be either short-lived or infrequent. (Two examples of prototyping tools are Savvy from Excalibur and Demo Program from Software Garden.)

The software productivity trends of the past decade have evolved through structured methodologies, nonprocedural languages, specification languages, automated development tools, prototyping, the use of Information Centers, and end-user computing workstations. The future will likely see greater movement toward the automation of automation through the "programmer's workbench" concept.

Design Workstation. Rather than meeting the growing need for software with more staff, many companies are doing it through higher productivity of existing staff. Design workstations are an important trend in this direction. New workstation (or workbench) products are now attacking the front end (systems analysis and design) of the systems development process as well as the back end (program code generators). The two are coming together to form powerful computer-aided software engineering (CASE) tools that can generate up to 80–90% of a system directly from design specifications, thus increasing programmer/analyst productivity 10X rather than 10%. An analyst's workbench generally refers to a programmer/analyst workstation equipped with a variety of software tools that offer the same productivity enhancements to programmers that CAD/CAM/CAE offers to design engineers. CASE workstations offload application development work from the mainframe and automate it on a PC, transferring a PC into a powerful application development workstation. A variety of CASE tools automate various parts of the design and programming process, ranging from compilers, to design tools, to program generators. Here are the three examples:

- Index Technology (InTech) of Cambridge, Massachusetts produces Excelerator, a designer workbench system design and documentation tool that generates applications design documentation from specifications. According to Index, a recent survey of users reported an average productivity increase in system design time of 35%, with some in excess of 100%, over conventional systems design techniques.
- Arthur Anderson & Co.'s Programmer Workbench was installed in a large reinsurance company that had estimated they would expend 15,000 workdays to create five new systems over 4 years. With the workstation they experienced a 50% reduction in the time needed to design, code, and test the programs, and a 22% reduction in workdays, saving 3300 workdays over the original estimate, and a year of development time.
- Hartford Integrated Technologies, Inc. (Hitech) in Hartford, Connecticut, an offshoot of the Hartford Insurance Group and Wang Laboratories, has The Solution, an applications development product line of programmer tools running on Wang processors with links to IBM mainframes. In this case, development is offloaded to a departmental minicomputer instead of a PC. This allows resource sharing among teams of programmers. Once programs have been coded and tested on the Wang, they are upgraded to the target host. Hartford claims to have boosted the productivity of their programmers with The Solution by nearly 30%.

Other makers of CASE products include Cadre Technologies (Providence, Rhode Island), Nastec (Southfield, Michigan), KnowledgeWare (Ann Arbor, Michigan) and some two dozen others at this writing.

The designer's workstation concept also lends itself nicely to telecommuting. Systems designers using a workbench workstation have all the resources they need to develop systems at home. In a city, this can tap programmers who live in the country. In the country, it can tap a lucrative city marketplace.

In the final analysis, the development center of the 1990s will likely be replaced by expanded versions of the programmer's workbench, which will move development to stand-alone micro workstations.

Communications Resources

> **IW 37—COMMUNICATIONS RESOURCES**
> Options for optimizing communications services at least costs.

When AT&T's long-distance business was separated from the Bell Operating Companies (BOCs) local phone service, many felt that large users would be the beneficiaries, because competitive pressures caused by deregulation would drive prices down almost to cost. It was expected that long-distance rates would decline while local rates would increase, again benefiting large companies who are the heavy long-distance users and who could afford to bypass local connections (i.e., directly connect a private network to long-distance lines).

This has pretty much been the case. The divestiture has increased competition and resulted in many more options to consider than in the past. New EOS opportunities have opened up, and new "bypass options" now offer communication managers many ways to increase productivity through communications. To gain competitive advantage from lower cost communications, managers cannot rely solely on the public network. New techniques and bypass options are needed to save money through new and better communications services.

Competitive Alternatives. The first way to seek communications productivity is through exploration of competitive alternatives such as the use of alternate common carriers, in-house PBXs, and packet switching, private, and virtual networks:

- *Alternate Carriers.* Such carriers as AT&T, MCI, and U. S. Sprint (formerly GTE Sprint) can offer opportunities to effect cost reductions by taking advantage of changing rates to different cities fostered by competition for business traffic. Discounts of 10–20% off regular long-distance rates are common. Companies with in-house PBXs should, in fact, put up several long-distance carriers, to take advantage of the lowest cost routing options as rates change through competition.
- *In-House PBXs.* Systems developed by AT&T, Northern Telecom, and IBM's Rolm are growing in popularity. In-house PBXs can cost less, give greater functionality, and provide greater in-house control. Digital PBXs are the trend. Wiring a building with digital wire enables computers, terminals, and telephones to be hooked up into a single network. An integrated voice/data network can provide a cost-ratio gain of 4:1. That is, the cost of separate voice and data channels will likely be four times that of a single integrated circuit, because data

rides almost free on the voice pipe—it uses so little bandwidth that 6–8 data lines can fit on one voice channel.

- *Packet Networks.* Telenet and Tymnet, for example, also offer lower cost opportunities over conventional long-distance lines. Packet switching has grown rapidly as a result. Packet switching breaks up messages into pieces. Message traffic is mixed up with other senders in packets and reassembled at the other end, much like a group being split up on several busses, then regrouping at the destination point. This shared use of communication lines results in more efficient and thus lower-cost communications traffic. This is what makes packet switching cheap and popular.

- *Private Networks..* In the past, the installation of private communications networks was prohibitively expensive, and was practical only for the largest companies. Recently, T-1 carrier service was opened up for use as commercial private networks, whereas previously only the phone companies used T-1 for public networks. This has created a whole new market for private networks. The T-1 circuits, operating at 1.544 megabits-per-second, literally offer a 24-lane communications superhighway (each T-1 provides 24 voice channels), integrating voice and data over the same network. The major advantage of T-1 is its ability to accommodate tremendous growth at a comparably inexpensive price. One T-1 link costs about three times as much as a 56 bito-bits-per-second channel, but because its capacity is 24 times greater, the cost/performance advantage over standard 56 kps is about 8:1.

- *Virtual Networks.* A "virtual" network is the use of a switched public network in a manner that gives it the appearance of a private network. Hence AT&T's virtual network called SDN (software defined network), for example, allows a user to have a virtual private line. That is, the user can define his own network and change it at will. There are no dialing or blocked calls, voice and data are integrated, and the user pays only a usage charge which is a fraction of the cost of a leased line. Companies offering virtual networks include AT&T, MCI, U. S. Telecom (now GTE), and Western Union. Virtual networks are an economical way to tie in low-traffic locations to a company's leased-line network without having to lease lines to each location.

Bypass options. In addition, there is the alternative of bypassing these alternate carrier services completely. The T-1 service mentioned above is an example. Other bypass options include microwave, satellite, fiber optics, cable, and mobile communications.

- *Microwave.* Used for short distances of up to 10 miles, microwave is fast becoming a popular option for companies with heavy voice and data traffic, particularly between two offices in a city that are within "line of sight" of one another. Microwave offers fast payback, often a year or so break-even over conventional leased lines, and a highly reliable service (up to 100 times greater than phone lines).

- *Satellite.* Although private satellites are still prohibitively expensive for all but the largest companies, alternatives are on the horizon. One promising alternative is the use of private micro earth stations, which share the cost of a transponder in the sky. Micro earth stations use small (2–3 meter) inexpensive dishes that hook up multipoint locations, ideal for companies with several offices located around the country that all need to talk to the head office. Although just getting off the ground (no pun intended), these small satellite systems can be cost effective and should show strong growth in the future as an alternative to private lines for data transmission.

- *Fiber Optics.* Although still a future alternative for most private corporations, some fiber-optics systems are already in place. Teleport Communications in New York, for example, has installed a 150-mile fiber-optic network utilized by 20 large users in the New York City area. Customers either connect to a satellite center on Staten Island or use the system to communicate between their own offices in the city, at higher capacity transmission rates than those provided by either copper wire or microwave.

- *Cable.* Direct cable connections represent one of the best long-term options for large-scale local telephone bypass. Most major cities will eventually offer cabled, providing the opportunity for more and more companies to connect several offices within a city via cable at very low costs. This should be a popular option in future years.

- *Mobile Communications.* The new cellular radio systems are a great improvement over the old single, high-powered radio transmitters that covered a whole city, and had poor quality reception and lots of busy signals. The new mobile communications systems divide a city into small cells, each with their own transmitter/receiver that allows cars moving from one cell to another to pass the calls over from one to the other, maintaining high-quality service levels. Not only is quality and service (few busy signals) better, but costs are dropping rapidly as well. In a few years, cellular car phones should begin to drop from a current purchase cost of $1500–$3000 (plus monthly charges averaging $30–$45) to packages one-tenth of that amount, making car telephones almost as ubiquitous as office telephones in the 1990s.

Although some bypass technologies, such as teleports, local area networks, and digital transmission services are still developing, bypass is one of the fastest growing segments of the telecommunications industry. *Fortune* magazine has forecast that the bypass market will be a $10–$14 billion market by the 1990s. Because of its productivity potential, every communications manager will be paying careful attention to bypass options in the years ahead.

Teleconferencing. Teleconferencing is not a communications bypass option, it is a travel bypass option. It is the moving of information instead of people. Whether audio or video, teleconferencing can save the hundreds and thousands of dollars in costs incurred by business people who travel to meetings in distant cities. The Stanford Research Institute has estimated that 20% of all business travel could be eliminated without loss of efficiency with teleconferencing. That represents a potential savings of several billion dollars per year in travel time and expense.

Audioconferencing is used more frequently than videoconferencing, primarily owing to convenience and cost. Everyone has a telephone, so setting up conference calls through the internal or external operator is relatively easy to do and is cheap (compared to travel). With an in-house PBX, a special conference-call telephone number can be established for access by anyone, anywhere. Conferees can join a conference call just by calling the special number. During installation of a Northern Telecom SL100 switch at Bank of Boston it was necessary to talk daily with the engineers in Dallas, Bell Northern Labs in Ottawa, and the installation folks in Boston. Each day at 1:00 PM all would call a special conference-call number and hold a status meeting. Even with individuals traveling around the country, it was easy to touch base with the entire "team" daily.

Videoconferencing has been slow to catch on. AT&T's Picturephone Meeting Service (PMS) maintains studios in a dozen major U. S. cities and even abroad (London). Using local PMS studios, a 1-hour videoconference between Boston and Los Angeles would cost around $1700; between Boston and Chicago, $1300; and between Boston and New York, $1000. Although this is more than audioconferencing, there are times when visual contact is needed and a videoconference is still cheaper than travel. This author has used the service a number of times—to avoid going to New York for a meeting, to eliminate having a consultant from Detroit come to Boston to make a presentation, to avoid visiting our offices in Los Angeles when a PMS meeting would suffice. Mainly, however, videoconferencing is used for one-way transmission. Hotels such as Holiday Inns offer broadcast (one-way) systems at selected hotels in major cities for use at sales conferences or seminars. A company president in Chicago, through videoconferencing, could speak to a gathering of company salespeople simultaneously in hotels in New York, Los Angeles, and Atlanta, thereby saving thousands of dollars in travel costs to hold a single meeting in Chicago.

EXTERNAL PRODUCTIVITY

CUSTOMER PRODUCTIVITY

Whereas innovation is generally focused externally, productivity is generally viewed as an internal process. Nevertheless, there are many opportunities to create productivity gains for *customers* that can result in competitive advantage. External productivity takes many forms. Better and faster service, a quality product, convenience, and value-added information are all forms of customer productivity. Productivity can come about through better use of resources serving outside markets, as a by-product of new customer products and services, and by broadening or narrowing competitive scope, in other words, anything that saves a customer's time and effort and/or delivers good value is productivity. A review of some of the earlier strategies and cases from Chapters 4–6 will illustrate this concept.

Productivity Through Leveraged Resources

> **IW 38—PRODUCTIVITY THROUGH LEVERAGED RESOURCES**
> Using existing resources to offer new customer services.

New business partnerships, such as joint ventures, mergers, or just the sharing of resources, often yield complementary products, skills, and other synergisms that result in productivity gains for customers. The two major ATM networks, Plus and Cirrus, for example, enable customers of small banks to conduct banking transactions throughout the country, not just in their local area (better service and convenience).

An often overlooked opportunity is putting resources to work more efficiently or to generate new revenue. Selling excess or unused capacity to customers, for example, can leverage resources to produce new revenue that would otherwise be lost. In the 1970s many major banks, recognizing that the systems and DP facilities developed originally for themselves could also be used productively by smaller banks who could not afford automation on their own, went into the correspondent bank DP services business. However, this is an EOS business. It's not enough to have a system; you need volume as well. One of the bigger players in this business is Mellon Bank. Mellon uses a distributed processing system to serve customer banks. Check data is captured at the customer's site using remote check processors connected via telecommunications to Mellon's computers in Pittsburgh. Mellon has developed the business by buying out competitors who did not have the scale to compete.

Companies with major in-place communications networks have learned to sell under-utilized network services to customers. J. C. Penney became an electronic highway toll collector when it began processing credit card transactions for Shell Oil and Gulf as a way to leverage its investment in its communications network. Recently, it formed a new subsidiary, J. C. Penney Communications, Inc., to offer a variety of communications services to institutional investors using excess capacity in facilities developed for internal uses. GTE Telenet used its in-place switching network to provide a natural base for its electronic mail service. Security Pacific Bank, McDonnell-Douglas (McAuto) and GE's Information Services Company (GEISCO) all leveraged in-place communications resources into new customer services.

The "frequent traveler" services offered by airlines came about as a result of computer analysis of unused seats in flights. By offering special discounts and free flights to business travelers, they have succeeded in generating new business at very little cost, since they are, for the most part, essentially filling otherwise empty seats. A similar tactic was used by the Red Lion Inns hotel chain. When a computer flagged persistently high vacancy rates at inns in several western states, the company sent a computer message to all of its hotels and to American Airlines Sabre reservations network offering discounts of up to 50% at the high-vacancy hotels. The result was fewer vacancies and more revenue at little extra cost (29). Another imaginative situation is the railroad industry's use of railway beds to allow communications carriers to lay fiber-optic cable between major cities.

Managers intent on getting on with the new often overlook the potential of converting underutilized existing resources into new revenue producers, and the effort and cost to do so is often small compared to the potential return.

Productivity as a By-Product

```
IW 39—PRODUCTIVITY AS A BY-PRODUCT
Productivity benefits as a by-product of innovation.
```

Competitive Support Systems. Competitive support systems often have a customer productivity advantage embedded within them. If we look through the strategy examples in Chapter 5 we see many examples of productivity by-products at the customer level. For example:

- *New Products.* Automated teller machines, when first introduced, created productivity gains for *both* banks and customers. Bank productivity was achieved through substitution of capital for human labor (tellers). Customer productivity occurred through the convenience factor; that is, customers could get cash and conduct banking transactions any time they pleased (24 hours a day, 7 days per week).

- *Extended Products.* Cullinet's EDP Auditor product became successful only after it was aimed at auditor's productivity, not DP productivity. By extending the product into a new market, a greater productivity need was found.

  An elevator company put terminals in the offices of architects who specialize in designing elevator systems. The architect enters data on load levels, number of floors, and so on, and the computer comes back with a suggested system design. The architect's productivity is leveraged with a minor product extension. As a result, the company gained a 5% share of market with a minimum of investment.

- *Substitute Products.* Many replacement products have increased productivity as a primary benefit, such as word processors over typewriters, PCs over calculators, and ATMs over bank tellers. Substitutes that offer greater convenience, speedier service, or improved quality all serve customer productivity. Wang's substitution strategy of replacing word processing terminals with Wang PCs is a good example. For the same investment, the customer gets added functionality to increase his/her productivity beyond just text processing into spreadsheets, graphics, and database management.

- *Differentiated Products.* Earlier we noted that differentiation can come from product innovation or process innovation. The latter particularly lends itself to customer productivity opportunities. Azco Coatings auto-body repair shop systems helps auto mechanics to produce faster estimates of repairs, and Bergen Brunswig's hand-held "scanner" speeds up the inventory-taking process in drug stores.

Super Systems. Since Super Systems usually bring great productivity gains to their developers in the form of lower-cost scale operations, it stands to reason they will do the same for any subsequent user. Companies that build Super Systems primarily for productivity rather than product differentiation reasons sometimes sell the product as a way of recouping high development costs. Lomas and Nettleton, one of the country's largest mortgage companies, for example, is reportedly planning to sell the $20 million mortgage orientation and processing system they have had under development for several years. Bradford Trust sold their mutual funds system to competitors just before introducing a brand new (and more advanced) system to serve their own customers. In other words, they sold the productivity remnants of the system, not the innovation, which was in the new product.

Custom Terminals. Putting terminals in customer spaces often encompasses all three of our competitive systems strategies: innovation, information, and productivity, not only for the provider but for the customer as well. McKesson's capture of prescription data as a by-product of its pharmaceutical order-entry system lifts the pharmacist's burden of preparing onerous insurance forms. Norton Co.'s order-entry system provides by-product information to distributors on the status of orders, pricing information, and data on catalog items that enable the distributors to quote delivery dates to customers over the phone, without wasteful callbacks.

Electronic Delivery. The Airline Reservation Systems (ARS) deliver productivity to the travel agents who use them. Electronic Data Interchange (EDI) systems automate the "chain" between suppliers, manufacturers, distributors, and retailers, making all parties to the transaction process more productive. For instance, International Harvester reportedly saved more than $80,000 in the first 18 months of EDI use, and helped reduce inventory by approximately 70% over period of 3 years (30). Electronic Funds Transfer systems (EFTS) enhance consumer productivity by saving time. The ATMs and home banking make it unnecessary to go to the bank to conduct business (convenience is productivity). By its very nature, "electronic" delivery implies faster service and distance insensitivity (speed is productivity). And paperless processing (from money transfers to corporate transactions to stock exchanges) means more volume can be handled in less time (efficient volume processing is productivity) and at less cost. An ATM transaction, for instance, costs 4 or 5 times less than a paper-based transaction.

Marketing Support. Computer-aided sales (CAS) tools are increasing salespeople's productivity (and thus customer service) through telemarketing, transaction terminals, and video screens, as described in Chapter 5. Portable terminals carried by sales staffs help plan sales calls, retrieve customer information, and place orders. Customer-service aids such as the loan phone process consumer credit applications in 15 minutes instead of several days.

Distribution Systems. Any system that results in faster delivery to the customer also delivers productivity, for example, the Lechmere and Bloomingdale's systems that enable goods to be delivered to the pickup counter faster than the customer can get there. Electronic delivery instead of physical delivery equals productivity, for example, bank lock-box services that short-circuit checks, transmitting payment information directly into corporate accounts, thus speeding up accounts receivable collection (time is money). "Electronic money" equals productivity—Sears' Discover card enables consumers to buy merchandise, often at discounts, all over the country, without cash, checks, or bother. Bank money-transfer systems instantaneously move millions of dollars around the world daily in the form of electronic "bits."

Productivity from Information Services

IW 40—PRODUCTIVITY FROM INFORMATION
SERVICES
Information services that increase customer productivity.

Management Support Systems. If MSSs can leverage internal managers, they can leverage your customer firms' managers. Putting those managers online to a proprietary database can have the same impact as an information center has for internal managers. Micros, because of their ubiquity and low cost of software, are a fertile ground for leveraging customer productivity. A "Big 8" accounting firm provides "template" spreadsheets to its clients to help them prepare balance sheets and operating statements. A major bank provides corporate customers with a package that helps corporations analyze their financial strengths and weaknesses and take corrective action. A midwestern university leverages its faculty through the use of computer-based (paperless) assignments, quizzes, and grading in its introductory Computer Sciences course, thereby increasing its student:teacher ratio. Bank cash management systems help treasurers manage corporate funds more efficiently. And Expert Systems offer great promise for the future. IBMs YES/MVS product and DECs XCON are both Expert Systems aimed at helping their DP customers increase their efficiency in managing operations and configuration management, respectively.

Information Brokering. The provision of information services to customers and client companies as discussed in Chapter 6 is another form of value-added customer service. Information brokering can not only be done internally, but the same resources can also be leveraged to serve customers. In Chapter 6 we discussed such banks as Security Pacific, First National Bank of Chicago, and Citibank, which offer by-product online information services to customers. TRW Information Services and Aetna Life also draw on existing databases to create new customer information services. Some, like Chase Manhattan Bank's Interactive Data Corp. (IDC) have become database producers and distributors. Others, like EDS, have become electronic publishers. There are numerous information business opportunities that can be leveraged or expanded from existing resources.

Productivity Centers. For help in finding new ways to use information services productively, both internally and externally, there are at least two dozen nonprofit productivity centers in the United States that can be most useful to the IW researcher. These organizations offer educational programs, seminars, and publications across the complete spectrum of productivity opportunities. Many are associated with educational institutions and frequently concentrate on geographical regions or specific topics (such as technology). The following is but a representative sampling: American Productivity Center (Houston, Texas); American Center for the Quality of Work Life (Washington, D. C.); Center for Effective Organizations (Los Angeles, California); Center for the Improvement of Productivity, George Mason University (Fairfax, Virginia); Commerce Productivity Center, U. S. Department of Commerce (Washington, D. C.) (31).

Productivity from Competitive Scope

> **IW 41—PRODUCTIVITY FROM COMPETITIVE SCOPE**
> Productivity from market expansion or contraction.

Competitive scope involves such things as leveraging resources, finding or creating niche markets, dominating a market, and creating new products and services out of old products. Whereas EOS operations are internally focused, competitive scope is external; it looks at how competitive advantage can be gained through broadening or narrowing market penetration; it involves the more productive use of resources in serving customers.

We have already seen how resources can be leveraged by adding new functionality to old products, by aiming at new markets, by selling excess capacity, or by putting resources to different uses (such as railroads that carry passengers by day and freight at night). Here, we examine how information resources can be used to effect *competitive scope* productivity opportunities.

Niches. Corporations define their SBUs around three dimensions: customer, product, and geography. When looking for a niche market, these three dimensions can be explored to find an appropriate niche. A customer niche aims at certain customer segments, for example, the Yuppie (young urban professional) market. A product niche aims at providing a unique, scarce, or low-cost product that gives more value than competing products. A geographic niche attempts to be dominant in a specific locality, for example, Boston, Massachusetts, or New England. As noted earlier, domination can be achieved by a unique product that fills the niche, leaving it unattractive for a competitor to move in. Information can also be used to help analyze markets to find the right customer or geographic niche.

An example that hits at all of these niche dimensions is Bank of Boston's supermarket banking system called Monec, which allows customers to cash checks for their food purchases and conduct other banking trans-action on terminals located in supermarkets. The supermarket chains that signed up (300 sites at this writing) for the service did so because it relieved them of being in the check-cashing business (and the losses attendant thereto). Other banks were invited to join the system (170 did) so the ser-vice could be extended to their customers for a fee as well. In other words, Bank of Boston "owned the railroad" and charged a fee for every passen-ger (transaction) that rode it. Monec has all three dimensions of a niche: unique product, specific customer segment (consumers), and geographic location (eastern Massachusetts)—and almost no competition.

But supermarket banking is an EOS business, and not all who enter this niche are successful. Consider this example: Giant Foods, Inc., a Mary-land-based supermarket chain in partnership with Suburban Bank of Be-thesda, Maryland, successfully operated ATMs in more than 100 Giant stores in the Maryland area. Safeway, the nation's biggest supermarket chain, unsuccessfully operated 90 ATMs in stores in the Washington, D. C. area. Docutel, the network's operator, after sinking $2–$3 million in the system, was still operating at a loss and looking for a buyer as of January 1986 (32). The difference between the Giant and Safeway operations was one of volume. Since the networks generate their revenues from fees that financial institutions pay each time one of their cardholders uses a ma-chine, low volume translates to low revenue. Giant food stores opened their machines to all the debit cards in the Washington market. Safeway only provided access to about half the cards in the Washington market. As a result, Giant stores averaged 3000 transactions per month per machine versus Safeway's 1000 per month per machine. One reached the breakeven point, the other did not. One survives, the other likely will not.

An example of niche domination is First Data Resources, an American Express Co. service bureau in Omaha, Nebraska that concentrates exclu-sively on credit card processing. By focusing on this niche market, First Data Resources has been able to provide an efficient low-cost service that banks cannot duplicate for the same money themselves. As a result, it has become the largest credit card processor in the country.

The software industry is a prime example of a niche-oriented market. Thousands of small companies find their niche by developing unique soft-ware products aimed at specific customer segments, geographic markets, or even types of computers (i.e., mainframe, minicomputer, or microcom-puter systems). Many package their products around specific minicom-puters so that they can be more easily sold as "turnkey" systems; others aim at the PC market (there are over 11,000 packages for the IBM PC alone); and still others go after specific industries with packages geared to serve segments of those industries.

Niches can be formed either as a little fish in a big pond or a big fish in a little pond. But to be a big fish in a big pond involves boundary expansion.

Boundary Spanning. The opposite of filling a niche (narrow market) is to broaden the market served (boundary spanning).

- Electronic transmission has enabled *The Wall Street Journal* to transmit the contents of its daily business newspaper to printing plants around the country so as to produce timely news on a national level. They are now broadening this further to a global strategy with Asian and European editions.
- Reuters Holdings PLC is a London-based company that began by offering financial information and stock quotes through special terminals installed in brokers' offices and banks. Then it began using its vast network to let customers talk back; that is, to use the worldwide network to trade in stocks, currencies, and commodities. Reuters was the leader in serving the world market for instant financial information and, as a result, it is now the biggest financial information network of its kind in the world. With a global network of 53,000 high-speed printers and terminals, Reuters network is another example of "owning the railroad," in this case, global financial news and trading data.
- Sears Roebuck is taking advantage of its thousands of retail outlets to broaden its services available at those outlets—not just retail merchandise, but financial services. It has the largest credit card operation in the country. It offers "banking" services, it sells insurance (AllState) and real estate (Coldwell Banker) and deals in brokerage services (Dean Witter). Sears' delivery system offers a formidable economy of scope that is hard for any competitor to match.

Sometimes, competitive scope is broadened through competitive rivalry. In the early 1970s, Bank of America came out with their Bankamerica (now Visa) credit card, which spread throughout their network of 1000 banks across the state of California. In self-defense, a number of other California banks banded together and created a competitive credit card called Master Charge (now Master Card). The rivalry between the two products quickly spread beyond California as both cards "franchised" their systems to banks throughout the country and then the world. In 10 years, Visa and Master Card grew to be the world's largest credit card operations functioning on a global scale—and all because of competitive rivalry.

Bundling. Creativity is partially defined as the ability to take two seemingly unrelated ideas and combine them into a new and unique innovation. The "bundling" of services to create a new product can be the business equivalent of this kind of creativity. A few years back, Merrill Lynch came out with their Cash Management Account (CMA). This service represented a bundling of different services—cash account, brokerage, and money market fund—into a single account and a single statement—a "bundled" new information service. The individual services were not new, but the idea of combining them into a single account, providing the customer with a total "financial management" service, was unique. Sears Roebuck now bundles financial services under their advertising banner, the Sears Financial Network: insurance, brokerage, real estate, and banking.

Bundling often requires an integrated systems infrastructure, which can be a formidable barrier to companies without integrated systems. On the other hand, it can sometimes be accomplished with amazing ease. A case in point is the "electronic window" strategy used by a major New York bank to "bundle" several information services into what appears to be a single service. A PC in the customer's office displays an umbrella "menu" of services. When the customer selects a service, he/she is routed by the bank's computer to the appropriate department (and computer) offering that service. Thus separate systems appear to be bundled as a single service offering.

References

1. Michael E. Porter, *Competitive Advantage*, The Free Press, New York, 1985, p. 62.
2. *Technology in Banking: Path to Competitive Advantage*, Salomon Bros., May 1985, p. 2.
3. Dale J. Hekhuis and Richard C. Raymond, "Productivity. Strategic Imperative for Banks," *Bank Administration*, Dec. 1985, p. 35.
4. Diane Crawford, "New Automation Strategies Dynamize Pru-Bache," *Wall Street Computer Review*, May 1985.
5. *Information Processing*, IBM, Winter 1986, p. 66.
6. Paper by Alan Paller, AVI Data Graphics/ISSCO, "Million Dollar Opportunities: Twelve of the Best Computer Graphics Applications in America," undated.
7. Paul Strassmann, *Information Payoff*, The Free Press, 1985.
8. *American Banker*, 12/19/85, p. 4.
9. Hekhuis and Raymond, p. 40.
10. Jim Mayers, "Merging Skunks and Possums," *Entrepreneurial Excellence*, Feb. 1986.
11. Daniel B. England, "Credit Productivity and Hudson's Bay Company," *Credit World*, Sept.–Oct. 1985, pp. 30–33.
12. Daniel M. Clark, "Have QCs Been Good for Operations?" *ABA Banking Journal*, Oct. 1985, p. 100.
13. Michael Haskew, "IMPROSHARE and Quality Circles: Teamwork at John F. Kennedy Medical Center," *Quality Circles Journal*, Sept. 1985, pp. 24–26.
14. *Information Week*, 5/26/86, p. 56.
15. Nolan Norton & Co., 1984. This figure is from NNCs proprietary portfolio assessment methodology.
16. W. F. Zachmann (IDC), as reported at the International Data Corp. conference in New Orleans, Nov., 1985.

17. *Information Week,* 8/5/85, p. 29.

18. *Information Week,* 8/12/85, p. 6.

19. *Telecommuting (TC) Report,* a monthly newsletter of Electronic Services, Ltd., undated.

20. Ibid.

21. *Management Review,* July 1986, p. 22.

22. Catherine Marenghi, "Managing New Work Options," *Infosystems,* Mar. 1986, p. 92.

23. Marcia M. Kelly, "Telecommuting: The New Workplace Revolution," *Information Strategy: the Executive Journal,* Winter 1986.

24. *Computerworld,* 12/23/85, p. 1.

25. *Information Week,* 8/26/85, p. 36.

26. W. R. Synnott and W. H. Gruber, *Information Resource Management,* Wiley, New York, 1981.

27. Carol A. Kamper, "Prototyping—New Tools for Cutting Through the Applications Backlog," *Computerworld Focus,* 9/18/85, p. 44.

28. *Bank Systems and Equipment,* April 1986, p. 95.

29. *Business Week,* 10/14/85, p. 112.

30. *Computerworld,* 2/3/86, p. 25.

31. *Bank Administration,* Jan. 1986, p. 55.

32. *American Banker,* 2/3/86, p. 2

33. *Business Week,* 10/14/85.

PART III

SUPPORTING THE INFORMATION WEAPON

8

INFORMATION RESOURCES
ARCHITECTURE

God did not play dice with the universe;
amidst the apparent chaos, there must be order.

ALBERT EINSTEIN

An overall architectural strategy is needed to deliver IW systems because CSSs must be able to combine products and services and deliver those services to any location; MSSs must be corporate-wide and compatible; and OSSs need to interface and minimize redundant and inconsistent systems. The technology architecture supplies the structure to support these information systems.

According to Webster's *New World Dictionary* architecture is "the science, art, or profession of designing and constructing buildings, bridges . . . any framework, system, etc." Information resources (IR) architecture is the art and science of designing supportive frameworks for a firm's technology infrastructure. The architectural framework, in turn, results in information policies and standards governing the selection and use of information resources.

A simplified definition of IR architecture then is:

Planning for the structure and integration of the information resources within a firm.

Information resources architectural planning has as its mission the design and implementation of information technologies according to a long-term plan and direction to assure a technology infrastructure which supports corporate and business unit objectives. Information resource management architecture seeks to avoid fragmentation. It defines components, functions, and structures, including systems interfaces and relationships between information resource components. It is, therefore, a method of illustrating a company's technological status, direction, and migration strategy. It shows where the company is headed technologically, and assures that the structure needed to get it there is in place or in process. Without an architecture in place, as computers continue to decentralize, the technology environment of organizations can become diverse, uncontrolled, and incompatible. Anticipating this, astute CIOs have begun to put into place architectures, policies, and standards to bring order out of what might otherwise be technological chaos. Diverse computers must talk to one another. Information must be able to flow and be manipulated and consolidated throughout the firm. Compatibility is the key, and IR architecture is the key to compatibility. Architectural planning is the second most important role and responsibility of the CIO. The first, integrated strategic planning, was the subject of Part II. As the reader will recall from Chapter 2, these represent the VALUE and STRUCTURE dimensions of the CIO's primary role in the organization. Here, in Part III, we deal with planning of the IR architecture (STRUCTURE).

This is not a technical treatise on architecture. Rather, I have attempted to address architectural planning from a business and management rather than a technical perspective. Just as information managers need to be involved in strategic planning to optimize information technology use in the firm, so business managers need to be involved in technology architecture at appropriate times and places to provide needed business direction. Architecture is too important to be left to the technologists. Figure 8.1 conceptually depicts how information managers and business managers need to view IR management. *Information* planning is a business-driven exercise with CIO involvement. The planning of information content leading to business value is primarily a business responsibility but, as argued in Chapter 3, the involvement of the information management people is essential to an effective technology support plan.

Likewise (information) *resources* planning is a CIO-driven task requiring business management involvement. The architectural plan forms the conduit that makes up the technology structure of the enterprise, but business mangers need to provide direction and support. Business needs and objectives form the basis for resource planning. The data, the application systems, the equipment, and the systems staff all depend on business input. Indeed, an architectural plan cannot be constructed without this business involvement. Thus, architecture is not something to be left to the tech-

Management focus ⟶	Information	Resources
Planning focus ⟶	Business planning	Technology architecture
Information focus ⟶	Content	Conduit
Objective ⟶	Value	Structure
Who leads? ⟶	Business driven	CIO driven

Figure 8.1. IRM's dual dimension.

nicians. Business mangers need to understand it, provide input and direction where needed, and most important, realize that *structure leads to value* and, therefore, needs to be appropriately supported by management.

ARCHITECTURAL PLANNING

Information resource management architecture is business and technology architecture integrated, just as strategic planning was business and information planning integrated. Thus the foundation for information resources planning is business plans and objectives. From these, information resources can be examined, one by one, as to their fit and adequacy to support business plans, additional needs can be identified, and a technology plan can be formulated.

As with strategic planning, the necessary ingredients to a successful architecture are shared vision, integrated planning, and leadership. The CIO must have a clear vision of the architecture and must communicate that vision to senior management in a way that can easily be understood so as to gain their support. The architecture must be built on a business foundation that management can relate to, not a technical foundation. For example, what is the value of compatible systems to the business? The CIO must provide the inspiration, motivation, and leadership to create and build the IRM program. The IRM program is built upon the business plan. Information resources are first fitted to the business plan, and then to each other, until they form a supportive information technology STRUCTURE designed to help business units reach their goals.

An IRM program covers the design and use of information resources throughout the firm, whereas an IRM plan refers to the consolidated plans of each information resource component of the program. These plans should view each architectural component from both a logical and physical perspective. A logical view looks at how data flows through the business, in and out of each technological component, and what the systems relationships are. A physical view looks at the location and makeup of architectural components (e.g., computers, peripherals, networks, and applications systems) as well as their interfaces. Logical design is concerned with *integration*, whereas physical design deals with *interfaces*, or connectivity, needs. There is a difference. Integrated systems share common data, avoiding data redundancy, whereas interfaced systems simply pass information from one to another; they are connected but data elements could be duplicated or defined differently in each system.

Although considerable interest and attention has been paid to the notion of IRM architecture of late, there is surprisingly very little literature describing IRM architecture. The Dooley Group (a management consultant consortium), in a recent survey of over 60 major corporations, found that on the subject of architectural planning many companies are talking about an overall technology architecture, but few actually have one. The Dooley study reported that about 30% of the surveyed companies reported that they had an overall technology architecture in place (1). The rest were either fragmented, just getting started, or wondering what architecture is all about.

Of course everyone has some form of technology architecture in place. The configuration of equipment in a data center constitutes an architecture; a communications network is an architecture; an applications systems is an architecture. The problem is that in the past most architectures were not documented, and long-term integration was not fully planned. The reasons for this are a throwback to the Computer Era. When most DP organizations were highly centralized, the DP manager had control of all information resources and made day-to-day decisions on how new hardware and software would be introduced into the scheme of things. For the most part, senior management did not ask about architecture. It was just something the DP manager did, and it was all in his/her head. The growing decentralization of information resources in the Information Era, by contrast, requires that technology architecture now be clearly documented and understood by all.

New decisions have to fit into the long-term architectural direction and they must be consistent with the technology infrastructure, because uncontrolled technology decisions can wreak havoc. The IRM architecture should be a collection of "building block" information resource architectures merged into a unified whole and, most important, should reflect a "to be" direction rather than just an "as is" status. The data center architecture must match the communications architecture which, in turn, ties in with applications systems architecture. And it must all extend corporate-wide, current and projected. For purposes of competitive advantage, we need a totally integrated architecture that has all technologies blending together to form a "system." The system is the conduit that carries the information content. Content is the key factor; but without an integrated, connected conduit, information management will flounder. Architecture "orchestrates" the delivery system. The order and structure of the individual parts becomes the orchestra.

An IRM Architectural Model

> **IW 42—AN IRM ARCHITECTURAL MODEL**
> Orchestrating the architectural components of technology infrastructure.

The architectural model presented here consists of seven components. As shown in Figure 8.2, the components are:

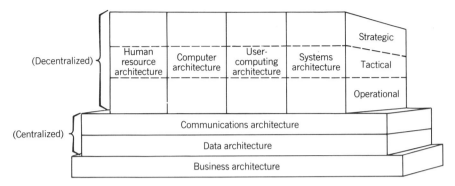

Figure 8.2. IRM architectural model.

1. Business architecture.
2. Data architecture.
3. Communications architecture.
4. Human resources architecture.
5. Computer architecture.
6. User-computing architecture.
7. Systems architecture.

The foundation of the model is *business architecture*. Business architecture results from the strategic planning process,[1] that is, what businesses the company is in (or wants to be in), the plans and objectives of those businesses, the organizational development of the firm around those businesses, and the information-technology needs assessment aimed at accomplishing business objectives. Business architecture is the foundation upon which the IRM architecture rests. The architectural model consists of a set of building-blocks of linked architectures which together form the basis for the technology infrastructure of the firm.

In Figure 8.2, data architecture and communications architecture are shown as horizontal bars because these are corporate-wide information resource components. They serve all business units. The four vertical resource components are business specific. The resources can be divided according to the business units they serve. That is, data and communications might be centralized resources, whereas human resources (professional systems staffs), computers, user-computing, and systems could all be decentralized resources to one degree or another. In a totally centralized

---

[1] If there is no strategic planning process in place in the organization to bring this about, the CIO can take the lead to develop strategic plans, based on interviews with corporate management, by forming an ad hoc planning team to conduct the interviews and develop business missions and objectives and technology support needs.

organization perhaps all but the user-computing component could be represented by horizontal bars. However, the degree of centralization/decentralization of the information resources is a matter of control, not architecture. The components, or building blocks, of the model apply regardless of organizational arrangement. This particular model is used because this author believes that the trend in the industry will be more and more toward decentralization, and thus the model is aimed at organizing and coordinating the decentralizing resources of the future firm.

Planning Levels

Planning for the IR architecture is done at three different levels: *strategic, tactical, and operational*. Strategic planning and design is a corporate view of how information resources are used to support the organization as a whole. It involves setting direction and missions. It is generally long-term planning (3–5 years).[2] Tactical planning is concerned with applying resources to strategic business units (SBUs). Given the SBU missions, tactical action plans are developed to achieve these missions. It is short-term planning (1 year) of the physical design and implementation of the strategic plan. Operational planning supports the products and services within business units. It is the day-to-day management of the implemented action plans, and the measurement and monitoring of the process. One way to sort out the difference in strategic, tactical, and operational architecture is to translate the three levels to what IBM describes as: *plan it, build it, run it.*

The main objective of architectural planning is to avoid chaos through uncontrolled implementation. The architectural plan provides guidelines for tactical decisions that promote consistency and compatibility as the pieces of the technological jig-saw puzzle come together. The architectural plan must be broad, flexible, and logical so that new pieces can be added without disrupting the entire structure. Detailed physical architecture changes constantly. That is why the architectural plan has to be broad to be flexible. It needs physical information, but concentrates on logical structures. The purpose of the plan, of course, is to make information readily accessible to managers and professionals to expedite decisions, facilitate planning, improve productivity and control over resources, and expedite the company's ability to respond rapidly to the marketplace.

In Figure 8.3 we see how this three-level planning process is applied to each information resource. The cumulative application of these 21 IW strategies results in a framework for planning the IR architecture. A brief explanation of the planning matrix follows:

---

[2]There are exceptions. Strategic planning could be short-term, such as when a quick strategic change in direction is dictated by the competitive marketplace. The change itself may persist for the long term, however.

Planning level architecture	Strategic	Tactical	Operational
Business	Create corporate organization structure, missions, objectives	Establish SBUs, missions, and objectives	Delineate products and services
Data	Link data planning to business information needs	Manage shared corporate data as a common resource	Assure database systems standards
Communications	Plan the corporate-wide communications structure	Implement integrated communications networks	Manage network access and control
Human resources	Allocate systems resources to SBUs	Allocate to development projects	Assign to specific application systems support
Computers	Plan the corporation's computer support resources	Install and interlink computers at all levels as needed	Assure uninterrupted computer service levels
User-computing	Integrate business professionals with technology	Leverage management productivity	Support controlled micro use and growth
Systems	Develop a long-term plan for the corporation's system portfolio	Develop new information systems and services	Maintain existing information systems

Figure 8.3. Architectural planning matrix.

- *Business Focus.* As stated, the business is the foundation for all architectural planning. At the strategic level, the corporate organizational structure, its plans and objectives, and its information support needs are the focal point. Individual business units are addressed at the tactical level. Support of the specific products and services of the SBUs occurs at the operational level.
- *Data Resources.* At the strategic level, strategic data planning (SDP) is done, linking the data architecture to the strategic planning output of information needs. Data administration (DA) takes over to identify,

define, and track data used at the tactical business-unit level, while data base administration (DBA) deals with data structure, access, and control at the individual database level.

- *Communications Resources.* As with data, strategic communications planning (SCP) begins with the identification of corporate networking needs and logical design alternatives. The physical design and implementation of networks is done at the tactical level, and network control (operations management) occurs at the third level of planning.

- *Human Resources.* The allocation of professional systems personnel to strategic business units is done at the strategic level. Allocation to specific application systems and development projects is at the tactical level. Allocation to product support (maintenance and enhancements) is at the operational level.

- *Computer Resources.* Because computers range from corporate mainframes to departmental minicomputers to personal computers, each has its own unique planning focus. Generally speaking, the strategic focus is on achieving economies of scale (EOS) or cost reduction. Data-center management (production, development, information centers) is at the tactical level. And computer operations (running the computers) is the third planning level.

- *User-Computing Resources.* Since the hardware is treated under computer resources, user computing deals with the use, or software side, of office computing. At the strategic level, our mission is to integrate professionals with technology. Management support systems (MSSs), that leverage management productivity represent tactical planning. Support of end-user computing use and growth occurs at the operational level.

- *Systems Resources.* As discussed earlier, the Portfolio Analysis planning methodology is an example of a strategic planning exercise aimed at lining up information resources appropriately, according to business missions. At the tactical level, these translate into specific systems development projects, and at the operational end, to resources devoted to the maintenance and enhancement of existing systems.

These examples of tier-level architectural planning are not meant to be rigid or exclusive, but merely illustrative. Each organization would tailor the model to fit its own individual needs.

Planning Steps

The following eight-step planning process can be applied to each of the architectural components:

1. Inventory. The first question to ask is: "Where are we now?" To answer this we start by taking a physical inventory of current information resources: hardware, software, people, and money. This need not be in

complete detail, but should be sufficiently developed to present to management an overall view of the status of information technology in the firm and the current investment in same (costs are an important ingredient in every inventory). Using existing sources for information as much as possible minimizes the task, but allows an information resources database to be built which can be used to present data in different ways, as needed, and can be easily updated periodically (annually might be sufficient).

2. Analysis. Following the data gathering phase, data are analyzed to find obvious strengths and weaknesses. Is the overall investment in technology appropriate to business needs and management's philosophy of the importance of technology to the firm? Are resources deployed appropriately to achieve corporate goals? What anomalies stand out in terms of profit contribution versus technology investment in the various business units? In effect, we are taking an IRM architectural audit of the technical health of the corporation.

3. Migration. While architectural planning defines and creates technology structure, the reality is that infrastructure exists at any point in time. Therefore, we must start with what exists (inventory and analysis) before planning a migration path forward. A migration path is not a detailed plan, only a direction, a vision. Where do we want to be in 3–5 years? What business needs must a long-term technology structure support? What are the cost implications? Will management support the direction— and the investment?

4. Alternatives. Like driving across the country, many routes are possible to a given destination. Architectural planning consists of continually selecting from alternative choices, then blending the selected choices together in a way that best fits the environment. Need, cost, availability, functionality, and futurity are some of the considerations in options analysis, which is an ongoing process.

5. Plan. The IR plan paints a logical picture for management. Like architectural design, which uses blueprints to guide builders, the use of schematic drawings to illustrate technology architectures can help management readily understand the plan (a picture is worth 10,000 words). A plan is developed for each information resource in the architectural model and general direction is translated into specific programs, projects, activities, and processes. Costs/benefits are determined. Resource needs are identified. General management support is sought.

6. Integration. Individual plans need be integrated into a common technology infrastructure. Where are the misfits? What must be done to ensure infrastructural fit? Are all the "bridges" in place, both logically and physically, to integrate the technological "islands?"

7. Guidelines. Once an architecture has been defined, information resource policies and standards are needed to assure that all information activities fit into the corporate architecture. Without such guidelines, the architecture is in danger of compromise. When a contractor renovates a

room, he doesn't pull a structural beam out because it's in the way. If he does, the building collapses. In the same way, technology architecture must be assured with corporate guidelines, policies, and standards that help to hold the technology together.

8. Compliance. Finally, some governance role is needed to oversee compliance with guidelines, information resource policies, and standards. Unless an oversight role is played by someone, there is no assurance that the architectural plan is being followed. This may or may not be a CIO's responsibility; it could be the responsibility of internal auditors or an independent compliance group.

Taken in order, these steps provide a useful planning guide that fits the three-tier planning process as follows: starting bottom-up, an inventory of what exists is taken and analyzed for strengths, weaknesses, and opportunities. This often results in projects at the tactical level to redo or enhance parts of the existing inventory to strengthen and capitalize on the underlying investment in existing information resources. Architectural planning at the strategic level then examines *new* opportunities for information resources that also become projects at the tactical level (all information resource projects join together at this stage). An implementation plan showing priorities, resource needs, specific individual responsibilities, and schedules forms the tactical plan. Finally, guidelines and monitoring activities are put into place to oversee implementation as planned and in conformance with architectural standards. This bottom-up/top-down process can be repeated with each component of the IRM architecture in the process of building the IRM architectural plan. In the process, careful attention is paid to the integration points among architectural components. The diagram in Figure 8.4 can be used as a building block for cross-referencing these integration points. For example, as the user-computing architectural model is created, its impact on the other architectural components can be noted under each. User-computing will need to address access requirements to internal and external databases, communications links, and specific computer systems. What are these connectivity needs and how will they be satisfied? What is being done under the other component plans to accommodate user-computing needs? By building up the matrix in this way, all of the integration, connectivity, and information delivery needs will be identified and addressed to assure the total integration of the IRM architecture.

In summary, the basic questions in which management is interested with regard to the IRM program probably boil down to these: Where are we? Where do we want to go? (sometimes referred to as "from–to's") How do we get there? What will it cost? What are the benefits? If the architectural plan answers these questions clearly and succinctly, it is probably a good plan. The model depicted in figure 8.2 has seven building blocks, three planning levels, and eight planning steps. Some of these can consume an enormous amount of time. Architectural planning does not occur

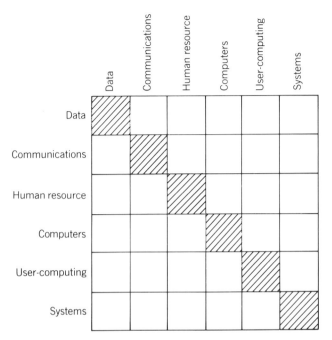

Figure 8.4. IRM integration points.

overnight. It is a long-term, ongoing incremental process. Getting the plan together is only a first step. Carrying it out, modifying it (as will be necessary) along the way, and refitting it to accommodate new business initiatives, new products and services, competitive moves, advances in technology, and changing business values and needs, is a never-ending process. With an architectural plan as a guide, all can keep their eye upon the doughnut and not upon the hole. Without an architectural plan, not only will efforts be wasted "fighting fires" and misallocating resources, but the ability to manage information as a corporate resource, particularly in the face of increasing technological decentralization, will be difficult, if not impossible. Rather than having order and structure, the company's technological infrastructure could, in fact, deteriorate to uncontrolled chaos.

BUSINESS ARCHITECTURE

> **IW 43—ORGANIZATION STRUCTURES**
> **Rationalizing the corporate and systems organizational alignment.**

Business architecture stands as the foundation of the IRM architectural model and plan. Just as a house cannot be built on sand, IRM architecture must also be built on the solid underpinnings of business structure and objectives. Business architecture, or structure, is usually a matter of tradition, corporate style and culture, and management preference. Radical change (in culture and/or organization structure) usually only occurs as the result of something traumatic: a crisis in the organization (e.g., huge losses) may trigger a corporate reorganization; a new CEO may have completely different views on how the organization should be structured and managed; a major strategic planning exercise (perhaps led by outside consultants) may trigger major change. Sometimes a shift to a strategic (market-driven) style of doing business can be the catalyst. Whatever the reason, organizational development seems to vacillate over time between two organizational extremes—centralization versus decentralization.

The Centralization versus Decentralization Issue

Whether it is best to centralize or decentralize is an age-old argument in organizational theory. As someone said: "Try as one may to make pancakes many different ways—they always end up with just two sides." John Leslie King (University of California) made the observation that to centralize or decentralize is a 20-year old debate. No universally approved arrangement has ever been found, primarily because the driving issues are not technical or economic; they are political. They hinge on the political considerations of organization structure and the issue of who should control resources (2). King argues there are three aspects to the decentralization issue: control, location, and function. Control refers to who makes the decisions. If centralized, control stays with top management; if decentralized, it moves to lower-level managers (which could encourage entrepreneurship). Location is where the resources are. If centralized, economies of scale often results; if decentralized to line units, autonomy may be offset by some unavoidable redundancy. Function has to do with functional responsibilities. Centralization can result in better performance, smoother operations, and lower costs; decentralization, however, can mean better cooperation between units and greater line discretion.

What we are seeing more and more of today is a compromise position (perhaps there *are* more than two sides to pancakes!). Centralization was dominant in the Computer Era (1960s and 1970s), mainly because of the complexity of computing (users didn't understand it), the cost of computing (centralization resulted in economies of scale), and the fear of loss of control. Today, users are more willing, even anxious, to take control of their information resources; the low cost of mini- and microcomputers has eroded the economies of scale argument; and computing is under sufficient control today that managers are not fearful of assuming its responsibility. As a result, the Information Era is seeing an increasing trend toward decentralization of information resources.

	Centralized	Distributed	Decentralized
Resource control	Central resources shared by all. Users control departmental machines.	Corporation provides central utilities. Users control departmental machines and systems staff.	Corporation provides some central utilities. User controls all dedicated resources.
Decision authority	Central control over all IRM decisions. IRM committee mediates as needed.	IRM committee approves major expenditures. Users make decisions within corporate limits.	Users make all IRM decisions. CEO approves major expenditures.

Figure 8.5. IRM control options.

The decentralization trend is being fueled by three forces: low-cost computing, more computer-literate managers, and the desire to use technology as a competitive strategy. However, recognizing some of the pros and cons of centralization/decentralization, many companies are seeking in-between arrangements that combine the advantages of both without the disadvantages of either. Distributed processing, characterized by an IRM program consisting of information resources dispersed around the firm but under some central guidance and coordination of the CIO, represents such an arrangement. Figure 8.5 shows various control options possible over IRM management. Distributed processing takes different forms. In some companies, it is limited to computers; that is, computers are decentralized (or dedicated) to line units, or central mainframes serve as a corporate utility, while departmental microcomputers are decentralized. (In the future, central data centers may restrict themselves to the processing of large corporate systems, serve as repositories of large corporate databases, and serve as the corporate information center for users throughout the company.) Many companies today are also beginning to decentralize their systems staffs to line units, bringing business and systems people closer to create new and innovative computer systems.[3] However it is carried out, there is more widespread understanding of the need for a central coordinator, an architect, a planner to pull together diverse resources into

[3] A survey of 250 attendees at an International Data Corp. conference which I addressed in New Orleans in November 1985 showed that 22% had decentralized systems functions in their companies.

an IRM architecture that avoids the pitfalls of uncontrolled implementation.

Organization Structure

Corporate Organization. An enterprise can be organized in a number of different ways, such as along functional lines (manufacturing, marketing, engineering, etc.), product lines, geographic units, or customer segmentation. The centralization/decentralization theory of organization, however, results in only two different types of corporate structures: *functional versus divisional*. Functional is centralized and divisional is decentralized (along product lines, geographic markets, and/or customer markets).

Functional structure, also known as pyramidal hierarchy (Figure 8.6A), revolves around an organization in which commands ripple down from the top and are acted upon by a widening number of specialists at each successive layer. Mountains of feedback flow from the bottom to the top. This type of organization structure is characterized by highly centralized control at the top. Although popular for many decades, functional organization began to give way after World War II to a growing propensity toward divisional structures. Divisional (decentralized) structure (Figure 8.6B) breaks up a large company into a series of smaller units, each headed by a manager with broad autonomy and authority to run the business, accountable for bottom-line results only. Divisionalized corporations are organized around the SBU as the building block of strategic planning. Each SBU has an identifiable market and mission with relation to that market. It has a set of competitors, and performance is measured against its mission. The SBUs have specific products and services to sell to specific markets. For example, a tire maker could sell a broad line of tires to all markets nationally, or it could sell a narrower line to specific customers (autos versus trucks) or geographic markets (the northeast region). An SBU could have a single product or several. The way in which a company's products and services are allocated to SBUs determines its organization structure. Many large companies (e.g., General Electric, General Mills, General Motors, 3M, Johnson & Johnson, Digital Equipment, Tenneco, and American Express) have decentralized along these lines in the last several decades. According to a report by McKinsey and Co. (management consultants), among the top 500 industrial firms in the United States, the proportion using decentralized management grew from 20% in 1950 to 80% in 1970.

The driving force behind decentralization in many large organizations is the conviction that it encourages creativity and innovation—in other words, *entrepreneurship*. The advantages are better responsiveness to markets, greater operational flexibility, clear accountability for results and, above all, innovation. In their book, *The 100 Best Companies to Work For in America*, Moskowitz et al. counted 30 entrepreneurial companies among their list of the 100 best (3). According to Don Gevritz, in *Business Plan for*

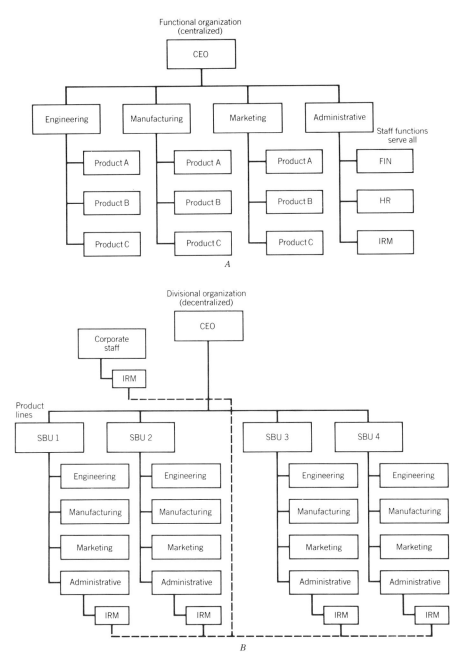

Figure 8.6. Functional (A) and divisional (B) corporate organizations.

America, the main reason for encouraging the small business entrepreneurial environment is:

> . . . entrepreneurially oriented small companies now create most of America's jobs, produce most of the innovation in the marketplace, and provide product diversity for customers and competition for old-line firms. (4)

Systems Organization. The information systems organization, of course, must follow corporate organization. If the corporation is centralized, it makes sense to centralize information resources; if it is decentralized, information resources must also be decentralized. To try to run a centralized IRM in a decentralized organization simply will not work over the long run. If we look at Figure 8.6A and *B* again, we note that under the *functional* or centralized corporate organization, the IRM function is centralized under a single entity. Administration, in this example, provides information services to all entities of the corporation. Under the *divisional* structure, the IRM function is decentralized to the line units, coordinated by the corporate IRM function at the staff level of the organization. IBM, for example, has only a small systems staff at the corporate level; most are decentralized into the line divisions. This staff coordination role is critical to the success of IRM decentralization. Companies that have attempted to decentralize their information resources without this control mechanism in place have had great difficulty moving information around the organization because of systems and vendor incompatibilities. Management information consolidation becomes an egregious task and redundancy abounds.

A couple of bank cases with which I am familiar illustrate the point. A large midwestern bank decentralized its systems organization in the mid-1970s. No corporate IRM function was established at that time. This subsequently led to so many coordination problems between the line units that the President of the bank decided to bring in someone from the outside to establish and head up a corporate systems (aka IRM) function to coordinate systems activities bank-wide. The new Corporate Systems Director reported directly to the President. Today the bank has decentralized systems, but operates its data center as a corporate "computer utility." The corporate systems group is responsible for corporate (centralized) IR activities such as telecommunications, corporate management information systems, systems assurance, the issuance of information resource policies, and general technology research. They issue systems architecture guideline documents to line units. A systems steering committee, headed by the President and cochaired by the Corporate Systems (IRM) Director, serves as a policy board and a resource allocation and funding committee.

In a similar case, a major northeastern bank similarly decentralized all of their systems and data processing activities. Over 100 individual units and a number of data centers were involved. In this case, a small corporate systems unit was established but, according to one source, "it issued standards that no one followed, had no top level support and was, therefore, ineffective at coordinating much of anything." As a result, three managers came and went into the position over a period of 10 years. They have made a lot of progress of late regaining control over the coordination of information resource decisions, but too much decentralization too fast, and without proper central control, created considerable integration and coordination problems which could have been avoided if the corporate IRM group had had "teeth" from the beginning.

These cases illustrate that establishing a strong IRM central unit with top management support is an important ingredient to success in a divisional (decentralized) organization structure. The central group provides a necessary coordination and control mechanism as information resources become decentralized throughout the firm. Although the IRM organization generally follows company organization, the long-term trend is toward distributing information resources along the entire spectrum of centralization/decentralization, as shown in Figure 8.7.

Because they are a broad corporate resource, the management of telecommunications and data tend to be centralized. Similarly, because they serve individual business units, system resources are, more and more, being decentralized into user areas. This includes applications systems, systems staffs, and user computing (three of the information resource components of the architectural model). Computers are both, ranging from centralized data centers to decentralized departmental minicomputers and personal microcomputers. Hence we consider these to be distributed (and networked) resources. Along this spectrum, the company has many options and possible organizational arrangements. For example, consider the *location* and *control* option of the company data center alone. The organizational location options are to centralize at the corporate level, centralize at the line level (an option not often considered), decentralize at the line level, farm out (service bureau), or use different combinations in different

Organization	Centralized (Efficiency)	Distributed (Balanced)	Decentralized (Effectiveness)
Corporate perspective	Economy of scale Management control Operations consistency Bureaucracy	Accountability Coordination Integrated IRM Committee mediator	Local autonomy Loss of control Loss of consolidation User control
Business unit perspective	Unresponsive Resource sharing Overhead assumption	Responsive Information sharing Overhead control	Responsive No sharing No overhead

Figure 8.7. IRM organization structure.

business units. There are at least four control options: centralized management, decentralize to the line unit, dedicated machines within the corporate data center, and facilitates management arrangements (user owns dedicated equipment that is run by someone else under contract).

The management of each component of the IRM architecture requires careful selection of organizational options that are consistent with the company's organization and needs. What works in one company does not necessarily work in another. As every amateur gardener knows, if you transplant something from one area to another, it might not grow. It could be the wrong soil, care, or environment (palm trees don't grow in Boston). Quality circles work better in Japan than in the United States because the Japanese culture (lifetime employment, participative management) support them better than does American culture. In the same way, organizational strategies, both corporate and systems, must fit the environment created by the corporate strategy and culture.

Information Resource Policy

> **IW 44—INFORMATION RESOURCE POLICIES**
> Establishing the policies and standards that will assure a sound technology architecture.

Another important part of business architecture from an information resource point of view is the company's information policy. Organizational development deals with how the corporation is organized to carry out its business mission. Information resource policy deals with management's support of the information resource and the policies and practices put into place to assure an appropriate and supportive technology infrastructure.

Management Support. The two cases cited earlier were examples of where senior management did not appreciate at the outset the importance of a coordinated and controlled IRM program, overseen by a CIO, with the solid backing of top management. The vision of competitive technology will best be reached by an effective IRM program that manages the firm's information resources not just as an asset resource, but as an integrated and synergistic asset. A champion, a CIO, is needed to lead the program, who requires not only the support of top management, but a clear role (authority and responsibility) to carry it out. That role is clearer in a centralized rather than a decentralized organization.

In a centralized organization, the two main issues of concern are whether control over information resources is fragmented and whether the CIO participates at a senior enough policy level in the organization. Fragmentation refers to instances when information resources such as telecommunications or office systems, even though centralized, may organizationally report to different areas of the organization. This obstructs "single-mind" planning of information resources. Top-level participation is important to assuring effective business and systems planning as well as architectural planning. The CIO that reports several layers down in the organization is at a decided disadvantage in being able to accomplish this.

In a decentralized organization, an added complication is that the information resources are under the control of users throughout the enterprise. Functional control is always weaker than physical control (possession is nine-tenths of the law). Therefore, in a decentralized organization, the CIO needs the strong support of senior management to avoid becoming a "toothless tiger" in the job. The best way to get that support is to educate management as to the value to the firm of leveraging its technology investment through an effective IRM program. As would be expected, the best IRM programs are driven from the top by CEOs who share the information weapon vision.

IRM Committee. Most organizations have some sort of steering committee to back up the information management function. An IRM committee, composed of senior management, is needed to provide policy direction and support to the CIO. Ideally, the CEO should chair the committee with the CIO as cochairman (as in the case of the midwestern bank presented above). The duties of the committee will, of course, vary with the organizational structure but, generally speaking, its responsibilities might include:

- Evaluating investment proposals.
- Mediating competing user priorities.
- Allocating scarce resources.
- Exercising a funding discipline over major expenditures.
- Providing better communication between the CIO and top management.

In decentralized organizations, a line-unit IRM committee may play a pre-screening role before presenting proposals to the senior IRM committee. A useful exercise to firm up "who does what" in terms of information resources decisions (acquisition, allocation, use) is to employ a decision matrix such as that shown in Figure 8.8. This helps to clarify the role of the IRM committee as well as senior management, line management, the CIO, and others. The matrix itself should be approved by top management (the CEO). The principal function of the IRM committee basically focuses around the allocation of resources. There are two models for allocating resources: committee-driven and budget-driven. As the name implies, the committee-driven approach has all proposed acquisitions and projects re-

	Inputs	Recommends	Reviews	Decides	Approves
Data Resources					
Corporate vs. line data	Anyone	User	CIO	Data Adm.	IRM Com.
Data definition	Anyone	User	CIO	DA	DA
Database selection	DB Adm.	DA	CIO	CIO	IRM Com.
Database standards	DB Adm.	DB Adm.	DA	DA	CIO
Data ownership	Users	DA	CIO	IRM Com.	CEO
Access control	Users	Users	DA	CIO	Line Mgmt.
·	·	·	·	·	·
·	·	·	·	·	·
·	·	·	·	·	·
Systems Resources					
Buy or build					
Systems design					
Package selection					
Contracts					
Use of consultants					
Project approvals					
Systems standards					
Project control					
Computer Resources					
Equipment					

Figure 8.8. Information resource decision matrix.

viewed by various committees covering the different types of resources (capital investments, information systems projects, strategic plans, etc.). Budget-driven resource allocation combines the budget process with projects review and resource needs as a single process. If the budget is approved, the associated resources are also considered approved. This approach requires that planning be done far in advance of the budgeting process so that projects and resources can be identified, prioritized, quantified, and included in the budget. Most companies do not have their act together well enough to do that kind of advanced planning. Consequently, even though the budget-driven approach is usually preferred, practicality results in the committee-driven approach as the usual method followed by most companies in the allocation of resources.

The CIO Role. As noted earlier, the CIO has two fundamental tasks: to bring *value* to the organization through the integration of business systems planning that results in new and powerful information weapons, and to bring *structure* to the organization through the architectural integration of technologies that synergistically support the enterprise's information systems and support needs. In a decentralized environment, the CIO has the added burden of managing centralized (corporate) information resources such as corporate utilities (data centers and networks) while, at the same time, coordinating and orchestrating the decentralized information resources not under his/her direct control. His/her staff role may include technology consulting, management of corporate (centralized) resources (e.g., telecommunications and data resource management), development of the technology architecture, issuance of information resource policies, coordination of decentralized systems activities, review/approval of major expenditures, and systems assurance. An architectural plan and assurance policies as well as a clear definition of role responsibilities are needed to procure the control necessary to manage effectively in this environment.

Before we discuss information resources control, let us establish a clear understanding of the *scope* of the information resources to be included in the IRM program.

In too many organizations the CIO is narrowly concerned with *computer-based* information (factual data). This addresses only a small percentage of the total information resources of the firm. An even larger portion is represented by *paper-based* information (textual data). But the real bulk of the information resource is *people-based* (verbal data). As Figure 8.9 illustrates, if the CIO controls the three main technologies of data processing, office automation, and communications, all three information mediums (sources) will also be automatically managed. Control in this sense does not imply the need to own or possess, merely to facilitate its use, that is, find the information, flow it where it's needed, and form it as required.

The Investment in Technology. One objective of information policy is to capture and track the company's investment in technology (i.e., information resources). This involves first defining what the information resource

Source:	Computer-based information	Paper-based information	People-based information
Technology:	Data processing	Office automation	Communications
Type:	Factual data	Textual data	Verbal data
Examples:	Data centers Small business computers Minicomputers Personal computers Databases Applications systems Workstations	Word processing Document transmission Electronic mail Microfiche Records management Libraries Graphics	Telephone systems Teleconferencing Videoconferencing Voice mail Audiovisual facilities Education and training Expert systems

Figure 8.9. Information management.

is and aggregating its cost. Management can then assess whether the investment appears to be reasonable in light of its overall technology strategy (conservative versus aggressive), as well as where the investment is in terms of which business units and which technologies. If the investment is too high or low overall or in specific areas, actions can be taken to bring it more in line with corporate desires. (In the past, 1–2% of sales spent on information resources was considered a reasonable investment. In the future, it has been predicted that investments of double and triple this level, 5% of sales, will be more common. Indeed, firms who share the vision of what information weapons can do for growth and profitability are already spending at that level.)

The issue of the "value of information" is an important one because more often than not management considers the dollar investment more than the perceived benefits when making investments. For example, a systems project may be cost-justified at the outset as returning a certain return on investment (ROI) over its useful life. However, after it is implemented, no one continues to track the benefits with the ongoing running costs. The result is that the business unit gets the benefits (reduced staff or new revenue) while DP costs rise. Management seldom equates the two. In the case of management systems, it is even worse. Generally, quantified benefits cannot even be shown up front. How do you measure the value of better decisions? With competitive information systems we have an opportunity to relate the investment much more positively to the return on increased business. We can invert the "funnel" effect, so to speak, that management generally perceives from

Finally, the total investment can be broken down into its components for a more detailed analysis. For instance, in a divisional organization, the profit contribution of each SBU can be compared to its technology investment to show where anomalies exist, as depicted in Figure 8.10A. Business units whose profit contribution are out of whack with their technology investment should either be justified by growth expectations or cutbacks must be considered. Figure 8.10B compares SBU missions with the percentage of *development* resources allocated to them. Again, the growth (LEAD and NICHE) businesses should be getting the bulk of these resources. Large development efforts in the other businesses would be suspect. Tracking the technology investment over time enables management to keep their pulse on what is being spent where and goes a long way

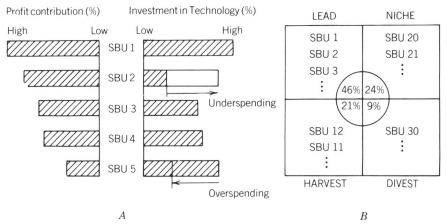

Figure 8.10. SBU analysis: (A) Profit contribution versus technology investment of SBU in a divisional organization; (B) Comparison of SBU missions with their development resources.

toward answering the three most-often asked questions of CIOs: Am I spending too little or too much on technology? Am I spending in the right places? Why am I spending so much?

Information Resource Policies

If the CIO's primary tool for forging technological structure is architectural planning, the primary tool for assuring that architecture is the issuance of information resource policies and the monitoring of adherance to those policies.

Each component of the IRM architecture model requires governing policies. What policies are needed generally falls out of the IRM architectural plan because it is necessarily custom-tailored to the specific corporate environment. Nonetheless, certain policies are required in every case. Only the content varies. For example, *security* is a generic requirement that fits every architectural component. Figure 8.11, lists a number of information resource policies as a general guide to the types of policies that can be issued.

The manner of controlling corporate policy issuance varies from company to company, again according to organizational style. In some, all policies emanate from one source. Others issue policies out of different functional areas (e.g., Finance issues financial policies; the Law Office issues legal and regulatory requirements, etc.). Still others leave it all to the line organization. The following describes the three-tier policies architecture

Category	Title
Information resource policies	Information resource policy (overview)
	Technology research
	Corporate investment in technology
	Information resource planning
	Information resource allocations
	Computer architecture
	Systems enhancements
Data resource policies	Proprietary information
	Data privacy and confidentiality
	Data resource policies (overview)
	Data ownership
	Database management systems selection
	Data administration policy
	Database administration policy
	Database standards manual
	Database architecture
	Data access control
Computer policies	Computer policies (overview)
	Security of computer equipment, software, and physical media
	Data access control
	Contingency planning
	Insurance coverage
	Selection/acquisition of computer equipment
	Selection/acquisition of application software
	Distributed processing
	Data processing—related expenses
	Data processing contracts (*NOTE:* This will also replace Data process-
	Use of outside computing services
	VDU/CRT replacement/purchase policy and ergonomic standards
	Computer architecture
	Vendor selection
	Vendor support
	Computer operations control
User-computing policies	Security of computer equipment, software, and physical media
	Office systems security and control
	Software piracy
	User-computing architecture
Communications policies	Communications architecture
	Planning/installing data communications systems
	Planning/installing voice communications systems
	Communications network security and access control
Systems policies	Trade secrets
	Project control
	Software piracy
	Vendor selection

Figure 8.11. Sample information resource policies.

218

Category	Title
	Systems architecture
	Feasibility studies
	Request for proposal—Software development
	Systems and programming standards manual
	Systems enhancements
	Systems bridges
Systems human resources policies	Systems personnel (PEP parity)
	Systems consultants

Figure 8.11. (Continued)

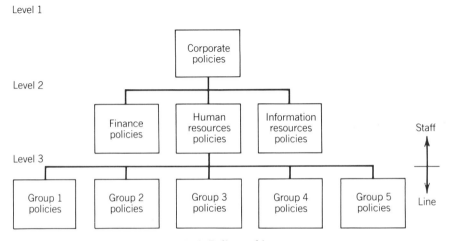

Figure 8.12. Policy architecture.

illustrated in Figure 8.12, as used by the Bank of Boston to control this important area of responsibility.

Because the bank is decentralized, policy responsibility is distributed between the staff and line groups. Level 1 policies cover corporate-wide issues that affect all line business units as well as staff support units. These are the responsibility of the Corporate Compliance Officer. Level 2 policies cover functional areas of responsibility, for example, finance, human resources, and information resources policies, that are also corporate-wide in nature. These are issued by the respective staff support units. Level 3 policies are germain only to the individual line business units and are, therefore, solely their responsibility. Regardless of who issues the policies, copies of all are maintained by a Corporate Compliance Officer for information and oversight purposes.

But the initiation and issuance of policies is only the first step. The second step in architectural assurance is the monitoring of policy compliance. This oversight responsibility is critical because to not exercise governance over policies negates their value. The CIO cannot know that decisions follow policy unless some sort of monitoring takes place. This need not be at a detailed audit level. It can be limited to a simple determination that a process is in effect to implement policy, that specific individuals are charged with the responsibility of overseeing it within each applicable area, and that routine internal audits are conducted by the line unit and/ or staff auditors from time to time.

Architectural oversight can cover a variety of areas, such as equipment configurations, data processing performance measurements, systems design reviews, tracking of systems projects (including post-audits), security and contingency reviews, network architecture reviews, and database planning.

In decentralized environments, where the CIO does not control all of these resources, a more formal review process may be needed to assure architecture. One simple technique for the CIO to follow is what I call the "sign-on/sign-off" strategy. From an architectural perspective, the important point in time for the CIO to be involved is at the very beginning, when ideas are generated and architectural options are wide open. This is where the CIO can make a real contribution in assisting systems managers and users alike to make sound architectural decisions. It is important for the CIO to "sign-on" at this critical early planning stage. "Sign-off" is the other end of the spectrum. Policies must be in place that require the CIO to "sign-off" on major technology expenditures. An automatic sign-off mechanism guarantees that nothing falls between the cracks. If the CIO was not signed-on in the beginning, he/she will be at the end—sort of a final assurance of initial sign-on.

This whole oversight process, while necessary to architectural assurance, especially in a decentralized company, can be a sensitive and political issue. When users have their own resources, outside interference will be resented. Yet corporate coordination and control is necessary. The CIO, therefore, has to walk the delicate line between control and support, cop or chaplain. The truly successful CIO is able to exercise the cop role in a chaplain's robe.

With a knowledge of the business architecture and the technology support needs of the organization, and with a sound information policy commitment from top management to assure the technology structure, we are ready to begin to build the IRM architecture plan. In the next two chapters I have divided the information resource domains into those resources that I believe should be centralized regardless of organizational structure and those that are decentralized or decentralizing. The material is further divided for each resource between the three planning levels of the architectural model: strategic, tactical, and operational.

References

1. A report by the Dooley Group (management consultants) to the Center for Information Management Studies (CIMS), Babson College, Wellesley, MA, July 1985.

2. John Leslie King, "Centralized versus Decentralized Computing: Organizational Considerations and Management Options," *Computing Surveys,* a publication of the Association for Computing Machinery, Dec. 1983.

3. Robert E. Levinson, "Why Decentralize?" *Management Review,* Oct. 1985.

4. Ibid., p. 51.

5. *Chemical Week,* 5/19/82, pp. 64–69.

9

CENTRALIZED INFORMATION RESOURCES

Good management rests on a reconciliation of centralization and
decentralization, or decentralization with coordinated control.
ALFRED P. SLOAN, JR.

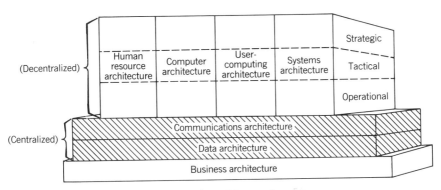

Figure 9.1. IRM architectural model.

The business architecture of the company (organization structure, strategic business units and missions, products and services) is the foundation of IRM architectural planning. Since every company has an existing architecture, architectural planning begins with an inventory of the firm's information resources. Assembling the various information resource components' inventories results in an "as is" picture of the corporation's technology structure. From this inventory, the CIO can analyze the strengths and weaknesses of the company's information resources, particularly as they relate to business information needs as identified in the strategic planning process. From this analysis one can evolve an architectural plan, which is a "to be" picture of where one wants to go and how to get there, not just a picture of the status quo.

The architectural model developed in Chapter 8 divided information resources into centralized and decentralized resources. This was meant to

223

address the trend toward decentralization in the industry, but at the same time recognize the need for central control over corporate information utilities, regardless of organizational structure. In Figure 9.1 data and communications are shown in horizontal bars because they represent information resources that cross divisional boundaries, are used by all, and thus should be under central management, even in decentralized organizations. Most companies have these information resource components under central control. System staffs and applications systems, on the other hand, are decentralizing in many organizations. Computers, by virtue of the rapid proliferation of small and inexpensive mini- and microcomputers in virtually all organizations, are decentralizing into distributed processing networks. End-user computing by its very definition is automatically a decentralized information resource. Hence, all of these are shown as vertical bars to represent information resources that are either already decentralized or are moving in that direction.

The reason for distinguishing between centralized and decentralized resources is that the management of centralized resources under a CIO's control is quite different from the management of decentralized resources under the control of users. The former is under direct control and can be mandated; the latter requires influence and persuasion, with control exercised primarily through information policies and standards.

Because the future focus of CIOs will, in this author's opinion, be directed more and more to the planning and management of the data and communications resources of the firm (and less to the computing and systems resources, which will be increasingly decentralized), this chapter goes into these two subjects in more detail than does Chapter 10 on the decentralized resources. This does not suggest that decentralized resources are less important; only that the management of them is shared so that these resources will likely not occupy as much of the CIO's primary interest and attention as the more rapidly growing areas of data resource management and telecommunications.

DATA ARCHITECTURE

Data architecture is the link between business plans and information systems. If one reads the textbooks, data architecture, or data resource management (DRM), should be a top-down process that begins with strategic data planning (SDP), understanding business processes and the underlying data used by the business. Strategic data planning is conducted by a data administration (DA) function composed of business-driven information specialists who build corporate data models and logical database designs. A database administrative function converts these to physical databases that are flexible, nonredundant and, presumably, navigable. The three basic functions of DRM then, should be strategic data planning, data administration, and database management, in that order. In actuality, theory and practice are reversed in most organizations. Instead of a top-down process, we generally find a bottom-up process. First, a database management system (DBMS) is selected and a database administrator is hired. The DA function often never gets established. (Even when it does, it is seldom business-driven.) Without DA, strategic data planning is seldom done. To quote Arnold Barnett, President of Barnett Data Systems:

> There are few companies—perhaps none—who have literally been through the whole top down process, defined subject databases, and implemented substantial portions of the associated applications. (1)

There are basically three problems: (1) DRM is a massive undertaking that cannot be done without top management support; (2) DRM requires a thorough understanding of the business that few data administrators possess; (3) DRM must basically be done by businessmen, led by a CIO. A review of the strategic data planning process will help to show why this is so hard to achieve.

Strategic Data Planning

STRATEGIC

IW 45—STRATEGIC DATA PLANNING
Linking data planning to business information needs.

In 1881 William Winchester, son of the famous rifle manufacturer, died leaving $20 million to his widow, Sara. During her mourning, she consulted a fortune-teller. The seer revealed that Sara's own survival depended on the construction of a house: as long as work on the house continued, Sara would live and prosper. Workers continued to add new wings and rooms until Sara's death 36 years later.

The still unfinished house has 160 rooms and covers six acres in San Jose, California. It has blind chimneys, doors that open into blank walls, stairways that lead to ceilings, windows blocked by later construction, and countless oddities that suppress any sense of the unity normally associated with the notion of a house. It's an interesting phenomenon, a freak, an example of on-the-fly design. The materials and workmanship of each room are the best that money could buy. But, built without an architectural plan, it cannot function as a house. (2)

Frank Sweet's above description of the Winchester House was meant to be an analogy to data planning. Without strategic data planning, there can be no overall plan or architecture for data, no understanding of corporate data and data relationships, and no consistency between information systems. Systems built one at a time without an overall plan tend to take on some of the characteristics of the Winchester House over time. Systems do not relate to each other, data is redundant or defined differently in separate systems, "feeds" to other systems become complicated, information consolidation is made more complex; in other words, the individual systems don't function as an integrated architecture any more than the Winchester House functions as a house.

Strategic data planning requires a thorough understanding of the business and heavy involvement of user management. Support of top management is vital because it is not a technical process; it is a business process. Therein lies the rub! The problem with top-down DRM planning is that it must first be *sold to upper management*. Very few companies have successfully sold this concept, and it can seldom be cost-justified on its own. Take a massive effort (multiyears, multimillions) that management does not really understand, add few companies that can showcase success, stir with murky cost-justification, and you have all the ingredients of a DRM program ready to fall of its own weight, like a "dropped" cake.

Nonetheless, information managers are heavy believers in DRM, as evidenced by a survey of MIS managers at a recent International Data Corp. conference which showed the following (3):

- 81% rated the need for a data administration function to be critical.
- 78% rated the use of a relational DBMS critical.
- 89% rated data integration through a data dictionary critical.
- 88% rated the use of fourth-generation languages critical.

If this survey is any indication, information managers are clearly sold on the need for DRM. The group that is *not* yet sold in most organizations is top management! The "education" of top management as to the need for DRM and the support they must provide it can be a long drawn-out affair. It has to begin with a CIO that is well versed in the subject. Many are not. They have treated it as a technical problem, hired a database administrator (or even a data administrator) and left it to happen. Experience has shown that this will not result in an effective DRM program. The CIO need not be technically proficient at SDP methodologies. Good consulting firms can be hired for this purpose. Nor does the CIO need to be a database expert. There are also good (though scarce) DBMS specialists that can be hired. The CIO does need to understand what has to be done, in what order, and by whom. He/she needs to know what is required of management, users, and technicians (the roles of each). Most of all, the CIO needs to gain management support to begin *somewhere*.

Lack of management commitment seems to be the single biggest problem in getting strategic data planning off the ground. In a study of the data administration function in business by the U. S. Department of Transportation, the researchers concluded that the major issue was management involvement.

> This was mentioned by nearly everyone. It is clearly something that cannot be overstated. . . . Without management support, data administration will never escape being branded as a DP boondoggle easily avoided. (4)

At a recent conference, Ronald G. Ross (R. E. Ross Associates) suggested that selling management on the need for an SDP program (what he calls the "missionary" phase), could take 6 months to a year of "informal meetings, hallway discussions, chalk talks, and idea memos" before acceptance of a program is gained (5). Once stated, he suggests moving rapidly with the initial study effort while management interest and enthusiasm remains high, and getting something implemented that has business value as quickly as possible. A protracted effort without demonstrable results, he suggests, can quickly degenerate into "post-SDP depression syndrome," a management attitude that begins with euphoria and ends in depression.

Avoid grandiose corporate-wide plans. As noted earlier, they usually don't work. Instead, start small, work incrementally, and find areas where quick results can be achieved that bring business value and credibility to the SDP process. Find a champion, a user who is sold on its value and willing to sponsor a study in his/her own area. Downplay the *process*. Bury it in the business solution. The user is buying information value, not technology.

In the early stages, it is probably wise to hire a data management consultant. There are a number of good ones around specializing in SDP. But don't just buy methodology; they all have a methodology. Equally important is experience and expertise in working with senior managers to define business functions and information needs and in helping to "sell" the business value of the program to users.

A number of firms have developed SDP methodologies that effectively integrate data planning with business plans (e.g., A. D. Little, Holland Systems, Index Systems, and Nolan-Norton Co.). The following two examples illustrate how these methodologies work to achieve business/data integration.

Methodology # 1 (6)

A. D. Little's Strategic Value Analysis (SVA) method is based on a 10-step process. This can be done on a corporate-wide basis, but in this author's opinion, it will probably be easier to start at the SBU level. A smaller-scale effort will make it easier to gain support, can be accomplished faster, and is easier to relate to individual business needs than a large corporate-wide endeavor. Another reason to start at the SBU level is that it enables the program to begin in the high-priority (LEAD) businesses. By setting up the program in this way, results can be demonstrated sooner where they really count.

Here is a summary of A. D. Little's SVA methodology:

1. Strategic business planning. Start by identifying business objectives. This will flow from the strategic planning process, if there is one; otherwise, the CIO must derive them from interviews with business managers. The relative importance of the objectives are weighted (i.e., if you had a dollar, how would you divide it over the objectives?).

2. Data-flow analysis. Define the business processes and data flows through top-down analysis of functions performed, unrelated to the organization structure. This shows both present (as is) and future (to be) views. Decompose down to successive layers of detail, showing objectives at each level.

3. Review existing systems. Develop both a user and information systems perspective of the efficiency and effectiveness of systems in place (and correlate the two). Understand the sources of data and the interdependencies between systems.

4. Assess information systems capabilities. Identify capabilities of in-place information systems in terms of how they could help achieve business objectives.

5. Design databases. Design the logical databases needed to support the "to be" data flows.

6. Synthesize systems. Synthesize the capabilities developed in step 4 into new systems.

7. Design the architecture. Design the logical and physical data architecture (what, where, connectivity needs, etc.) needed to accomplish business objectives. Keep it broad and logical, not detailed (whether the system is to be built, bought, or an existing system fixed).

8. Create projects. Define needed projects.

9. Develop the plan. Alternative plans are developed for management approval which detail priorities, costs/benefits, schedules, and resource needs.

10. Maintain the plan. Use and keep the plan current (an important follow-up process).

Methodology # 2 (7)

Holland Systems Corp. suggests that DRM consists of three elements: a management philosophy, analytical methods, and implementation guidelines that enable a firm to integrate and share information resources. By management philosophy they mean managing information as a corporate resource. Analytical methods analyze and define business actions (every business action has information requirements associated with it) as well as information use and interdependencies. Implementation guidelines are the architectural plans to build the "house."

Holland's data planning methodology is called Strategic Systems Planning (SSP). It is supported by software that consists of three pieces: the business model, the data architecture, and the information systems architecture (see Figure 9.2).

1. The business model is meant to be a functional representation of the business broken down into a series of business actions taking place in the organization (or business unit being studied), which are determined through a rigorous interviewing process. The business actions are defined in terms of business functions, which incorporate processes that are composed of activities.

2. The data architecture looks at each business activity and seeks to determine what information is needed to perform that activity. These information requirements are condensed into a small number of business subjects called entities (customers, accounts, invoices). The SSP software keeps track of the information requirements, the entities and their relationship to activities, as well as where the entities are used throughout the business model. The data architecture defines the business use of information and the data that can be shared by more than one activity. This results in a set of subject databases aimed at optimally structuring business information.

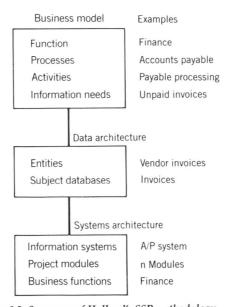

Figure 9.2. Summary of Holland's SSP methodology.

3. The information systems architecture examines the business activities of the model and determines groups of activities that produce major information output. These groupings are called "project modules." These project modules add up to the information systems requirements of the business. These information systems are independent of the subject databases but share the information contained in them.

Holland's SSP methodology is followed by an equally rigorous and formalized tactical systems planning (TSP) process, during which projects are identified and implemented according to priorities, and a logical database design (LDD) phase, which focuses on development of logical data models.

As noted earlier, getting management support for data planning is often more difficult to achieve than the methodology used to bring it about. This is why many favor an incremental approach. Ways include: (1) finding a receptive area to "pilot" a small study that brings fast results, (2) building prototype systems that have quick turnaround, (3) starting a corporate information center, (4) downloading to departmental information centers (or PCs), (5) creating a front-end corporate MIS as an interim system for management.

Data Administration

TACTICAL

> IW 46—DATA ADMINISTRATION
> Managing shared corporate data as a common resource.

Data administration (DA) is the function that carries out strategic data planning. Therefore, before SDP can be undertaken, a data administrator must be in place. The data administrator is not a technical position; it is a business position with a technical specialty. The mission of the data administrator is to develop the data architecture for the corporation as a whole. The data administrator is charged with managing data as a resource. He or she does this by developing business data models (how businesses use data) and developing and maintaining nonredundant databases.

The purpose of a DA function is to establish the plan, policies, and procedures for the management of data as part of information resource management. To do this, the data administrator conducts strategic data planning, creates technical plans for database implementation, and oversees or works closely with the database administrator to manage and control database systems. The DA function is expected to define policies for corporate data, manage the data analysis effort, identify data-sharing opportunities, and define standards for use in database design. The major

DA activities are development of plans for corporate data management, institution of data policies and standards, identification of strategic corporate data, identification of data-sharing opportunities, and control over data integrity and security.

In many organizations, even those with database management systems, applications are developed individually, with separate databases for each, and often with data dictionaries that are not controlled through a common dictionary. James Martin calls this a "Class II environment," in which many databases are developed containing high redundancy levels and maintenance costs. These companies are not achieving the major advantages of data management. By identifying corporate subject databases which are independent of applications systems and are shared by many applications, much redundancy can be avoided and data management optimized. Martin calls this a "Class III environment" (see Figure 9.3). Since databases form the foundation of future data processing, the control of corporate (shared) data through data administration is a critical need in all modern organizations. Too often the administrator is a technical person far removed from the business enterprise and the senior business managers who run it, which accounts for many of the failures in getting DRM off the ground. As a result, many advocates suggest that the DA function should be a user-driven activity headed by a businessman. The problem with that approach is that it often results in splintering the overall responsibility for information resource management; that is, different people are responsible for information (content) planning and information resources (conduit) planning. Unless the two report to the same individual, problems can re-

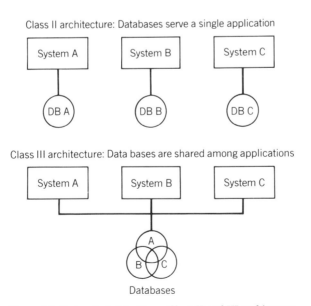

Figure 9.3. Data administration—Class II and III architecture.

sult. There is also often confusion between the role and responsibilities of the data administrator and the database administrator, with both possibly reporting to different people in the organization.

Although many organizational options are possible, in this author's view, single-minded management works best in data architecture planning, and the CIO is an appropriate person to exercise it. Figure 9.4 shows several different options for organizing the DA/DBA functions under the CIO. Figure 9.5 illustrates some of the main differences in the DA and DBA positions. As can be seen, the DA position is very business-oriented, global in scope, and long-term in perspective. The DBA post is technical, localized, and has a short-term view of the use of data. The DA function is concerned with what goes into a database and DBA with *how* it is implemented. Both functions are typically small. In reporting on the results of 11 different surveys on the subject of DA taken between 1970–1983, one researcher reported that

> . . . numerous DA groups consist of only one person, the largest size reported was 75. More typically, however, the surveys determined that a large

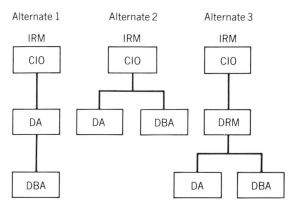

Figure 9.4. Options for organizing the data and database administration functions.

Function	Data Administration	Database Administration
Mission	DRM	DRM
Function	Manage information	Manage data
Role	Managerial	Technical
Scope	All databases	Specific databases
Skills	Business planning	DB technology
	System development	DBMS
Primary contacts	Management	Technical staff
Planning focus	Strategic data management	DBMS management
Concerned with	Metadata (information about data)	Data
Data management	Data dictionaries	DBMSs

Figure 9.5. Comparison of responsibilities of data and database administrators.

DA group has seven or eight people, and a small group, two or three. These figures have not varied over the years. (8)

James Odell, in an article in *Data Base Newsletter,* described seven DA roles that might serve as a model for a large company's DA function as shown in Figure 9.6 (9). Historically, the need for DA has arisen because of DBMS; that is, most DA groups have been formed after the introduction of DBMS, the typical sequence being DBMS, DA, and data dictionary. Displacement of the DBMS by the data dictionary (DD) as the focal point for data planning came with experience. The realization of the importance of the common DD took a while. Dr. George Schussel, in a paper prepared for POSPP (Profit Oriented Systems Planning Programs) noted that the DBMS started out as the focal point of data management with other developments surrounding it. However, in later years, the DD replaced the DBMS as the focal point of data management, as shown in Figure 9.7 (10).

The data administrator has four fundamental responsibilities: data strategist, logical database designer, corporate dictionary custodian, and issuer of data policies and standards.

1. Data strategist. The fundamental responsibility of a data strategist is to define the information plans of the enterprise. This begins with creation of *business data models,* which serve as the architectural plan or blueprint of corporate (shared) data. They show what and where data exists and how it is used, acting as a directory to corporate data. They describe data simply in business terms. They show where data is redundantly stored and maintained, which assists in the formulation of data-sharing policies. They doc-

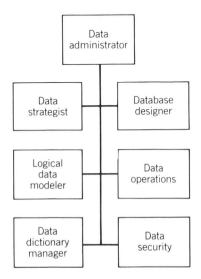

Figure 9.6. Data administration organization—large company.

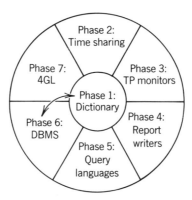

Figure 9.7. Data management evolution. Adapted from G. Schussel (10).

ument conflicting definitions, resulting in standard terminology. Business models are, therefore, a critical tool for moving toward a Class III architecture. There can be one overall corporate model or a number of business unit models that eventually integrate into a corporate model. I favor the latter approach. By starting small, by business unit, one can show value more quickly, gaining credibility to move on. Business models need not be more than a one-page diagram that describes the business's data in terms of entities and the relationships between them.

Figure 9.8 shows a simple model of a bank business unit called Loan Placements. The business of placements involves identifying loans on a bank's books that are currently unattractive and packaging them for resale to investors. This frees up funds for alternative investments. Level 0 of the model lists the business unit and the external forces affecting it. Level 1 shows major business functions performed. These are further broken down in Level 2 "processes." Level 3 (not shown) would then decompose the *processes* into their various *activities*. While the procedure seems simple, in practice it requires a great deal of work by knowledgable business managers to reduce a business to a one-page diagram that identifies the major databases required to support the business's information needs. But once done, the model is not likely to change over time and thus serves as an excellent foundation for database design and implementation. Without a business data model, it is likely that a company will remain with a Class II architecture.

2. Logical database designer. Logical database design flows from business data models. Logical database design is essentially a map of the data used in the business written in business terms. Its goal is to develop independent, sharable, and stable databases that will not be impacted by organizational changes. It is done concurrently with data flow analysis, one leads to the other. The steps involved are:

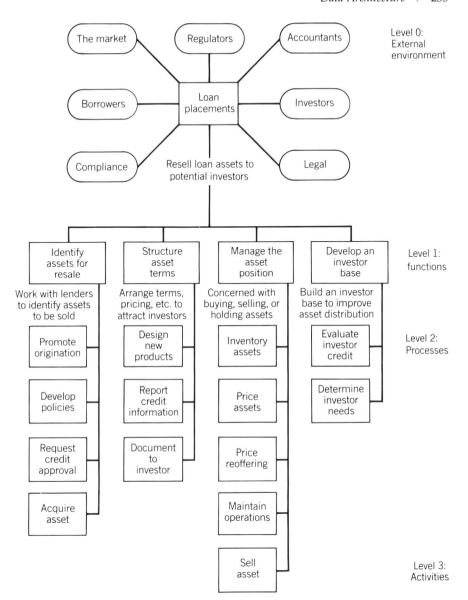

Figure 9.8. A business model (SBU level).

a. Identify entity classes and establish clear definitions of each. Entities are people, places, things, or events (e.g., employees, geographic locations, products, or purchase orders).
b. Create a data structure diagram for each class. Each entity needs its own data structure diagram in the logical database design.

 c. Prepare data definitions that are agreed to by all. Each must be unique and clear.

 d. Evaluate entity classes. Look for opportunities to combine, split, or add entities.

 e. Perfect data structure diagrams. Add elements and definitions, assign domains.

 f. Finalize the documentation.

 3. Data dictionary custodian. The key to data coordination is the corporate DD which is maintained by the data administrator. Data developed while building a business model is defined and put into the corporate DD. Every data element contained in application database dictionaries is also contained in the corporate dictionary (without duplication). The major advantage of the corporate, or common, DD is that elements are defined once and do not need to be redefined again for another application. The first application defines the data element and subsequent applications simply reference the data element without having to create new data elements for each system. The goal is to have all definitions of data elements in a common DD, rather than in application code. Nonredundant data definitions are critical to a sound data architecture. Most DBMS today have a data dictionary already built in, making the task easier. Active DDs are integrated with the other components of the DBMS, whereas passive DDs require intermediate processing and, therefore, store less useful information. Some objectives of a common DD are:

 a. Facilitate database migration.

 b. Establish agreed upon definitions of data elements.

 c. Minimize redundancy.

 d. Create standard documentation of information systems.

 e. Make information about data (metadata) more easily available.

 f. Reduce system development time.

 g. Reduce system maintenance.

 h. Establish programming standards with respect to data use.

 This work is facilitated today by the use of automated data dictionaries that catalog standard data definitions and how they are used, and automated data modeling tools that synthesize data into formalized data structures.

 4. Issuer of policies and standards. Finally, the data administrator needs to initiate the necessary data resource policies and standards needed to assure that individual database projects are implemented in a manner that is consistent across the corporation. These range from general business policies such as data ownership and access control to detailed standards about the structure and design of databases. The main objective of policies and standards is architectural assurance. In a decentralized en-

vironment where the administrator does not control the development process, such standards may be the *only* way to control data integration, hence they are critical to data architecture.

Database Management

> **IW 47—DATABASE ADMINISTRATION**
> Assuring database systems standards.

Database technology separates data from systems to create a flexible but stable integrated structure for the data resource, regardless of how business organization structure may change or what information systems are developed. Without this data link, one can only continue to build systems one at a time, perpetuating data redundancy and minimal ability to share data between systems. This is not only costly and inefficient, but ineffective in using the potential of information as a resource. Each system serves a specific business function without regard to any others. To pass data from one system to another requires writing special programs to extract the data from one file and reformat it for another (exacerbated by mixed data definitions). Creating management reports from consolidated data from several systems becomes laborious. Communication and integration across departmental lines is difficult, as is consolidation for top management. Yet this is the way systems were built in the first 20 years of business computing. The problem with file systems is that they create much redundancy, are inflexible and costly to change, and do not easily permit corporate information consolidation or analysis. This can be a particularly sore point with management that does not understand why they cannot get the information they need—"Everything is automated. We know it's in the computers somewhere. Why can't we get at it?"

The answer lies in the problems of file systems versus the database approach. In the mid-1970s, the notion of database management, separating data from systems, moving away from the file-system approach, began to take hold. But many mistakenly thought that it meant building one gigantic "intergalactic" database in the sky. Considerable work went into attempting to design the total MIS approach in some organizations. It never flew. The all-or-nothing approach generally resulted in nothing. Gradually, many companies realized that there would, in fact, be many databases in an organization. The important thing was to standardize the structure and data elements so that one could navigate between them. Databases built with common data descriptions, defined in a common DD, and using a common design methodology result in linkage between systems and a corporate-wide data architecture.

Many companies began installing DBMSs in the late 1970s. Many of these early installations, however, had no common dictionary and no DA function. Many simply added a front-end DBMS to a file system. Even when a DD was in place, the dictionaries in each database were often not coordinated into a common one. Many companies simply used a DBMS as a front-end access system for each application system. In such cases, duplicate data still existed and integration was still not possible. And many failed to create a DA function. This meant that the DBMS strategy became a technical task rather than a business one. Management and users were not involved; hence they viewed the DB specialist as merely another technician and the database approach as simply a technical methodology. Data resource management should provide the way to migrate from the Computer Era's disassociated file systems to the Information Era's total data architecture, in a logical and incremental manner. It is not unlike rebuilding a city (a continuous process in old established eastern cities like New York and Boston). You do it building by building, but all under a long-term urban development program with architecture and guidelines to give concerted direction to the individual projects.

The evolution from files to databases is necessarily a slow and tedious process because it is done as systems are rewritten or replaced. Since a system's life is generally on the order of 10 years, database migration is a long and painful process.

A number of alternative solutions to database migration exist:

1. Start from scratch. Look for start-up opportunities where no system yet exists. (After 30 years of computing, there aren't many.)

2. Convert all file systems to database systems. This is costly and time-consuming, and little new functionality will be perceived.

3. Gradual conversion. This is most commonly done as systems need to be rewritten, but takes 10–15 years to complete.

4. Replace with packages. Possible, but one needs to be careful that the package (and database) fits the corporate architecture.

5. Build "bridge" systems. Create a front-end DBMS to a file system. Backward compatibility may be required, however, to preserve existing programs.

6. Provide an interim solution. Most commonly done in the form of a corporate Information Center.

Alternatives 3 and 6 are probably the most popular, that is, gradual conversion to a common DBMS using the information center concept as an interim solution. Generally, this is accomplished by dumping the files to a nonproduction machine, and facilitating access to the data through use of a fourth-generation language (4GL) such as Focus, Ramis, or Mark IV. The problem is that raw data must be massaged to be useful, 4GLs are not really that "user friendly," and the files still contain much redundant data.

Because of these problems, some companies have begun to build front-end corporate MIS systems for their managers that contain preselected management data (an institutionalized information center, if you will).

What is the best DB architecture? In the 1960s, hierarchical versus network architecture was the debate. In the 1970s it was inverted file architecture. Now, it's relational.[1]

The market is dominated by a handful of products that include IBM (IMS, DB2), which has 50% of the market, Cullinet (IDMS/IDMS-R) with 20%, and lesser shares for other market leaders such as Applied Data Research (Datacom), Cincom (Total, Supra), and Software AG (Adabas) (11).

Finally, there is the question of database machines. A database machine is a specialized combination of hardware and relational DBMS software. The market leaders, Teradata Corp. (Los Angeles, California) and Britton-Lee (Los Gatos, California), have only installed a relatively small number of machines to date. One reason is probably that IBM has not tipped its hand yet regarding a database machine and many wait for Big Blue to support a technology before they consider it viable. So, while database machines may play a larger role in the future, it is a future consideration that should not affect a DBMS selection decision today.

The formula for database success in an organization may be summarized as follows: (1) adopt the IRM concept for data management, (2) establish a data administration function, (3) develop a solid database staff, and (4) get some automated tools to help do the job (e.g., modeling tools, data dictionary, and DBMS).

COMMUNICATIONS ARCHITECTURE

The second centralized information resource to be architectured is *communications*. Telecommunications, both voice and data, need to be under single-mind management to make all the pieces fit together. Ten spiders do not make a web. If voice and data are to be integrated into a company-wide, even worldwide, network, centralized management is paramount. Communications is the "electronic highway" of the firm. If communications planning and design is not centralized, it would be like allowing the individual states to build the U. S. highway system. Richer states would have four-lane highways changing to dirt roads at the border of poorer states—or roads would end at the borders, or at rivers without bridges. A nationwide highway system requires coordinated planning. A company-

---

[1]Relational DBs display data in files that consist of tables of rows and columns (similar to flat files). Data in different rows can be selected using the verb SELECT. Data in different columns are extracted using the verb PROJECT, and rows and columns from different tables can be brought together with the verb JOIN. All the user needs to learn to retrieve data is the name of the tables, the name of the rows (primary keys), and the name of the columns.

wide "electronic highway" also requires centralized coordinated planning to be effective.

Until recently, telecommunications management was largely a matter of choosing among AT&T offerings to provide needed service at the lowest cost. But on January 1, 1984, all of that changed. That date marked the court-ordered divestiture of AT&T into 22 companies regrouped as seven large regional phone companies. From that moment on, telecommunications managers had a new role: serving as an in-house AT&T, choosing among many options of communications services not previously available. Decisions involve selection of communications channels, common carriers, communications protocols, capacity, responsiveness, and linkage access between layers of computing ranging from corporate mainframes to departmental minis to personal microcomputers. The divestiture created widespread uncertainty. Many felt that large users would benefit from competitive pressures to drive costs down, that long-distance rates would drop and local rates would rise, again to the gain of large companies who are the major long-distance users. This has since been borne out. Two years after the divestiture order, Sam Simon, executive director of the Telecommunications Research Action Center, a consumer lobby group, reported that local telephone rates had risen 20–30%, while long-distance charges declined about 15%. He also noted that the imposition of the $6 per line access charge to connect to the local telephone loop virtually wiped out any potential gains to small businesses from the cheaper long-distance rates. Furthermore, he predicts a bigger shock is coming in that the Federal Communications Commission, responding to local telephone companies' requests for local rate hikes to offset lost business from "by-pass," is planning to boost access fees to about $11 per line by 1990. (12)

The economics of divestiture, coupled with dissatisfaction with service, is pushing telecommunications managers to other options, including ownership of equipment (telephones, wiring, PBXs) rather than leasing as in the past. This has fostered tremendous competition. At this writing, there were at least 70 manufacturers of telephone equipment, and the long-distance market was being served by over 400 companies (13). (Experts, however, expect a shakeout in the industry will soon reduce this to a small number of large carriers.) With change comes opportunity! The divestiture of AT&T resulted in confusion through increased competition and many more options for communications managers to consider. But with that came the opportunity to build better service networks, create significant economies-of-scale facilities, and even turn telecommunications services into new revenue-producing information weapons. All the telecommunications manager needs is education, that is, he/she needs to know and understand the options available and to select the choices that best fit the communications architecture of the enterprise and its environmental needs.

Strategic Communications Planning

STRATEGIC

> **IW 48—STRATEGIC COMMUNICATIONS PLANNING**
> Planning the corporate-wide communications structure.

All information resource architectures involve choosing among options, but because of the divestiture, communications architecture has become mainly a matter of choosing among alternatives. "Options analysis" can be both strategic or tactical.

At the strategic planning level, *logical* options are those that involve decisions as to "What is be done?" At the tactical planning level, *physical* options deal with choosing among competing products and vendors, or "How will it be done?" A decision to wire a building with your own wire instead of the phone company's is a strategic option because it leads to greater future control over functionality and architectural direction. The choice of wiring (coaxial cables, shielded twisted pair, or telephone-type twisted pair) is a tactical option on how to get it done. A decision to go "in-house" with a PBX telephone switching system instead of leasing the phone company's Centrex system is strategic; the choice of vendor (AT&T, Northern Telecom, Rolm) is tactical. A decision to "bypass" is strategic; how to do it is tactical.

Strategic communications planning is essentially network planning. And network planning divides into local area network (LAN) and wide area network (WAN) planning.

Local Area Networks. The options available for LAN planning are PBXs (private branch exchange) or LAN (or both). A PBX can either be a voice only (analog) switch or (preferably) an integrated voice/data (digital) switch. A digital PBX is, in fact, a form of LAN. A LAN is a wired network that links up office computers and other equipment. Today, only about 20% of U. S. companies have gone the in-house PBX route, and another 10% have LAN services. That leaves 70% still undecided. Waiting for the ultimate solution is probably unwise with the fast payoffs offered by today's equipment.

1. PBX. Installing a company owned and operated PBX communications switch can offer cost savings, ease in adding new functionality (e.g., voice mail), and greater control. It also has potential pitfalls. With your own switch, *you* are now the in-house AT&T. The settling-in period will likely be underestimated. Users will demand 100% up-time (not 99% as in computers). Since this will not be possible, the communications manager's visibility in the firm will be high and perhaps uncomfortable. The amount

of training needed will be underestimated by everyone. Nonetheless,the benefits can far outweigh the problems. An integrated voice/data network can provide a cost ratio gain of 4:1 over separate voice and data channels. That is why the integrated voice/data PBX is fast becoming the favored choice among communications managers.

2. LAN. Local area networks that connect up computers and terminals within a department, building, or campus are the second most popular LAN alternative. However, installations in 1984 and 1985 were essentially flat at about 16,000 per year. This is hardly tapping the market. As mentioned earlier, 70% of the market is still waiting. The leading LAN, Ethernet, backed by Xerox, Digital Equipment Corp., and others, has over 25,000 installations. Now IBM is pushing its "token-ring" network[2] and AT&T is backing a product called Starlan.

These industry leaders are followed by dozens of third-party LAN suppliers. LANs are also being developed by private firms such as General Motors, which is pushing, and gaining acceptance, for its Manufacturing Automation Protocol (MAP), a standard for factory LANs, and Boeing Computer Services Co., with its Technology Office Protocol (TOP), a standard for office systems. (15)

Those who are hesitating to dive into LANs fear the risks of technology coupled with obsolescence; hundreds of components, terminal devices, gateways, protocol converters, and miles of cable increase the chances for failure. Notes one observer:

> With installation costs ranging from $500 to $6,000 per port, LANs don't come cheap, and many managers believe the risk of obsolescence is too great to justify the cost. (16)

However, great strides are being made and more and more users are sticking their feet into the water, starting with departmental, if not corporate-wide LANs.

Wide Area Networks. Wide area network (WAN) planning deals with the installation of high-speed communications facilities between long-distance geographic locations, both domestic and worldwide. There is no single network solution. Each company must decide on its network configuration based upon its own internal needs. WAN architecture offers many options from different vendors, supporting varied communications protocols, that makes integration and compatibility difficult. Architecture must necessarily evolve gradually, attempting to fit into industry standards as

---

[2]IBM's LAN strategy is somewhat confusing. Its token-ring strategy will fit primarily into the SNA world rather than as a general purpose LAN. IBM is also selling Canvas Systems' Omninet, Nestar Systems Plan, and Orchid Technology's PC Net (14). IBM does not seem to have a clear unifying plan. Those who are looking to IBM for direction may have a long wait.

they, in turn, evolve. Separate networks are a reality. Universal communications standards are not likely to ever happen (just as Esperanto never became the universal language). The challenge is to provide appropriate interfaces between them. Gateways are needed to provide these interfaces. We can install LANs within our own buildings but, once outside our walls, we need gateways to access the outside nonhomogenous world. Vendors like Tymnet and Telenet partially fill that gap, providing the linking protocols between systems. But vendor incompatibility still prevails. As a disillusioned manager once observed to me: "Getting IBM and DEC to talk to one another is like trying to make an elephant and a bird dance." The number of communications options available has grown rapidly owing to both technological progress and competitive choices spurred by the divestiture of AT&T. Building WAN architectures involves a combination of strategies incorporating both local loop services and long-distance alternatives.

"Bypass" options are also the vogue. In simple terms, "bypass" generally refers to any communications alternative that avoids, or bypasses, the telephone company network. In-house PBXs and LANs are examples of bypass options at the local level. At the WAN level, one can choose among a number of telephone company offerings as well as a variety of alternative communications paths (bypasses) in building a firm's communications architecture. These include different common carriers, T1 carrier service, private microwave links, fiber-optic cable, and satellite transmissions. (A more detailed discussion of these options is in the section that follows.) Most companies use a combination of service offerings in building their wide area network architecture, as illustrated by the following example.

Bank of Boston's WAN architecture consists of two parts: a backbone domestic network called FIRSTNET and an international network called IBX (international branch exchange), as shown in Figure 9.9. FIRSTNET is an integrated voice/data network that is based on the use of high capacity (1.544 MB), all-digital T1 circuits running between major high-traffic New England and other U. S. cities. The nodes in each city consist of multiplexors from Network Equipment Technologies (Menlo Park, California) that route traffic to other nodes in the network. FIRSTNET thus acquires transmission capacity at wholesale prices, reducing existing corporate interlocation expenses by up to 40%. Should a circuit go down between any two nodes, traffic is automatically rerouted via a different node in the network, making the failure transparent to users. Finally, a private microwave circuit runs between the bank's headquarters in downtown Boston and its primary data center 4 miles south.

The IBX network consists of IBM Series/1 minicomputer nodes located in Boston, London, and Hong Kong, which handle data traffic between overseas locations in a store-and-forward mode. Access to the nodes is a combination of packet nets, leased lines, and dial-up, according to what is most economical in the area. Customized software in the Series/1s pro-

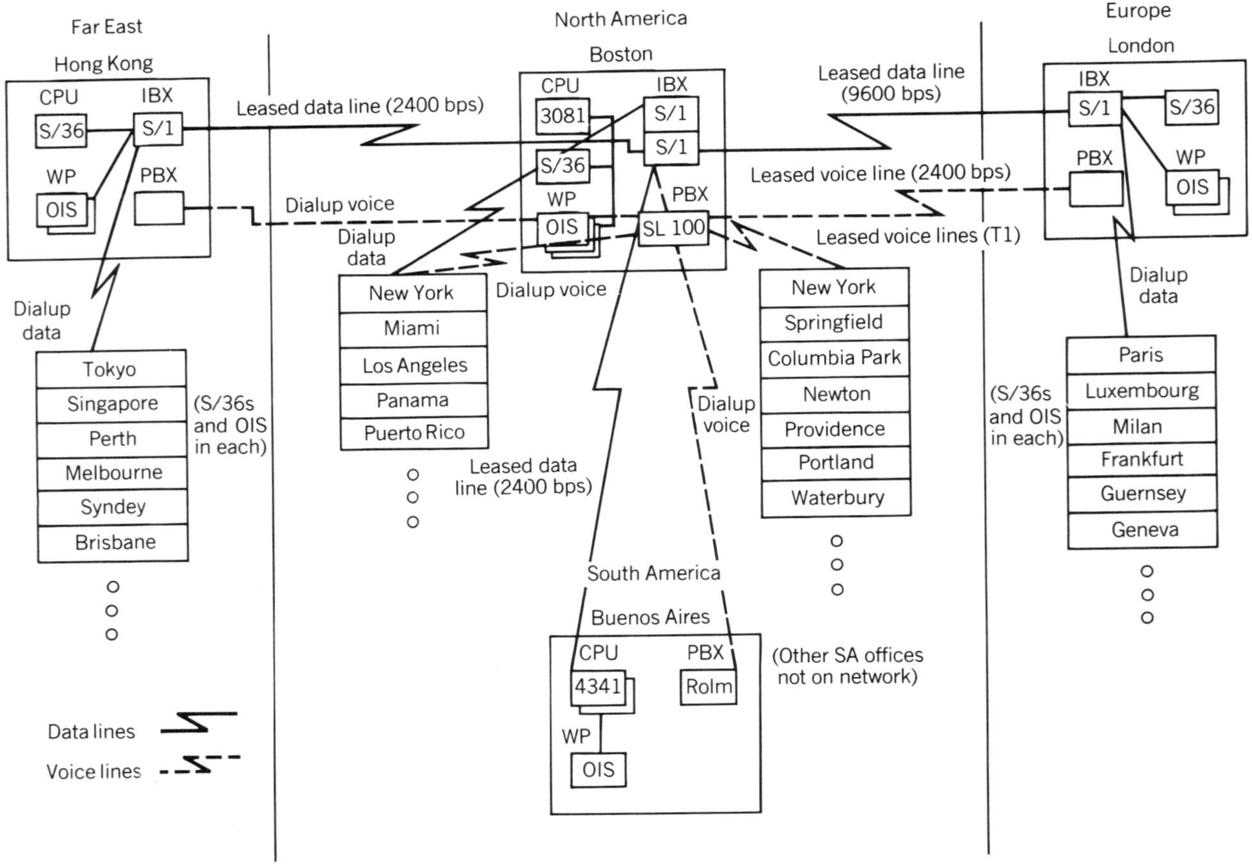

Figure 9.9. Bank of Boston's wide area network.

244

vides interconnectivity between IBM host mainframes, IBM S/34–36s in the branches, and Wang VS machines and word processors. The system permits data transfer and consolidation of financial, customer, and management information from overseas offices overnight as needed. Documents created in one office can be printed out in any other office on the network, literally within minutes. The flexibility of the system allows new offices to be attached to the system easily and inexpensively.

Virtual Networks. One of the most important developments in WAN options is the so-called virtual network. Virtual networks go by different names. AT&T's is called the Software Defined Network (SDN). MCI Communications calls theirs the Virtual Private Network (VPN). The basic idea is to tie small company facilities into the corporate leased-line network using dial-up connections. It is an economical way to support low-traffic locations which can't justify a leased line. Users tie in to a switched public network that looks like a private network, providing a "virtual" private line (series of pipes) in which the user defines his own network, paying only a usage charge, which is a fraction of the cost of a leased line. Virtual networks are the new rage in the long-distance industry. To date AT&T, MCI, US Telecom, and Western Union have all announced versions of a virtual network.

Network Planning

TACTICAL

IW 49—NETWORK PLANNING
Implementing integrated communications networks.

At the tactical level, physical network planning takes place—the selection of vendors, products, and services needed to carry out the strategic communications plan.

PBX. If a decision has been made to go to an in-house PBX, an RFP (request for proposal) is usually prepared and given to a number of telephone equipment companies. The five top companies selling PBXs in the United States today are AT&T, Northern Telecom (of Canada), Rolm (now a subsidiary of IBM), Mitel, and Nippon Electric Co. (Japan).[3]

Experts agree that buying your own telephone system is probably the cheapest way to go in the long run. Here is a summary of their advice (17).

---

[3]In terms of digital switches installed in telephone company central offices, AT&T and Northern Telecom were about even as of this writing, with the two giants locking up over 85% of the market.

1. Find out how well your present phone system is performing through user interviews, especially receptionists.

2. Decide on the performance and management features desired (e.g., speed dialing, call forwarding, conferencing, automatic redial, long-distance controls, least-cost routing).

3. Analyze your present telephone costs and calling patterns. Give these to alternate long-distance carriers to find out what the service would cost using their rates.

4. Issue a RFP to a number of telephone equipment suppliers and get their bids for a system design and prices.

5. Satisfy yourself about the long-term viability of the company and its service and support capabilities in your area.

6. Look at other devices and services that are offered to save time and money (e.g., pagers, cellular telephones, telemarketing).

LAN. A decision to buy a LAN also involves a lot of options and care must be taken to find the solution that best fits the environment.

In general, LAN networks fall into three categories: general-purpose (Ungermann-Bass, Bridge Communications, Sytek); PC (3 Com Corp., Corvus Systems, Novell, Nestar Systems); and back-end (Banyan Systems, Britton Lee, California Network Systems). Back-end LANs provide only a piece of the network, such as a file server (Banyan) or software (Network Systems) (18).

Many communications managers are waiting for the resolution of a variety of connectivity issues in the areas of implementation, management, and applications. Implementation issues involve LAN standards, cost-justification, product/vendor integration, and wiring the building. Management concerns have to do with running the network, including end-user access, monitoring, troubleshooting, resource allocation, and security. Applications include electronic mail, access to mainframe databases, and file sharing (19).

Different vendors also embrace different topologies. Some are star structures; others are ring strategies (IBM); and still others are bus systems (Ethernet). The difference between these topologies is summarized in Figure 9.10. Some experts think that Ethernet will become the small-company standard and IBM token-ring strategy will become the big-company standard.

Many companies start small and install a departmental LAN as a prototype before investing heavily in LAN technology. Bank of Boston, for instance, started with a Banyan (Westboro, Massachusetts) virtual network-server in selected departments where clustered PCs had a need to talk to one another, share memory and printers, and connect to host mainframes for database access. The system provided a X.25 gateway to outside databases and connected to other Banyan servers internally.

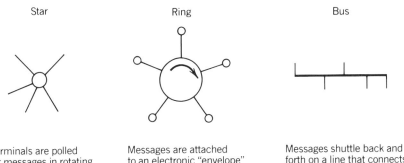

Star	Ring	Bus
Terminals are polled for messages in rotating fashion.	Messages are attached to an electronic "envelope" that continually moves around the ring.	Messages shuttle back and forth on a line that connects all components of a system (a collision detection technique is used to avoid message collisions).

Figure 9.10. Basic LAN Methodologies.

Other companies have bitten the bullet and gone with corporate-wide LANs. Two such companies are Mountain Bell and Brown University. Both have installed Sytek, Inc. (Mountain View, California) broadband-LANs to service their corporate-wide connectivity needs. Mountain Bell serves four downtown Denver locations and some 4000 potential users. Sytek handles the backbone network: a coaxial cable that links all buildings and floors. Telephone-type twisted pair lines are used to get the data from the phone closet on each floor to individual terminals (20).

Brown University (Figure 9.10) uses a Sytek Local Net 20 broadband coaxial cable to interconnect up to 150 buildings and 3000 users in every office and dormitory room. Three different networks are accommodated; broadband subchannels serve faculty (using IBM PC net), engineers (CAD/CAM applications serving on Ethernet attached to a Digital Equipment Corp. VAX minicomputer), and students (using Macintosh terminals and Apple talk) connected to host mainframes (21).

A decision to install a LAN requires answers to many questions: type (facility-wide, departmental, or local PC LAN)? vendor? size (small baseband application or large broadband)? topology (star, ring, or bus)? Some may ask: Why a LAN? Why not go directly to a mainframe? The answer is that a mainframe is an expensive file server. The goal is to keep overhead off the mainframe and thereby delay having to upgrade to a bigger machine as long as possible. As communications standards come into place over the next few years, these questions will become easier to answer, diminishing the risk of technological complexity and obsolescence; this should push more and more communications managers to move into PBXs and LANs as the foundation of their local area network architecture.

Wiring. Before we leave the subject of local area networks, a word on wiring is necessary because the wiring of a building is an important deci-

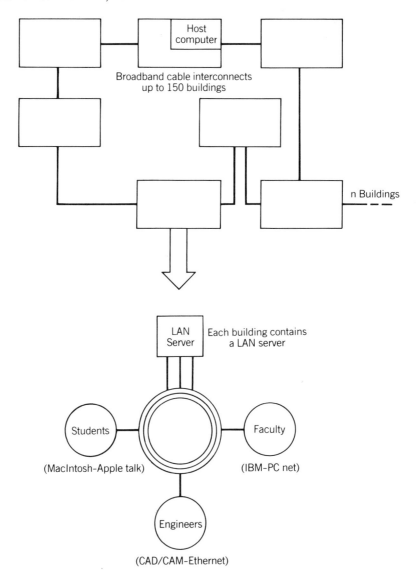

Figure 9.11 Brown University's LAN.

sion. There are four types of wiring: coaxial cable, fiber optic, shielded twisted pair, and standard telephone-type twisted pair. Coaxial has been the standard for years, but it is 10 times more expensive than twisted pair and more difficult to install. Fiber optic is generally used in conjunction with other wiring systems [e.g., AT&T's Premises Distribution System (PDS)]. Shielded wire was originally believed necessary to protect data signals from outside electrical interferences (e.g., fluorescent lights). Conversely, it was believed that the energy radiated from nonshielded wire could interfere with other electrical devices. Recent experiments, however, have demonstrated that nonshielded twisted-pair wire can be used to support synchronous terminals. Northern Telecom's new headquarters building in Nashville, for example, was wired with ordinary twisted-pair digital wire to support 150 IBM 3270 terminals, 160 Northern Telecom 585 devices (minicontrollers), and 70 NT Meridien 4000 terminals (these emulate IBM 3278 displays and have integrated digital telephones) (22). IBM surprised (and confused) everyone when they reversed their policy and conceded that twisted-pair telephone wiring is adequate for data transmission. In the beginning, IBM told users that they would have to install shielded-type wire to support data devices and future IBM local-network products. Later, they announced a new Type 3 nonshielded wire for the IBM Cabling System which costs one-sixth as much as the former Type 2 shielded cable (23).[4] The two major industry standards for wiring buildings today are AT&T's PDS and the IBM Cabling System.

Networking Options. The communications manager has a number of options to choose from in building the company's wide area network (WAN) system.

1. T-1 carrier service. Although T-1 carrier service has been around for some time, until recently it was only available on the public network. Now that it is available for private networks, usage is growing rapidly. AT&T expects T-1 to increase by an annual rate of 200%. The Yankee Group, a Boston-based market research firm, observed that in 1985 the number of leased T-1 lines increased 500% over 1984, and they predict this level of demand will continue well into the 1990s (24). A T-1 line is a circuit that operates at 1.544 megabits/second, integrating voice and data over the same line. Each T-1 circuit provides 24 voice-frequency channels. Since many companies' data transmission requirements are growing at rates of 50% or more annually, the major advantage of T-1 is its ability to accommodate growth at low cost. As noted earlier, one T-1 link costs about three times as much as a 56-kilobits/second channel. With a capacity 24 times greater, the cost/performance advantage over standard 56 kbps is about 8:1. Companies providing products to support multipoint T-1 networks include Network Equipment Technologies, Cohesive Networks, Network Switching Systems, and Spectrum Digital.

2. Microwave. Private microwave systems have been around for two decades, but their use commercially has been relatively slow to catch on. One reason is that the technology has only provided cheap short-haul ra-

---

[4]IBM also said that existing imbedded wire in many buildings could serve their token-ring network. In fact, many buildings have inadequate wiring; some is actual twisted pair and some is not.

dio. It is, however, now fast becoming a popular short-haul (the last mile) option for companies with large data and voice traffic, particularly between two offices within "line of sight" of each other. Microwave usually is used for distances up to 10 miles for voice, data, and/or video traffic. It offers low cost over conventional leased lines and high reliability. As an example, Bank of Boston has had a microwave link between its headquarters building in downtown Boston and its primary data processing center (four miles south) for over 15 years. The initial installation paid for itself in 1 year. Downtime has almost been nil and the system has paid for itself many times over.

3. Satellite. Satellite transmission is expensive. Only the very largest corporations can afford to own their own transponder in the sky (Citicorp is one). However, *shared* satellite service is something else. A number of large companies have formed consortiums to buy into satellite transponders. Also, certain private firms sell "pieces" of satellite transponders to corporate customers. A recent and promising development in this area is the use of micro earth stations (also known as very small aperture terminals (VSAT)). These multipoint satellite networks allow many locations to share the cost of a transponder. Until recently, these low-powered systems, with their 2–3 meter VSATs, were just available as receive-only services, suitable for publishing firms and other companies with time-sensitive transmission needs (such as sending closing stock prices to brokerage firms). Federal Express, for instance, contracted with M/A-Com for up to 25,000 micro earth stations, which they plan to use to effect worldwide electronic document delivery. Federal Express plans to use its network of on-premises terminals to transmit millions of messages per day (25). Two-way VSATs today provide a low-cost satellite system, ideal for multiple sites that all want to talk to a central location. As private line rates continue to climb, these small satellite systems will become cost effective for many companies and should show strong growth as an alternative to private lines for data transmission. A leader in micro earth stations has been Equatorial Communications Co. (Mountain View, California). Other vendors include Comsat, M/A-Com., Harris Corp., Telecan General, and Vitalink.

Two other trends in shared satellite service are the use of urban teleports and wired buildings. Teleports are communications centers established in major cities selling satellite services to subscribers in that city. For instance, the Port Authority of New York, in partnership with Merrill Lynch and Western Union, built a teleport communications center on Staten Island in New York to provide bypass satellite communications to subscribers in downtown Manhattan. A fiber-optic cable connects the teleport facility to the Manhattan subscribers. The satellite service can be used either to transmit to a teleport facility in a distant city or to a private corporate satellite facility. Similar teleports are installed in the San Francisco Bay area and Houston. Wired buildings are new buildings that are wired during construction to provide tenants with built-in communications links to a shared satellite roof-top dish. Although these are pretty much limited to new construction in major cities, they are becoming more popular and may well become standard fixtures in future urban construction.

4. Fiber-optics. The telephone companies' terrestrial answer to satellites is fiber-optic transmission (electrical impulses translated into light and carried over glass cables). Its advantages are that it won't rust or rot, carries high capacity, has a huge bandwidth, is secure, and requires low maintenance. Its major disadvantage is that costs at each end are high. A number of cities now have operational high capacity fiber-optic installations. The major bottleneck is the recabling required, which will take some time to spread broadly across the country. Therefore, fiber-optic links, as a bypass option, will necessarily remain confined to small pockets for a while. The telephone companies themselves are the prime users today. However, by the 1990s, watch for a major battle between IBM (satellite) and AT&T (fiber-optic)—communications "star wars."

5. Cable. As more and more U. S. cities are cabled-up, driven by the cable TV entertainment business, the opportunity to tie-in to local cable companies to link various offices within a city is growing. Cable handles considerable traffic, plenty of unused capacity remains available, and the cable companies are searching for new avenues of revenue. As a result, direct cable connections represent one of the best long-term options for large-scale local telephone bypass.

6. Packet networks. Packet switching networks, such as Telenet and Tymnet, offer an alternative that can save money over traditional long-distance data-transmission facilities. Packet switching has grown rapidly and today is in widespread use, not only in the United States, but in most other countries as well. Packet switching works somewhat like a railroad. Picture one track and a lot of cars. As passengers fill a car, it is sent on its way. At the other end, as the cars unload the passengers, those in your group are reassembled. In a communications sense, breaking your message traffic into pieces, which are shared with other senders in packets and reassembled at the other end, results in more efficient (shared) use of communications lines, making packet switching a cheaper alternative.

7. Long-distance carriers. On the voice side, a number of alternative carriers have sprung up to provide long-distance calling service within the United States. The principal ones are AT&T, MCI, and GTE Sprint, with 85%, 5%, and 2.5% of the long-distance market, respectively, as of this writing (25). But at least a dozen more are in hot competition. The AT&T settlement, in fact, has fueled this competition by requiring the ex-Bell operating companies to ask customers to pick a carrier for their long-distance calls. It's no longer a monopoly; therefore, the use of alternate carriers will grow as a communications option.

8. Cellular radio. A bypass of growing interest for people who like to stay in touch while traveling is cellular radio, or car telephones. The first

commercial cellular radio–telephone system came on line in Chicago in October 1983. Before then, car phones were only available on a very limited basis depending on a single, high-powered radio transmitter for a city. This severely limited the number of calls that could be handled at one time, causing lots of busy signals. Cellular radio divides a city into small hexagonal grids, or cells, of 6–8 miles in radius. Each cell has its own transmitter/ receiver and its own set of FM radio frequencies. As a car moves from one cell to another, the call is "handed over" to the next cell. This system can handle many more calls at once, at the same quality level as a home phone. Car telephones are dropping rapidly in price and should be at a level that most people can afford, especially business firms, by the early 1990s, which should make cellular radio an exciting and widely used bypass telephone option in the 1990s.

9. Teleconferencing. An underutilized bypass travel option is teleconferencing. Actually, audioconferencing is proving to be a more popular alternative than video, primarily because of cost. Videoconferencing is fairly expensive to use as a private system (only 20 or so corporations in the United States have private systems today) but, once again, shared alternatives are possible. AT&T's Picturephone Meeting Service (PMS) can be rented by the hour, or one can tie-in from a private studio to PMS to transmit to another studio in a distant city. As noted earlier, some hotel chains now offer broadcast (one-way only) systems at selected hotels for use for sales conferences and company meetings, thereby avoiding the necessity of moving a speaker repeatedly from city to city, or bringing everyone to one city to hear the speaker (e.g., a company President addressing a sales convention). Considerable time and money can be saved in either event.

10. Connectivity products. Products that provide multivendor connectivity are now provided by a multitude of third-party vendors. Since it is unlikely that most companies will ever settle on a single vendor, or that the vendors themselves will standardize to effect transparent connectivity between each other, the recent growth of third-party "bridge vendors" to provide micro–mainframe connectivity, selected multivendor connectivity, and even "any-to-any" connectivity is now an important source for connectivity solutions. (Because these are hardware- or software-based rather than communications products per se, they are treated in more depth in Chapter 10 under User Computing.)

By 1990, most major corporations will combine a variety of communications options to form fully connected, distributed information resource networks as a way of providing information service at the lowest possible cost. Although large firms have the most to gain (government agencies, *Fortune* 500 companies, banks, major utilities, broadcasting companies, etc.), because they have the highest volume communications needs, small firms can also benefit from the use of the multiplicity of communications networking options available today.

Network Design Tools. Finally, network design can be aided by the use of automated network design tools such as the Network Design and Management System (NDMS) from DMW (Ann Arbor, Michigan), available on time-sharing, or Multipoint Network Design System (MNDS) from Connections Inc. (West Bridgewater, Massachusetts), an IBM PC/XT software package. Such software tools assist in network designs in such areas as point-to-point circuit pricing under different carrier tariffs, definition of multipoint network topology in their various traffic and cost constraints, performance analysis of a multipoint data network under various protocols, development of a network database reflecting the existing network configuration (useful for measuring the impact of future carrier price increases), and automatic coordinate hookup with city and Lata (area code) designations and AT&T serving offices.

Network Control

OPERATIONAL

IW 50—NETWORK CONTROL
Managing network access and control.

Network control consists of running the networks and monitoring and controlling performance to assure high customer-service levels. The goal in network control is to maximize mean time to failure (MTTF) and minimize mean time to repair (MTTR). Although network control systems have been around for years, many companies still do not make adequate use of such tools. A random poll by *Computerworld* of communications managers, for instance, found that managers listed selection and installation of a network package as their department's most important objective (26). Giving impetus to the trend toward in-house network management systems is the increasing importance of the communications network in most companies. *Computerworld* recently noted:

> Today, a number of financial, airline and information businesses rely on networks so greatly that when a network goes down, a company cannot function until it is restored. For example, if a stock brokerage house went down for 5 minutes, the loss could be catastrophic. (27)

By controlling the network in-house, communications managers can better fine tune it to maximum efficiency. All that is needed is a competent staff and the right network control tools. Principal control activities include:

- Network resource control—involves taking and maintaining an inventory of communications resources—PBXs, LANs, equipment vendors, software architecture, protocols used, and so on. The inventory is used to track costs, to plan add-ons, and to ensure physical connectivity.
- Network systems control—introduces monitoring devices, diagnostic equipment, and statistical performance gathering, measurement, and reporting.
- Network architecture control—has to do with working within industry standards, choosing specific network architectures for the company, and establishing in-house standards for the physical design of networks, equipment selection guidelines, protocol options, and so on.

Not much more need be said about network resource control, but network systems control and architectural control bear further discussion.

Network systems control is aided by a variety of tools. Some are built in such as in-house PBXs that track problems, perform automatic diagnoses, automatically switch to redundant processors in the event of problems, and report both problems and performance statistics on operator consoles. Others are supplied by third-party vendors to aid control over data center operations. Take data network control systems, for example. According to Dataquest (28), a marketing research firm, there are at least four different types of control systems: performance monitors, network switches, response-time analysis systems, and network management and control systems. Vendors include:

- Monitors—Tektronix, Atlantic Research, Data Management Sciences, Hewlett Packard, Northern Telecom.
- Switches—Northern Telecom's Spectron Division, Avant-Garde, Codex, Dataswitch, Dynatech
- Response-time analysis—Avant-Garde, Connections, Data Management Sciences, IBM, Paradyne, Textdata
- Network management and control—Paradyne, ATT, Codex, Digilog, General Data Comm., IBM, Northern Telecom., Racal Milgo.

Network architecture control is a matter of standards. The key to communications architecture is connectivity. And the key to connectivity is open architecture (any-to-any connections). Open architecture is, in turn, dependent on standards. Industry standards, therefore, are the linchpin to communications architecture. A lot of work has, and is, being done by various standards organizations to achieve standardization, but much still remains. Take the well-known International Standards Organization (ISO) model for open systems interconnection (OSI), as shown in Figure 9.12.

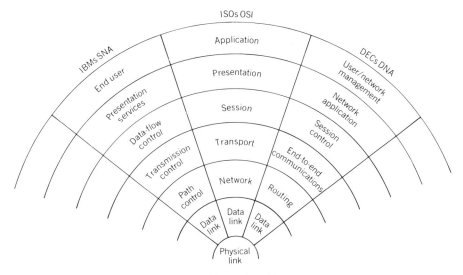

Figure 9.12. Network architectures.

Only the bottom four layers of the ISO architecture are actually in place; the rest are still being defined. Therefore, vendors like IBM and DEC have developed their own architecture that parallel ISO's bottom four layers and fill in the remaining layers with their own architectures (that fit their own equipment). Even the defined lower layers leave room for interpretation, so that one OSI product won't necessarily talk to another; X.25 (the CCITT International standard that fits the lower 3 layers), for example, has run into standardization problems, because its range of interpretations is so broad that its implementation by the various vendors often results in failure to communicate with one another. There is also a confusion of standards: ISOs OSI, IBMs SNA, DECs DNA, DODs (Department of Defense) TCP, GMs MAP, and CCITT's ISDN, to name but a few. To go with OSI or TCP is to pit yourself against IBM's SNA. Moreover, many standards in the industry are de facto standards based on IBM architectures and products, since more than 80% of the mainframe market is IBM or IBM-compatible. Yet General Motors has also shown that users can take an active role in setting standards by promoting their own standards called MAP (manufacturing automation protocol) and getting other large companies, and suppliers, to go along with it. Many of the leading industry vendors are now coming out with MAP-compatible products.

Finally, there is the promised land, called ISDN (integrated services digital network), which is an evolving international standard for a worldwide digital network for voice and data transmission. ISDN promises to transform telephone lines from 2-lane country roads to 24-lane super highways. ISDN is to be implemented in three steps (29):

1. All BOC-central office switches will be replaced with digital switches. This will be a long-term process because of the cost and effort involved (although MCI says it will be completely digital by 1990).
2. Hardware and software will be added to the stations to provide narrowband ISDN (the splitting of phone lines into three high-speed digital channels carrying simultaneous voice and data).
3. The switching stations will be upgraded to broadband capability (telephone lines will be divided into 24 channels totaling 1.544 megabits/second).

According to the Yankee Group, within 2 years everybody will be providing ISDN—AT&T, Northern Telecom, Bellcore, Siemens, the regional holding companies, and the PBX vendors. All the European countries are also planning to introduce ISDN and Japan is pushing its own version called INS. Within the next decade we should see these major trading areas of the world—the United States, Europe, and Japan—all linked through ISDN networks. The real importance of ISDN in the future will be to facilitate intercompany networks, a growing requirement for future communications (30).

In 1985 progress toward vendor product standardization was given a big push with the formulation of the Corporation for Open Systems (COS), based in Washington, D. C. A 100 member nonprofit organization made up of computer manufacturers (including IBM) and major users, COS overseas standard-making bodies like ISO and CCITT, publishes standards specifications, and conducts product testing and certification to support industry standards (31). In the end, we may all be interconnected (PBX, LAN, terminals, databases, computers) on a worldwide basis. But we're a long way from there today, leaving the communications architect to choose among multiple and confusing options to fill the gap until industry standards are sorted out and vendors build totally integrated ISDN networks.

Technology advances have almost given communications managers *too* many options. The best road map doesn't tell you where to go; it only gives you options. The trick is to pick options that produce winners, rather than those that become career limiters. Whatever options are chosen, these must be transmitted into in-company standards to guide and assure the communications architecture for the enterprise as it stumbles forward through the murky communications waters ahead.

References

1. Arnold Barnett, in an interview with *Data Base Newsletter,* Jan./Feb. 1985.
2. Frank Sweet, "The Winchester House Syndrome," *Datamation,* April 1984.
3. *Computerworld,* Dec. 2, 1985, p. 2.

4. Richard Baumer, "A Survey on the Subject of Data Administration and Database Administration," U. S. Dept. of Transportation, Cambridge, MA, 3/29/85.

5. Ronald G. Ross, "Gaining (& Keeping) Organizational Acceptance for Strategic Data Planning," Strategic Data Planning Conference, Washington, D. C., April 1985.

6. Robert M. Curtice, "Strategic Value Analysis: A Modern Approach to Systems Data Planning," an A. D. Little, Inc. publication, Jan. 1985.

7. Holland Systems Corp. promotional material, Oct 1984.

8. Jay-Louise Weldon, "The Elusive Data Administration Function," *Journal of Information Systems Management*, Nov. 1984.

9. James Odell, "Organizational Structure for Data Administration," *Data Base Newsletter*, Nov./Dec. 1984.

10. Dr. George Schussel, "Planning for Data Management/DB/4GL," POSPP, publication # P24–4, June 1984.

11. Thomas J. Murray et al., "Hot Tickets of High Tech," *Duns Business Month*, June 1985.

12. Karen Berney, "How the Split Hits Small Firms," *Nation's Business*, Jan. 1986, p. 80.

13. Ibid, p. 81.

14. Brian Jeffery, "IBM's Local Net Policy: When Will it surface?" *Computerworld Focus*, 8/29/85, p. 18.

15. Gary Stix, "Users and Vendors Think Links," *Computer Decisions*, Dec. 1985, p. 52.

16. J. B. Miles, "Plateau in the Landscape," *Computer Decisions*, 6/18/85, p. 91.

17. Berney, p. 82.

18. *Information Week*, 8/12/85 p. 37.

19. Claire P. Fleig, "Information Managers Caught in Web of PC LAN Confusion," *Information Week*, 8/12/85, p. 37.

20. Paul E. Schindler, Jr., "Mountain Bell Switched to Sytek's Local Area Network," *Information Week*, 9/19/85, p. 37.

21. *Information Week*, 4/1/85, p. 46.

22. *Computerworld*, 12/16/85.

23. *Computerworld*, 11/4/85, p. 1.

24. Julie King, "MIS Finds Corporate Uses for AT&T's T-1 Technology," *Information Week*, 11/25/85, p. 26.

25. Guy M. Stephens, "Big Business, Small Dishes, *Satellite Communication*, Feb. 1986, p. 20.

26. *The Wall Street Journal*, 6/26/85.

27. *Computerworld*, 8/12/85, p. 13.

28. *MIS Week*, 9/18/85.

29. Judy Getts, "ISDN: Network of the Future?" *PC World*, Jan. 1986.

30. *Yankee Ingenuity*, a newsletter of the Yankee Group, Vol. 7, No. 5, Jan. 1986.

31. *Communications Week*, 2/10/86, p. 1.

10

DECENTRALIZED INFORMATION RESOURCES

There they go; I must hurry; I am their leader!
—Dr. Michael Hammer

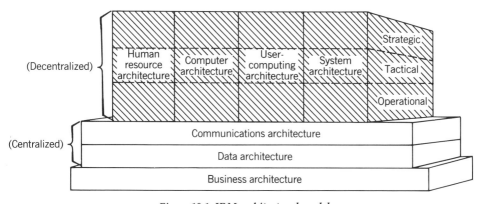

Figure 10.1. IRM architectural model.

The architectural model above shows the remaining information resources—human (information professionals), computers, end-user computing, and information systems—as vertical bars to denote decentralized (or decentralizing) resources. The trend towards decentralization is likely to continue because it follows a similar trend in corporate organization structure.

The rapid proliferation of mini- and microcomputers is resulting in de facto decentralization of computing. The central data center(s) continues in place, and will likely continue to play a vital, but different, role than in the past. End-user computing, by its very nature, is automatically decentralized, although more and more it will be networked. In many organizations, systems (staff and applications) is also being decentralized. Companies with decentralized organization structures customarily distribute

259

systems resources to the various business units. But even centralized companies are slowly migrating systems responsibilities to business units to provide business managers with direct control over their support resources. After 30 years of computing, business managers are becoming comfortable with the use and management of computer resources. And as the competitive potential of these resources becomes more fully appreciated by business managers, they will be more frequently asking for, and getting, control over their information systems resources.

In the Information Era, the architectural management of decentralized information resources will represent a much different challenge than the centralized management style of the Computer Era. When resources are directly controlled, architecture can be mandated; it is a matter of day-to-day decisions over the assimilation of new technologies and resources. But when these resources are in the hands of end-users, architectural planning has to be accomplished through influence, persuasion, and collegial cooperation. This organizational difference requires that the CIO have finely-honed interpersonal and political skills, the ability to deal with managers from a business, not a technical, perspective, and the skill to convince management of the need for the architectural policies, guidelines, and standards that assure that information resources are usable, shareable, and available to support business needs. This is quite a different role from the DP manager of the past.

In this chapter, some technology architecture considerations for these four decentralizing information resources are reviewed from the three planning perspectives of the architectural model: strategic, tactical, and operational, which translates to planning, implementation, and maintenance. First, the future technology structure must be envisioned; this is the planning phase. Second, all the bits and pieces must be worked together like a jigsaw puzzle; this is the implementation phase. Third, it all must be maintained during the maintenance phase. Likewise, the initiation of governing policies is a strategic activity ("what" is to be done); the issuance of procedures or standards is tactical ("how" it is to be done); the monitoring of conformance with both is operational control.

Because architectural planning is necessarily unique to every business, and because decentralized resources are driven by specific business needs, it is not possible to deal with specific architectures here. Instead, I focus on broad architectural planning, implementation, and control issues applicable to all entities, but from a decentralized management perspective.

HUMAN RESOURCE ARCHITECTURE

Organization of The Information Systems Function

STRATEGIC

> **IW 51—SBU STAFF ALLOCATIONS**
> The allocation of systems professionals to strategic
> business units.

The principal focus of human resource architecture in this section is with "systems" human resources, to be defined as all technical/professional people devoted exclusively to information technology work (e.g., systems, data processing, telecommunications, etc.).

The strategic planning of these resources includes such things as determining the number and quality of the systems staff needed, how the systems function is or should be organized, how systems human resources are to be allocated to business units, the effectiveness of the human resource management programs, and the formulation of human resource policies. The basic principles of management—planning, organizing, staffing, directing, controlling—are applicable here. Planning and organization are strategic activities, staffing (recruitment) is a tactical one, and directing and controlling staff activities are operational.

Organizational Change. Many systems organizations are undergoing revolutionary change today due to corporate reorganizations, mergers and acquisitions, or management changes. Principal among these changes is the trend to decentralization of systems resources. Decentralization dramatically changes not only how systems are organized, but how they are managed. As noted in Chapter 8, the information systems organization must follow corporate organization. If the company is highly centralized, then systems should also be centralized. Conversely, a decentralized company generally moves systems resources into the hands of the business units along the lines shown in Figure 8.6B.

In the past, information systems organizations were mostly centralized with control in the hands of a single information manager. Most information managers have had a good deal of experience dealing with this kind of controlled resource organization. But today, the trend is toward decentralization—of business *and* systems—and the role of information managers and CIOs in the management of professional/technical personnel is changing to one of indirect, advisory participation (with line management) in information resource management, including human resources.

Examples of companies that have decentralized systems resources are numerous, including such giants as Kaiser Aluminum, Metropolitan Life

Insurance, Citibank, Chase Manhattan Bank, IBM, General Motors, Deere and Co., First National Bank of Chicago, Bank of Boston, and many others. Some key issues in the decentralization of systems human resources are how resources are allocated, the role and reporting relationships of staff versus line units, and the establishment of policies to standardize and preserve parity across the organization.

Resource Allocation. The strategic level of systems staff allocation addresses the overall size of the staff and how it should be allocated among SBUs. The total that is appropriate is a matter of the relative aggressiveness of the firm with regard to its investment in technology, the information systems support needs of the various business units, and the relative profitability of the units. Three useful measurements in this regard are: industry comparisons, SBU profit versus technology investment, and SBU mission versus development resources.

- Industry comparisons measure systems staff levels compared to other companies in the industry and to overall industry averages (often available from trade groups). These include broad company measures such as percent of systems staff to total staff, systems staff growth rate, total costs per systems employee, and total sales/expenses/profits per systems employee.
- Profit versus investment relates the overall investment in technology, by SBU, to its overall profit contribution to the firm (see Figure 8.10*A*). Imbalances should be reviewed carefully for reasonableness or indicated changes.
- Mission versus development resources maps the allocation of the systems development resources to SBU missions (Figure 8.10*B*). This tells whether development resources are appropriately allocated to the growth businesses (too high a percentage in DIVEST businesses would be a red flag) and whether individual SBUs seem to have the right numbers relative to their systems development efforts.

Role Resolution. In a centralized organization, boss–subordinate relationships are clear and direct. When decentralized, staff versus line roles are much more vague and hard to define. The relationship of the CIO to management and the line organization in such an environment is critical. Does the CIO represent the CEO office in technological decisionmaking? Must the CIO approve all major investments in technology? What is the CIO's responsibility over decentralized systems? What are the line systems managers' responsibilities? Must they include the CIO in their systems planning efforts? The respective role of the staff CIO and line systems managers is necessarily a customized activity, but at a minimum, should include the planning process, the decisionmaking and approval process, and certain implementation activities.

Matrix management (reporting to two bosses) may be an inescapable part of decentralization. In this sense, matrix reporting relationships involve horizontal rather than vertical management; that is, while the CIO has functional, or technical, responsibility over information resources that spread horizontally across the firm, the individual systems organizations may report directly to the business units to which they are assigned. The degree of direct versus indirect control can range from tight control to loose coordination. Some firms decentralize systems staffs but leave them on the CIO's payroll, others leave only the systems managers reporting to the CIO, and still others have only a "dotted line" relationship. Whatever the reporting relationship, roles and responsibilities must be made clear because matrix management will be considerably more difficult to operate under than simple hierarchical management.

A simple but expedient concept for managing in a matrixed environment is what I call my "sign-on/sign-off" strategy. Most people understand sign-off. It means having final authority to sign-off, or approve, major technology decisions. The problem with sign-off is that it is usually too late to raise real issues without upsetting the project's sponsors. Architectural input should be given in the planning process, not at final approval time. This is what I call the sign-on stage. At the time a major project or equipment acquisition is first proposed is when the CIO, or architectural planner, should be "signed-on," not at the end when it is all but a fait accompli. Sign-on is a much more effective way to involve the CIO than sign-off. The only good thing about sign-off is that it is the final audit of sign-on; that is, if you weren't signed-on in the first place, you'll know it when you have to sign-off.

Architectural Policies. To ensure information resource architecture, particularly in a decentralized firm, policy guidelines and procedures (standards) are imperative. In the case of human resources, these would cover such things as hiring policies, training, compensation, benefits, recognition programs (performance ratings, promotions, instant awards), and career pathing (job postings, dual career paths). Much of this will be done by the Human Resources Department, but specific focus on systems human resources is needed when they are decentralized in order to achieve parity treatment across the organization and facilitate movement between SBUs. The CIO needs to work closely with the Human Resource Department to ensure a united systems view to human resource planning. The development of policy is a strategic exercise; the issuance of operating procedures and standards spelling out how to carry out policy is tactical; the monitoring of compliance with policies and procedures is an operational activity. This applies to all information resources, not just human resources.

A three-tiered policy issuance architecture suitable to a decentralized environment was discussed in Chapter 8 (see Figure 8.12).

Employing the Human Resource

TACTICAL

> **IW 52—DEVELOPMENT STAFF ALLOCATIONS**
> The allocation of systems professionals to development
> projects.

Systems Projects. Having allocated the systems staff to SBUs, the next step is their allocation to specific development efforts and/or the support of existing systems. The starting point is an assessment of the minimum resources needed to maintain the existing systems. This represents a fixed and irreducible base; everything else is optional. The information manager determines the information systems requirements of business managers and translates these into the number of human resources needed to deliver the products. When this is matched against the existing staff, there will either be an excess or, more likely, a shortfall of staff. The IRM Committee can then evaluate the demand versus the supply and authorize staff adjustments or additions accordingly. (The function of the IRM Committee was discussed in Chapter 8). Attention should be paid at this juncture to the balance of systems (i.e., operations, management, or customer support) to ensure that requested systems are in concert with the missions of the business units. A standard method of computing costs–benefits over the life of the system is also important to provide the committee with a consistent way of looking at project justification.

Human Resource Management Systems. Decentralized systems resources require coordinated programs to ensure equity and parity across the organization. Without this, the different SBUs will establish their own programs, leading to inequities and imbalances that can cause in-fighting, "raiding" of personnel, and demoralization of staff.

The areas of human resource management in which the CIO needs to foster consistency and cooperation between units include recruitment, skills identification, staff development, performance evaluation, and compensation and reward.

- *Recruitment.* A consistent hiring policy, standard starting salaries for given jobs, and a collaborative recruiting effort between business groups are needed to present a standard, unified "face" of the company to potential employees.
- *Skills Identification.* A staff profile system is needed to quickly identify potential candidates for open positions, not only within business

units, but between units as well. There must be opportunities to move between units for the good of the individual as well as the corporation.

- *Staff Development.* A standard education and training program is needed to assure consistency in systems design and transportability of people between units without retraining.
- *Performance Evaluation.* A standard way of measuring and recording performance is another important need to assure consistent and fair treatment of people across the corporation.
- *Compensation and Reward.* Salaries must be based on standard job descriptions, job grades, and salary ranges corporate-wide. Bonuses and promotions, while decided at the line level, are then consistent in terms of corporate guidelines.

Career Pathing. Logical career paths are necessary in every organization, but in a decentralized company, it is even more important to ensure that staff members perceive opportunity, not only in their own unit, but elsewhere in the corporation. Two human resource strategies that can be used in combination to ensure logical career paths are dual career ladders and job posting.

- *Dual Career Ladders.* Some companies are adopting dual career ladders for managerial and professional (technical) personnel in recognition of the fact that the skills and requirements of the two ladders are markedly different. Managerial and technical roles are, in many ways, incompatible; one is people-oriented, the other is thing-oriented. Each has different motivations. People with a managerial bent enjoy working with and through people. People with a technical bent enjoy technical challenges and personal accomplishment. A technician should not have to default to a manager's position simply because it is perceived to be the only way up. You don't want to lose a good technician only to gain a poor manager. Yet, that is precisely what many companies are getting with single career ladders. In such companies, there seldom are high-level technical positions equal to high-level managerial positions.

  A dual career ladder might look like the diagram in Figure 10.2. As people reach the exempt level, job ladders break into a managerial and a professional track. Job descriptions are written for all unique positions on both tracks and these are then rated according to the key dimensions of the job (e.g., know-how, problem-solving, and accountability). Based on this comparison, positions with similar responsibility levels, both managerial and technical, can be grouped together in job grades. Each job grade is assigned a salary range reflecting the value of the positions within that group. These ranges are based on the "going rate" for similar positions in the marketplace derived from

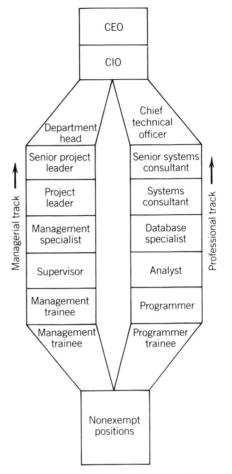

Figure 10.2. Dual career pathing. Position titles are for illustrative purposes only.

salary surveys. Thus, whether an individual chooses to follow a managerial or a professional track, there is opportunity to advance and be rewarded similarly on either track according to comparable worth.

- *Job Posting.* With a dual career ladder in place, a job-posting program can provide the mobility for staff members to move laterally or upward not only within their own business units, but between business units as well. In a job-posting program, job openings are "posted," or listed internally, to give existing employees the opportunity to apply for the job. Only when and if the position cannot be filled internally does outside recruitment begin. This not only provides mobility options, but promotion opportunities as well, because people can apply to higher positions as long as they meet the qualifications criteria. The combination of a dual career path and job posting can provide a very satisfactory career pathing program, which is especially important in a decentralized organization.

Monitoring the Human Resource

OPERATIONAL

> **IW 53—APPLICATIONS SUPPORT ASSIGNMENTS**
> The assignment of systems professionals to specific applications systems.

Inventory. The operational (control) level of human resource architecture deals with understanding the makeup of the resource and providing appropriate monitoring and control mechanisms that foster uniformity and standardization across the corporation. To get a handle on what the resource is, one can start with a staff inventory system (SIS). This exercise becomes more necessary when the information technology people are decentralized, but it is also useful in centralized organizations as well. The inventory should be coded so that data can be collected as to resource allocations by SBU, by projects, by application system, and by information resource (i.e., how many people in systems, data processing, telecommunications, etc.?). Each of these, in turn, could provide successive layers of detail as needed. Systems could be further broken down, for instance, as to the number of people in development versus maintenance work (to see if the 40:60 rule applies).

Another important ingredient to the inventory is career profile data. This could be carried on a separate career profile system (CPS), or could be a part of the SIS. A CPS is really an automated resumé. It carries information about each staff member's career history such as jobs held, skills, education, title history, performance history, and EEO (equal employment opportunity) data. The CPS can be used to track programs, match talents to needs, or plan career development. In a decentralized company, it can also help find the best candidates for openings without being restricted by organizational arrangement, and thus it is beneficial for both the individual and the corporation. A combination SIS/CPS inventory can be an excellent human resource architecture starting point.

Human Resource Monitoring. So far we have dealt with monitoring what the staff is, where they are, and what they are working on. Other areas of interest include their education and training, time management, and performance/reward issues:

- Education and training should be a standardized process. In a decentralized company this requires getting general agreement on what is to be taught and how (classroom training, videotape instruction, etc.); otherwise, training will not only be haphazard but inconsistent. People transferring from one area to another will have to relearn all over again and, what is worse, nonstandard systems development creeps in, complicating systems architecture. A standard systems development life cycle, for instance, should not only be adopted, but the roles of both systems people and users must be clearly articulated and understood throughout the project. The steps of the project life cycle are fairly standard in the industry. Many books have been written on the subject. Few, however, have defined the roles and responsibilities of the systems and user people involved in the process. In my previous book I presented a diagram that does just that. It s reproduced here as Figure 10.3. Each step in the process delineates the roles and responsibilities of the systems people and the users so that everyone is clear about who does what all along the way.

- Time management, in this sense, refers to tracking where the time goes rather than how to be most efficient in its use. A project control system is useful in providing such data. Two typical reports, for example, might be a personnel time analysis and a project time analysis. The first shows, for each staff member, where his/her time has gone, broken down by the number of hours charged to various projects (typically averages 70% of total time available), hours spent on education and training, vacation time, administrative duties and so on. The second report shows, for each project, who charged time to the project for any given period. The two in combination enable managers to track time management for individuals and projects.

- Performance/reward in a decentralized arena is generally done at the SBU level. However, it is important that the CIO have some input to this process if his/her authority is to have any clout at all. If a formal system is in place, the performance rating of each of the decentralized business unit's systems managers should be done jointly by the SBU head and the CIO. Likewise, salary and bonus recommendations should be agreed to by both parties. In this way, the CIO's influence and authority has some teeth. Without such participation, the CIO's influence over the decentralized systems organizations will be considerably weakened. Finally, the hiring or replacement of SBU-level system managers should also be a joint decision between the CIO and the SBU manager.

These examples do not by any means exhaust the human resource monitoring process, but are meant to serve as illustrations of things that are appropriately overseen by the CIO architect.

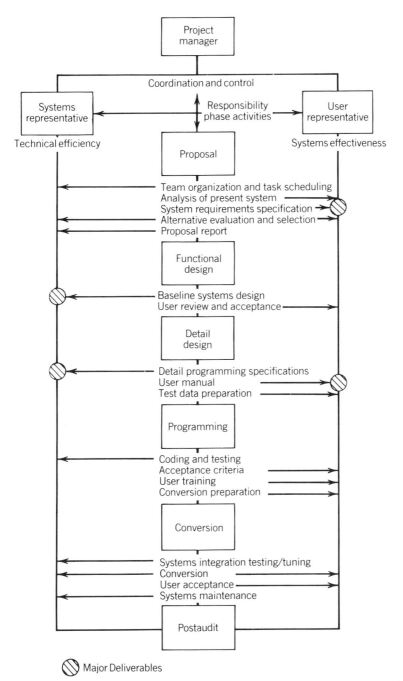

Figure 10.3. Project life-cycle responsibilities (from W. R. Synnott and W. H. Gruber, Information Resource Management, *Wiley, New York, 1981, p. 278).*

Policy Oversight. Policy oversight is the process of ensuring architecture through the issuance of governing policies and the monitoring of compliance with those policies. As noted earlier, the human resource policies we are interested in from an architectural perspective are those that aim at consistency and equity across the organization: consistent starting salaries for undergraduate and graduate candidates, standardized training programs, market-driven salary adjustments that apply across the board and not just to a single business unit, job-posting programs, transfer opportunities between business units, standard job descriptions and salary ranges.

Two thoughts are offered in overseeing this process. The first is the establishment of an "affinity" group, composed of the CIO and the line group systems managers, who would meet regularly to create needed policies and administer their implementation. This affinity group is a sort of association, with common interests such that all stand to gain from a collaborative effort. The second is the establishment of a compliance network, such as that described in Figure 8.12. In that example, compliance personnel are designated at both the staff and line levels to oversee the implementation of policy within their respective areas. This includes monitoring compliance with external regulations as well as internal policies.

COMPUTER ARCHITECTURE

Computer Integration

STRATEGIC

IW 54—COMPUTER PLANNING
Planning the corporation's computer support resources.

In Chapter 8 it was suggested that computer architecture in most companies is rapidly moving toward distributed rather than decentralized processing. The distinction is important. Decentralized processing implies stand-alone operations, whereas distributed processing suggests a number of geographically dispersed machines linked into a network that enables the sharing of information, if not computers. The traditional data center has long been recognized as a shared resource. But departmental minicomputers are often seen as stand-alone unshared resources. Yet information must still pass between applications; the output of one system may be the input of another, and information must be consolidated from many sources, including departmental systems, for management purposes. This is also true of microcomputers.

Uncoordinated processing leads to redundancy, cost escalation, and functional isolation. The integration of systems, the downloading of corporate databases, and information consolidation will all ultimately be stopped in its tracks without an integrating architectural plan. Computer architecture represents the information processing power of the enterprise. Thus how it is organized and integrated is a vital strategic planning issue.

Today's online processing theoretically allows the computer to be physically located anywhere, but logical organization is something else. Organizational control options include centralizing processing at the corporate level, centralizing it at a line level (i.e., operated as a central utility by a SBU), decentralizing processing to the line level, out-of-house (service bureau) processing, or all of the above. Most mainframe processing, because of its capacity and economy-of-scale potential, is still centralized, although large companies frequently have dedicated data processing departments for major business units. Most minicomputers, on the other hand, are decentralized, the computers being located near the point of transaction origination. Microcomputers, by their very nature, are all decentralized. The challenge to the technology architect is to build the connections between the four layers of computing illustrated in Figure 10.4, regardless of location or organizational ownership, to facilitate information movement between all layers of computers, even if they are from different vendors and use different software systems and communications protocols. The problem is exemplified by a recent survey by A. D. Little which found that the top two vendor problems today are (1) the lack of product line integration and (2) incompatibility with other vendors' products (reported by 83% and 68%, respectively, of survey participants) (1).

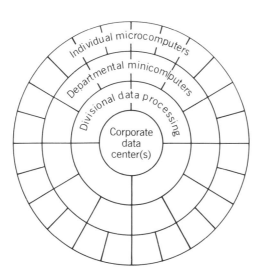

Figure 10.4. The four layers of computing.

As noted in Chapter 9, the work of the standards organizations, and particularly the newly-formed Corporation for Open Systems (COS), may eventually solve the problem of integrating diverse and incompatible vendor systems represented in the four layers of computing. But meanwhile, it is necessary to continue to build bridges between systems. These bridges have mostly been in-house efforts; that is, programs written to extract data from one system and reformatted to be acceptable as input by another. Of interest to technology architects is the recent birth of a new crop of vendors—the so-called "bridge" vendors. They provide products that facilitate the passing of information from one system to another, whether mainframe, mini, or micro, regardless of vendor. (In the section on End-User Computer Architecture that follows, this integration strategy is discussed further.)

Computer Planning. Architecturally, the primary concern regarding the planning for a computer is the type of computer that represents the best solution under the circumstances. This doesn't mean what vendor; that comes next. The first decision is should it be a mainframe, minicomputer, or microcomputer solution? Issues to consider include the budget (how much can be spent?), time frame (long or short), technical support (who will provide it?), beneficiary (individual, department, or corporation), type of system (OSS, MSS, CSS), proprietary versus shared data, frequency of expected use, and a myriad of other considerations. There is no easy or set answer. A general guideline to the architectural planner is suggested by the matrix in figure 10.5.

Some choices are clear: a Super-System is a mainframe application; a spreadsheet suggests a micro solution; a stand-alone special purpose application is probably a minicomputer choice. But there are a great many applications in the gray zone; they could be solved by a mainframe or mini, or by a mini or micro, or by all three. In such cases, Figure 10.5 might be a useful guide to the architectural planner.

Contingency Planning. Another vital part of computer architecture is the emergency backup of vital computer processing—keeping it in place once it's in place. The reliance on computers in most organizations today has reached the point where a prolonged outage could be catastrophic. Therefore, planning for the continued operation of the computer resource in emergency situations is a necessity. (In fact, all financial institutions are under federal mandate to have disaster contingency plans in place.)

As with computer planning, contingency planning covers all three planning levels. The strategic level deals with a determination of how the contingency backup of critical operations will be provided. The choices include hot sites, cold sites, development sites, and other users' sites:

- A hot site is a complete data center facility equipped with compatible computers, ready to move into. These are usually provided by com-

HARDWARE

SOFTWARE

Architecture	Mainframe	Mini	Micro	Mainframe	Mini	Micro
Application (who served?)	Corporation	Department	Individual	IS Professional	Business management	Individual user
Function	Transaction processing	Single-application SBU	Personal support	Back-shop support	Single product support	Task automation
Strength	High-capacity EOS	Specialization autonomy low cost	Managerial productivity	Risk	Customized	Friendly
Weakness	Long life cycle	Vendor support dependence	Limited data	Complex	Specialized	Limited
Uses OSS	High	Medium	Low	High	Medium	Low
MSS	Medium	High	High	High	High	High
CSS	High	Medium	Medium	High	Low	Low–medium

Figure 10.5 *Characteristics of architectural choices.*

mercial companies for a fee to subscribers. Some examples are Sungard (Wayne, Pennsylvania), Comdisco (Rosemont, Illinois), and Data Processing Security (Fort Worth, Texas), who provide IBM hot sites, and Digital Equipment Corp. and ComCare, Inc. (Billings, Montana), who provide DEC hot sites.

- Cold sites are "shells," empty data processing facilities, environmentally prepared, but having no computers installed. The customer is responsible for getting and installing the equipment in an emergency.

- Development sites are second data centers, common with *Fortune* 500 companies, that are fully equipped sites normally used for program development and information center support. In an emergency, such work is dropped and the site is converted to a backup production site. The site is often a mirror of the primary production site.

- Other users' sites refer to arrangements for backup at other local data processing organizations on a "best efforts basis." Generally speaking, these represent a weak and unsatisfactory backup alternative.

For those who can afford it, the development site approach is probably the best contingency arrangement possible, since it fully duplicates the production site and is under your direct control, not someone else's. In any event, all options should have one thing in common: *off-site* backup. On-site backup, in the form of multiple computers, is not considered adequate contingency planning; it protects from a single computer failure, but nothing else.

Governing Policies. Once again, the necessary policies need to be put into place to ensure the computer architecture. These would include policies governing equipment acquisition, funding (buy or lease), vendor standards, connectivity requirements, security, contingency backup, insurance coverage, distributed processing guidelines, contract negotiations, and use of outside services. All four layers of the computer architecture must be covered by appropriate policies personalized to the specific organizational structure and environment.

Computer Implementation

TACTICAL

> **IW 55—COMPUTER MANAGEMENT**
> The installation and interlinking of computers at all levels of the organization.

The four layers of computer architecture require different implementation and support strategies. The issues facing a data center are quite different than those for a departmental minicomputer installation. And a PC installation is certainly considerably less complex than a mainframe computer. The role of the CIO also differs in each case.

- *Data Center(s).* Whether in a corporate data center or a business unit data center, the issues with mainframe processing are similar, except perhaps for the critical mass of in-house expertise available to support the installation. Thus, from a CIO's point of view, the architectural issues are the same. A start-up data center is obviously first concerned with location and size, what operations will be housed there, adjacency requirements, communications needs within and without the company, security issues, contingency backup, staffing levels, and so on. Once operational, implementation issues turn to equipment configurations, systems software decision planning, long-term capacity planning, workload balancing (not just production, but also development and information center needs), network installation, education and training, and so on. The degree to which the CIO is involved in these matters obviously depends on the organization structure. Involvement is total if the data center reports directly to him/her but, if decentralized over a number of business units in diverse geographic locations, the involvement may be indirect; that is, participation in planning activities and decision making, final approval authority, and/ or perhaps an oversight, or monitoring, role. From an architectural perspective, the CIO needs to have some control over hardware and software acquisitions. Therefore, his/her minimum (or base level) involvement should probably include capacity planning, equipment selection, computer connectivity requirements, and acquisition approval (as an architecture control mechanism more than for dollar control).
- *Departmental Minicomputers.* The primary difference here is that more CIO guidance is needed even though the resources are out of his/her hands. This is because of the degree of technical sophistication resident in the user department which usually starts out at nil. Someone is brought in to run the operation, but the support staff is most often thin at best, necessitating continued reliance on the software (most mini systems are bought rather than developed in-house) and hardware vendor over the life of the system. Issues of concern to the CIO are preparation of the initial, vendor selection (and overall viability of the vendor), contract terms and conditions, oversight of the vendor development process, acceptance testing criteria, and adherence to in-house company standards, including connectivity bridges to other in-house systems. Once installed, the issues shift to technical support (and vendor dependence), database management security and control, and contingency backup (especially if the operation is critical). Again, the CIO need not be intricately involved in these activities, only assured that they have been properly addressed.

• *Individual Computing.* The further computing decentralizes, the less the CIO is involved. Individual computing includes word processing, information center use, and personal computers. The chief concerns of the CIO here are in promoting architectural standards that facilitate corporate-wide use and interchange of information while, at the same time, being concerned with the security, control, and integrity of that same information. The hardware side of this is primarily the establishment of vendor standards and connectivity solutions (i.e., micro-to-mainframe connections). The software side addresses issues of effectiveness, accuracy, security, and control. Because of the importance and rapid growth of individual, or end-user, computing to the organization, it has been given separate treatment as a decentralized resource in and of itself in the section to follow.

Computer Assurance. One of the principal roles of the CIO in any company, regardless of organization structure, is computer assurance. Computer assurance differs from one firm to another but, in general, it is concerned with assuring that resources will be planned far enough in advance that computer support is not seriously degraded because of a lack of resources, that the computing resources are adequately protected, and that emergency conditions will not result in cessation of vital computer support. Thus, three critical concerns of the CIO are capacity planning, computer security, and contingency planning:

• *Capacity Planning.* The purpose of capacity planning is to forecast needed resources in advance of demand so that the right "horses" are in place when needed and service is not unnecessarily degraded. The capacity planner estimates the resources that would be needed to process the workload over a range of possibilities and calculates performance figures (resource utilization, throughput rates, response times) to determine the optimum configuration needed to guarantee good service. There are various methods for doing this, ranging from the rule-of-thumb method (guesses based on past experience), the linear projection or "eye-balling," method (extrapolated trend lines based on past performance), and bench-marking. The latter uses an analytic model to convert guesses into precision, allowing the capacity planner to forecast most accurately the resources needed to optimize service levels and costs.

Benchmarking is fast and easy to do. Capacity planning charts of both batch and online work help to plan equipment upgrades far enough in advance to avoid capacity "crunches" and assure smooth, continued operations. The criticality of good response time on productivity can be seen in Figure 10.6. Poor response time slows both production and development. In terms of production, the amount of work done per hour rises sharply with shortened response time. In

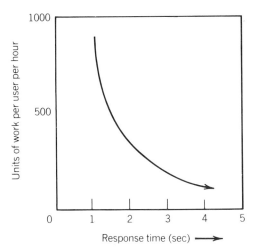

Figure 10.6. Criticality of response time. Production work measured in numbers of transactions; development work measured in number of interactions.

terms of development, each extra second of response time costs a second or more of think time, slowing development work accordingly.

- *Security.* Security encompasses every information resource; data, communications, personnel, computers, physical premises, end-user computing, and applications systems. Computer security covers mainframes, minis, and micros, whether centralized or decentralized. It also covers a variety of risks dealing with the theft, destruction, alteration, or disclosure of intellectual property (e.g., software, databases). The subject is too broad to be treated in any detail in this small space. Whole books and libraries are devoted to this one subject. The important thing to note is that the responsibility of the CIO is to see that *baseline* security is in place throughout the organization. Baseline security is that level of security deemed minimal to provide reasonable protection over valuable information assets. Whatever that is deemed to be, it must be built into company security standards and monitored for compliance by someone—the Auditor, the CIO, compliance officers, or others.

- *Contingency Planning.* As noted earlier, the importance of assuring uninterrupted computer service in an emergency dictates that contingency planning be at the top of every CIO's "must" list. Whatever solution is chosen (hot site, cold site, development site, etc.), the implementation stage deals with putting the plan into action. At the least, baseline contingency involves segregating all applications into priority categories, for example, A = critical, B = important but not critical, C = less essential. Off-site contingency backup and recovery of at least the *critical* applications is mandatory. Three things are needed at a minimum: the site must be determined and arranged in advance; emergency procedures (not just for computer operations but user operations as well) must be documented; and the backup system must be tested for each application, before the contingency plan can be considered adequate. This applies not just for the data center(s), but for every critical minicomputer application as well. (Because of the general proliferation of micros in the organization, backup is generally not a concern for these devices.)

Operational Control

OPERATIONAL

> **IW 56—COMPUTER OPERATIONS**
> The assurance of uninterrupted computer service levels.

Inventorying. The starting point for all resource management is an inventory of what is currently in place. In the case of computer architecture, this includes a compilation of all computers, be they large data center-based mainframes complete with peripheral equipment and systems software utilized, or simple PCs on individual desks. It is important to record them all, for they are all part of the computer architecture. Just because a $5000 PC is small doesn't mean it is any less important to track. As the power of PCs grow, they will be the source for more important work and decisions, the demand for connectivity to corporate databases will increase, and the sharing of data between machines will also grow. Thus the architectural planner needs to inventory *all* machines, large or small. Cost, location, owner (SBU), type and model, software used, connections to other systems and databases, are all important information.

The inventory is not just hardware; it also includes software (though micro software could be excluded), which is a vital part of computer architecture. This includes operating systems teleprocessing monitors, DBMS software, utilities, and production aid tools. Because systems software fits between the hardware and the application system, careful attention must be paid to its architectural fit. A map or diagram of the company's logical computer connectivity is also a very useful aid in architectural planning, an example of which is shown in Figure 10.7. In this example, solid lines between machines indicate automated information transfers between systems, dotted lines show tape-to-tape or other semiautomated transfers, and no lines means the computer is stand-alone, that is, it does not currently feed or receive data from any other computer. The computer inventory is a reference document that can be used across the planning spec-

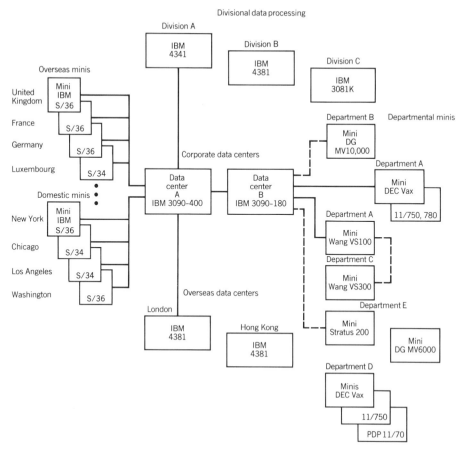

Figure 10.7. Logical computer connectivity.

trum to plan, implement, and monitor computer usage throughout the enterprise.

Operations. Data center computer operations may or may not be a responsibility of the CIO, depending on organizational arrangement. If it is, then operations such as scheduling, equipment utilization, network control, and productivity aids and utilities are a normal part of the CIO's planning activities. But if it is not, the CIO should at least be satisfied that appropriate control mechanisms are in place, such as an automated scheduling package, equipment utilization reports that show management how the machine resources are being utilized around the clock, capacity planning reports of projected computer usage, and network control systems like those described in Chapter 9. If nothing else, the CIO needs these to monitor operations and to satisfy himself that no major surprises are going to surface to senior management without forewarning. This applies to minicomputer installations as well, especially since these are often not as professionally managed as are data centers.

Monitoring. Once again, the CIO's monitoring role is a matter of management preference. In some organizations, it will include monitoring data center activities but not minis or micros; in others it will involve monitoring all computer usage; in still others, the CIO will do no computer monitoring, sticking to planning activities only. Areas that probably should receive at least minimal supervision, even in a decentralized operation, are standards, contingency plans, micro use, charge-out systems, and service levels.

- Standards for computer acquisition, installation, and operation are part of overall information resource standards. The CIO is responsible for establishing such standards, and may also be responsible for monitoring adherence, though the latter might be delegated to others.
- Contingency plans, as previously discussed, are really a part of standards monitoring. An overall evaluation of the status of contingency plans, for every critical site and application, should probably be prepared for senior management at least annually.
- Micro usage surveys are useful for management to understand not only how these devices are being used, but to satisfy themselves that they are cost-justified. (See PC Surveys under End-User Computing Architecture.)
- Charge-out systems should be validated as to their accuracy and fairness by a responsible third party. This could be the CIO, CFO , or Auditor. This is helpful because most charge-out systems are still expressed in computer resource units (CPU cycles, tape mounts, disk space used, lines of print, etc.) rather than in business resource units (cost per account, per transaction, per report) and, therefore, business managers have a hard time understanding the charge-out system.
- Service levels can be assessed in terms of service statistics, such as percent of systems uptime, response time, and ontime report delivery (efficiency measures) or by user satisfaction surveys (effectiveness measures), or both. No matter how good the service provider may think the service is, the proof is in the pudding, that is, it's what the user perceives to be important. It is perfectly possible to be rendering good service but have it perceived as poor service. The goal should be to give good service that is perceived as good service. When this is the case, a temporary slip in service will not immediately be perceived by users, permitting time for corrective action. But when good service is perceived as bad service, some good public relations and communications are in order. Good communications is needed to separate myth

from reality. This is an area where information organizations do not generally do a good job; hence it is an area where the CIO can play an important public relations role.

END-USER ARCHITECTURE

STRATEGIC

> **IW 57—EUC INTEGRATION**
> The integration of business professionals with technology.

The *strategic* goal of end-user computing (EUC) is to integrate business professionals and managers with technology so as to greatly leverage productivity and decisionmaking in the business office environment. Although office technology consists of many products, the three major components of EUC architecture for our purposes are office systems, information centers, and personal computers.[1]

Office Systems. Office automation (OA) began modestly a decade or so ago as word processing for secretaries. Before architecture could even be considered, the turf issue as to who would be in charge of OA had to be settled. Most organizations ended up rolling it into the Information Manager's or CIO's bailiwick. Next, the issue was how to cost-justify it. Many an analyst slaved over the numbers trying to demonstrate how many secretaries, or parts of secretaries, could be saved using word processing. Much of this proved to be a futile exercise. Most businesses that have installed word processing simply believed in its productivity value; I doubt that the numbers made them believers. A case in point is the way Bank of Boston management was sold on word processing back in the mid-1970s. After striving in vain to demonstrate cost-justification to management, a different tactic was tried. Three areas where *management* productivity benefits had been realized from word processing were employed to illustrate the value of word processing, not to the secretaries, but to the professionals they served. The Law Office testified as to the value to lawyers of editing lengthy legal documents and contracts without having to reread the entire document (only the changes had to be checked). Finance said they saved valuable CPA time by letting the word processor's math function automatically cross-total financial statements without having to do it manually. The Audit Department showed how the system helped auditors create lengthy and confidential audit reports faster and easier. The man-

---

[1] One could also include PBXs, especially if used as local-area networks, or when telephones are integrated with workstations. However, since PBXs were treated in Communications Architecture in chapter 9, they have been excluded here.

agement committee was impressed—they never again asked about cost-justification for word processors. Over the past decade, office systems have expanded from simple word processing for secretaries to a new focus on managerial productivity, not just from word processing, but from electronic mail, information centers, and personal computers. Today when we talk about office automation, we generally mean to encompass all office technologies from bottom to top, that is, from the clerical force to managers and professionals, to senior management, and even the CEO.

Information Centers. As noted in Chapter 7, the original concept of the information center (IC) was to copy production files to another machine which could then be accessed directly by users using fourth-generation languages to extract needed information. This is still a popular IC strategy. In addition, many businesses download specific databases to departmental minicomputers serving as local ICs. The downloading of selective data to PCs at the individual level is also becoming increasingly popular. The technology architect needs to determine where and how ICs will be used in the future to plan for the connectivity needs and tools necessary to provide support.

Personal Computers. Since the birth of the Apple PC in 1976, microcomputers have spread across the office landscape with unbelievable agility and speed. PC dollar sales in the United States already exceed mainframe sales and the industry is now producing PCs faster than we produce people (1 every 10 seconds). This is nothing short of phenomenal growth of an industry that didn't even exist 10 years ago. If, indeed, most managers will have a workstation of some kind on their desk by 1990, as experts predict, PCs clearly will transform the office of the future. By 1990, it is predicted that PC power will grow by a factor of 10X, which means that there will be what amounts to a data center on every desk. Clearly, this will need careful architectural planning. As suggested earlier, there is no such thing as a personal computer in a business office. All office computers are business computers that are part of the computer architecture. Ultimately, they will be shared and networked; thus planning for their connectivity and the advanced uses of this technology as it continues its evolution in the office is the strategic challenge. The PC revolution, in this writer's opinion, has at least three identifiable strategic phases, as suggested in Figure 10.8:

- Phase I, the hardware phase, is the introductory period. It is the hand-holding, hardware-oriented, education–experimentation phase of PC introduction into the firm. Most leading U. S. firms entered into this phase of PC evolution beginning around 1982.

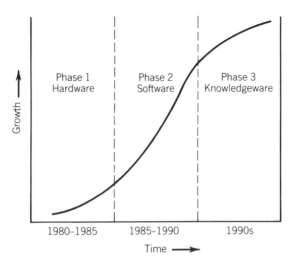

Figure 10.8. The PC revolution.

- Phase II, the software phase, follows with rapid acceleration and pro-liferation as computer literacy and usage spreads across the organiza-tion. In leading firms, this phase began around 1985. Today the first wave of saturation is being felt, and the growth curve is slowing as companies try to assimilate the technology they have and attempt to leverage their investment through multiple uses and a shifting focus to software and communications that enable the sharing and network-ing of these machines.
- Phase III, the knowledgeware phase, introduces artificial intelligence in the form of natural languages and Expert Systems that promise to turn the computer from a productivity tool to an automated assistant. This highly sophisticated but easy to use technology is still evolving, but holds considerable hope for the 1990s, not only as a management support tool but as a competitive weapon in its own right. Organiza-tional productivity from the use of PCs depends on linking them into the overall architecture. This long-term integration must be planned up-front, even as stand-alone PCs are installed. The user will focus on the individual PC; the CIO must focus on how individual PCs will network to form a cohesive architecture.

Strategically, these three technologies—office systems, information cen-ters, and personal computers—combine into an end-user computer archi-tecture that plans for its evolution, interconnection, and compatible exis-tence—all custom-tailored to the environment in which it must function.

Management Support

TACTICAL

IW 58—EUC SUPPORT
Leveraging managerial productivity.

The tactical side of EUC deals with the implementation of office systems, information centers, personal computers, Expert Systems, and other office technologies designed to leverage managerial/professional productivity.

Office Systems. Although office technology includes a wide array of products (e.g., copiers, reprographics, facsimile, and output devices), the two essential workhorses of office systems are still word processing (primarily for secretaries) and electronic mail (primarily for business managers). The tactical support for these activities has focused on vendor selection and standardization, installation support, the development of standards and procedures, and technical support. Many companies maintain office systems support groups to provide this kind of ongoing support. Word processing has pretty much saturated the office today with terminal-to-secretary ratios approaching 1:1 in many companies. E-Mail, on the other hand, has been slower to grow because it is aimed at the managerial audience where the terminal ratio is not yet as high. But this is changing and every leading manufacturer offers an E-mail product (e.g., IBM's Profs, Wang's Office, DEC's All-in-1). Voice mail has been adopted as an alternative strategy by many companies, especially for higher level managers. With office systems approaching a mature state in the office, most of the implementation attention today addresses information centers and PCs.

Information Centers. A centralized architecture would have a single IC operated by the corporate data center as one of its three processing functions (the other two are production and development). A decentralized approach would have a number of departmental minicomputer-based ICs. A third alternative is to have both, an interconnection of corporate, departmental, and even personal information centers. In this latter scenario, the idea is to try to satisfy as much of the management information needs as possible through the IC rather than through conventional systems development and COBOL programs. Even production transaction systems can separate its management reporting needs from operations. One may feed the other, but they can be developed and maintained separately.

A number of vendors provide IC support architecture. Here are a few examples:

- Cullinet's Information Center Management System (ICMS), for example, provides a way of managing information in mainframe sites having information center requirements. The system consists of an IDMS information database, end-user computing facilities, and an "open-system" architecture. Software links provide a bridge between the mainframe database and end-users using either dumb terminals or PCs, and the open-system architecture connects to Digital Equipment, Wang, and Data General minicomputer products as well as IBM mainframes.
- Digital Equipment's VAX Information Center is a comprehensive portfolio of integrated hardware and software that links end-users with VAX-based (minicomputer) databases. The "VAX Toolbox" consists of a group of integrated software tools that enable end-user access to external databases, data analysis, graphics presentation, statistical modeling, and online queries. The system works on the premise that mainframe data will be downloaded to a departmental VAX machine serving local end-users.
- Pilot Executive Software, Boston, has the Command Center, a graphics-based IC package designed for ease of use (mouse-driven) by high-level executives. With this package, data can be resident on a mainframe or down-loaded to a departmental IC. The data can be organized and dynamically graphed and presented on display screens in high-quality color presentation graphics, can be printed, or can be transmitted or sent by diskette to remote offices.

Advances in the power and functionality of desk-top computers in the years ahead will put enough power and storage at the individual workstation level so that corporate and departmental ICs will likely change their role. The corporate data center will function primarily as a downloader of information databases, and the departmental IC will probably become a local-area network server housing a shared database, accessed by clustered PCs. In some cases, the data will be downloaded directly to an individual PC. Implementation planning today must have a long-range migration plan to facilitate the transition to these future architectures.

Personal Computers. The personal computer has, in just a few short years, literally pervaded the business office. The PC invasion cannot be stopped, nor can it be ignored. It must be led. The PC is here to stay; it is a very important part of the corporate technology architecture; and it requires leadership. Personal computers are not toys or calculators. They can be abused, misused, and underused. Management is rightfully concerned with the strategic issues of control, cost, security, and data integrity in the use of PCs in the office.

To provide leadership over what potentially could be a large uncontrolled resource in the corporation, a growing number of companies have established corporate personal computer (PC) centers as a tactical implementation control strategy. Variously called PC centers, information centers,[2] in-house stores, the function of the PC center is to serve as an in-house computer store and laboratory, an internal "computerland" if you will, where managers and professionals can get help in learning how to use PC's to solve business problems (see IW 30—PC Centers).

During Phase I, the hardware stage of the PC evolution, the PC center served as an introductory agent, a facilitator, an educator/trainer. During Phase II, the software stage that most U. S. companies are now in, the primary focus has shifted from hardware to software leverage. The PC center in this stage works to promote multiple and advanced uses of the PC with users and strives to provide the necessary connectivity links to promote information movement and exchange. These links occur at three levels: individual, departmental, and corporate, as shown in Figure 10.9.

- *Individual Workstations.* The first level of EUC connectivity is the individual. Just as the Computer Era was the time of the mainframe computer, the Information Era is the time of the PC or, more precisely, the integrated individual *workstation*. As noted earlier, the ratio of terminals to managers (at least middle managers) is expected to approach 1:1 in the 1990s. The architecture of these integrated workstations will have to be easy to use, incorporate standard functions such as spreadsheets, word processing, and electronic mail, provide for user-installed products that customize the machine to the individual user, and access both internal and external databases.

  The next wave of integrated multiuser systems will provide multiaccess, that is, access to multiple databases and the ability to display several screens simultaneously. Adoption of a standard workstation addresses PC architecture at the individual level.

- *Departmental LANs.* The second level of EUC connectivity is work groups served by departmental local area networks (LAN). Architectural planners must weigh the pros and cons of multiuser shared logic systems (the traditional mini) versus multiuser PC-based LANs. The advantages of the PC-based LAN include greater flexibility, availability of off-the-shelf applications, and the value of local intelligence at the user level. In time, powerful micro shared-logic systems that also run applications and work as file servers for a LAN will be available, bring-

---

[2]This is a different role than the information center concept discussed previously. However, many companies have combined responsibility for both under the same management and thus use the same term to cover both activities.

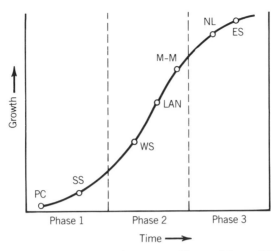

Figure 10.9. EUC architecture. PC, personal computer; SS, spreadsheets; WS, individual work-stations; LAN, department LANs; M–M, micro–mainframe connections; NL, natural languages; ES, expert systems.

ing the advantages of both in one system. A typical departmental LAN consists of a network server attached to a cluster of PCs via a cabling system (e.g., Ethernet) or asynchronous communications links for remote PCs. Personal computer users share disk files and printers. The back end of the server will usually provide remote connectivity to a host mainframe computer, public data networks, and other LAN servers.

Many LANs use micros as servers. 3Com, for instance, uses an IBM PC XT as its Ethernet file server. Others use specially designed servers, such as Banyan Systems, a front-runner in LAN development. The Banyan Server is divided into three parts: a front end that interfaces with PCs (via Ethernet); a back end that accesses host computers, public networks, and other Banyan servers; and a processor that provides a variety of services (file, print, mail, backup) to PC users. Other departmental LAN providers include IBM's PC Network, Ominnet, Proteon Inc.'s ProNet, Datapoint's ARCnet, 3Com systems and Novell Inc.'s network products (2).

- *Corporate Connectivity.* The third level of EUC connectivity is the corporate micro–mainframe connection. The linking of microcomputer to mainframes is probably the most important single architectural connectivity need of end-users. The problem is that everyone is looking for a universal "cookbook" solution where none exists. There is no single industry solution. The dozens of companies that sell micro–mainframe links present the information manager with a bewildering task of sorting out and finding the best solution for the company's needs. It is unlikely that a single vendor will be settled on to resolve this problem because the reality is that few companies will use the same vendor—even IBM—for everything. Even if they could, there would still be the problem of eventually having to connect to outside sources where vendor selection cannot be controlled.

The hardware, software, communications connectivity problem is so acute and is such a nightmare to everyone, that a whole new business has emerged to address vendor incompatibility problems: the third-party "bridge" vendors. Simply put, bridge vendors are companies that provide hardware and/or software products that enable incompatible systems to talk to one another. Forrester Research (Cambridge, Massachusetts) notes there are two kinds of bridges: physical and logical. Physical bridges deal with conduit; logical bridges deal with content. A physical bridge, for example, would be a DEC to IBM connection, or a 3270 terminal emulator. A logical bridge would be an application to application connection, or a connection to IBM's system network architecture (SNA). Forrester classifies bridge vendors into three groups: *systems* vendors (DEC, DG, Wang), which provide physical bridges to IBM networks and logical bridges to IBM applications (DISOSS, DB2); *physical* (conduit) bridge vendors that offer protocol converters, LAN links, and terminal emulation (e.g., Bridge Communications and Jupiter Technologies); and *logical* bridge vendors that focus on document compatibility and communications interfaces, mainly to IBM (e.g., Software Research Corp., Softswitch) (3).

Software Research Corp.'s (Natick, Massachusetts) product, called Strategic Network Environment (SNE), for example, is a software bridge that allows dissimilar mainframe, mini, and microcomputers to exchange various types of information with one another. Specifically, it can transfer files and messages between IBM MVS/VM, DEC VAX, Wang/VS, and IBM and compatible PC computers. At this writing, pilot versions were running at Bank of Boston, Chase Manhattan Bank, John Hancock Insurance, and GE Credit.

Bridge vendors may yet fill the architectural connectivity gap left by the lack of industry standards and thus could be an important part of the technology architect's connectivity "tool kit."

Expert Systems. Phase III of the EUC evolution, the knowledgeware stage, will see the introduction of commercial artificial intelligence in the form of natural languages and Expert Systems (ES). Expert systems are beginning to come out of the artificial intelligence labs and into commercial use. Most of the major computer companies (e.g., IBM, Digital Equipment, AT&T, and Xerox) are investing heavily in the potential of Expert Systems. Early systems were in the professional areas—medical diagnosis, geological analysis (oil and gas drilling), genetic engineering, and so on. Now business uses are emerging—financial and estate planning, marketing research, and investment management. The architectural planner needs to keep up with ES developments in order to plan its introduction into the future workstation environment. He/she needs to know the players in the field, the applications, and how they will be used. Major hardware players to watch include Symbolics, Xerox, DEC, Lisp Machines, Software-Intellicorp, Applied Expert Systems, Teknowledge, Inference Corp., and IBM. Leading ES development package vendors include Teknowledge Inc., Intellicorp, Carnegie Group, and Inference Corp.

In the 1990s, end users will not just use computers; computers will be their administrative assistants, their automated mentors, if you will. By the end of this century, I believe we will have completed the transfer of technology to users through the three phases of growth—hardware, software, and knowledgeware—depicted in Figure 10.8. The architectural planner will need to anticipate and provide leadership through all three phases to optimize EUC for managerial effectiveness and competitive advantage.

EUC Support

OPERATIONAL

> **IW 59—EUC CONTROL**
> Supporting controlled EUC use and growth.

Even though the pace of PC growth has slowed recently as managers grapple to assimilate what they already have, the end-user to terminal ratio is still fast becoming 1:1. The PCs are cheap, autonomous, responsive, and easy to use. But they can also be redundant, isolated, and unstandardized; they can spew out unreliable data, be difficult to integrate, and create control and security problems. As PCs multiply and users "do their own thing," EUC information management will become more and more difficult to control. The PC software industry has fueled the problem by an explosion of generic inexpensive software readily available to users. The best of it is easy to use and amenable to rapid customization. It supports independent work and is cheap (mostly under $500). But it is also deceptively individualized, which fosters isolation and contradicts the basic notion of integration. To provide leadership for the intelligent use and growth of EUC, an operations support strategy is needed. At a minimum, this includes a support organization, architecture, applications support, education and training, control mechanisms, and policies and standards.

Support Organizations. An appropriate support organization is needed to provide leadership and direction to end-user computing. The central PC center strategy described earlier is the favored strategy for supplying this, but it is not the only strategy. A PC coordinator can be established in each business unit, who is responsible for providing all necessary aid and assistance. The PCs can be centralized into a common pool shared by all, as many schools have done. However it is arranged, it is important that some kind of support organization be put in place; PCs should not be allowed to drift uncontrolled. The information systems organization has 25 years of working experience that can and should be drawn on to help PC users avoid making all the "big iron" mistakes on "little iron."

Architecture. This begins with an inventory of all EUC hardware and software. A mechanism is needed to track acquisitions in order to maintain the inventory. At Bank of Boston, this was initially accomplished by having the PC center serve as the in-company "store," that is, all PCs and accompanying software were ordered through the PC center, which was controlled by the information systems organization. Later, when the PC center had served its initial purpose as a facilitator for the introduction of EUC in the bank, this function was turned over to the purchasing department. However, an arrangement was made to have copies of all EUC purchase orders sent to the PC center so that inventory control could be maintained. An EUC architecture was adopted (as in Figure 10.9) to support the logical progression of EUC through the phases of the PC evolution. Inventory knowledge enabled the support group to know where and how to promote the chosen architectures.

Applications Support. An inventory of PC *usage* is also needed. One way this can be done is through periodic, perhaps annual, surveys of PC user/owners. The survey shown in Figure 5.4 is an example. The nine classifications used in that survey basically showed that 72% of all uses were for individual task automation applications (word processing and spreadsheets), 19% were departmental applications, and 9% represented more innovative uses of PCs. A similar PC survey taken at Pacific Bell showed that 47% of their PC usage was exclusively word processing, 18% was for spreadsheet applications, 15% database management, 11% graphics, and 9% all other uses (4). From these and other surveys it appears that word processing and spreadsheet applications still make up the bulk of PC usage in most organizations. This means that there is an opportunity to leverage the PC investment by helping users find additional uses for their machines. A second use (for the same user) of a PC doubles the investment leverage, a third triples it, and so on.

Education and Training. The EUC leader has a responsibility to educate potential and existing users. During Phase I, that is mainly introductory training on hardware and basic packages (e.g., spreadsheets); in Phase II, advanced software (applications) training is important; Phase III will be concerned with the introduction and use of Expert Systems. Training can be done in-house or outside. If in-house, it could be managed by a PC center, a human resource training center, or an outside consultant. The purpose is not only to make users proficient in the use of the hardware and software, but also to help them understand such things as risk exposure and the user's responsibility for security and control over corporate information assets.

Control Mechanisms. Traditional control mechanisms such as project teams, specifications, milestone reporting, testing, and documentation will not work in the PC environment. New control mechanisms are needed. Why is this important? Because users new to computers do not understand what can go wrong, and what the impact can be on the organization. Most novice PC users don't think to use reasonableness and validity checks, audit trails, and the other error detection/data validity checks used by information services professionals for years. Sometimes they don't even back up files or, if they do, they file the copies and originals together. There are dozens of war stories about PC controls. Headlines like "A Slip of the Chip on Computer Spread Sheets Can Cost Millions;" "No More Million Dollar Mistakes;" and "Microcomputers Threaten Central Data Control" (5), all attest to the potential problems of data integrity which companies face today and which they must get under control before they lose control.

Policies and Standards. One control mechanism over EUC use is the issuance of governing policies and standards. This gives auditors something to audit against. Such policies might cover PC physical security (equipment, software, diskettes, data), access controls (authorization and use of IDs and passwords), vendor standards, software piracy, encryption, and so on. To be effective, standards must (1) have top management backing, (2) be custom-tailored to the environment, (3) be reasonable (or people won't follow them), and (4) be enforceable.

SYSTEMS ARCHITECTURE

Systems architecture at the strategic level involves the long-range planning of the application systems needed to run the business and support corporate objectives. Implementing those systems is the tactical planning dimension. Providing ongoing support, the maintenance and enhancement of existing systems, represents the operations and control phase.

Strategic Systems Planning

STRATEGIC

> **IW 60—PORTFOLIO ANALYSIS**
> Developing a long-term plan for the corporation's systems portfolio.

Chapters 3–7 dealt in depth with the strategic systems planning process. Therefore, this strategy focuses on the organizational responsibilities of the various parties in a decentralized (or decentralizing) systems organization, rather than on "what" is to be done. A CIO in full control of information resources carries direct responsibility over the entire systems life cycle. But in a decentralized organization, the CIO's role can range from passive to proactive, depending on the management style and culture of the organization.

Roles and Responsibilities. Figure 10.10 shows the typical system life cycle broken into the three phases alluded to above: planning, implementation, and support. The planning phase, although it may only constitute 5% of the project's life cycle, is the most important part since it determines how the other 95% of the resources will be employed. A push in the wrong direction will not only be a waste of scarce resources, but will fail to support the business. The implementation phase makes up some 95% of the project life cycle, covering conception to birth. The support phase is concerned with ongoing maintenance and enhancement of the system over its life. The role of the CIO in this life cycle (again assuming decentralized systems resources) can vary from limited to participative to authoritative, as illustrated in Figure 10.11.

- *Limited Model.* In this mode, the CIO's responsibility is architectural only, that is, he/she issues systems policies and standards and then stands back out of the way and lets the SBUs do their thing. There is little or no control beyond the standards "glue" designed to guide a consistent architecture.
- *Participative Model.* In the participative management model, the CIO plays a consulting and advisory role, and the business unit systems managers have at least a dotted-line (functional) reporting relationship to the CIO. The CIO will have some form of "sign-on/sign-off" responsibility over the system process, as described earlier. The degree of sign-on/sign-off authority varies widely from company to company according to individual preference and management style.
- *Authoritative Model.* The authoritative model, while decentralizing systems resources to the line units, would keep the systems staff (or

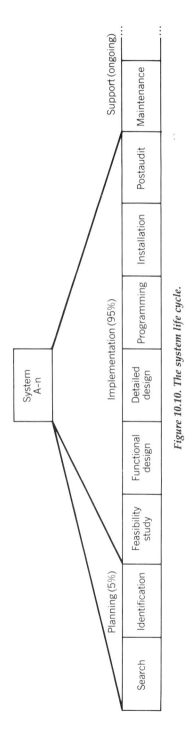

Figure 10.10. The system life cycle.

Model	CIO Responsibility	Reporting Relationship*	CIO Role in Life Cycle		
			Planning	Implementation	Support
Limited	Issue policies and standards	None	None	Systems development standard	None
Participative	Consulting/advisory	Dotted line	Sign-on authority	Sign-off authority	Monitor architectural impacts
Authoritative	Manages systems resources	Solid line	Lead the planning effort	Control over project management	Responsible for maintenance

*Relationship of CIO to SBU systems managers.

Figure 10.11. CIO role in system architecture.

at least the line unit systems managers) on the corporate CIO's payroll. Thus the CIO continues to exercise management authority and responsibility over systems planning, implementation, and support, even though it is decentralized.

Of these models, the trend seems to be more toward the middle ground. The limited model is usually too passive and results in a CIO position with no teeth in it. The authoritative model, on the other hand, can be too heavy-handed in trying to exercise centralized control over decentralized resources. In the participative management role, the CIO becomes more of a strategist than an implementor, and is more concerned with strategic and architectural planning than day-to-day computer and systems management.

Systems Portfolio. Once the issue of who does what, when, and how is resolved, the long-term systems portfolio can be developed. This consists of a combination of existing and planned new systems resulting from the planning process.

- *New Systems.* For each new system that is planned, a number of architectural steps are required. The business opportunity (technical and competitive) inherent in each proposal must be assessed; the resources needed to implement the system must be determined together with an assessment of its reasonableness in light of the business mission; the funding of discretionary systems to the areas of greatest potential return must be prioritized; a buy or build decision must be made; the architectural impact of needed systems interfaces must be considered; the risk/return associated with each project must be assessed; and proposals must be prepared for review by the company's IRM committee.
- *Old Systems.* Starting with an inventory of existing systems, each must be assessed as to its relative strength and weakness to determine whether it has a long life or is a candidate for major updating or replacement. The automation penetration survey suggested in Chapter 7 can be effective for this purpose. The idea is to determine the relative efficiency and effectiveness of each system, the interfaces between systems, and information about the composition of the portfolio, so as to determine the replacement or enhancement needs of the existing portfolio of systems.

Systems Implementation

> **IW 61—SYSTEMS DEVELOPMENT PROJECTS**
> Developing new information systems and services.

Analytical considerations for systems development activities include the project approval process, project management, project oversight, and implementation standards.

Project Approval. Generally, three parties are involved in the project approval process: the user proposing the system, the CIO, and some management body, such as an IRM committee. Factors considered for new information systems should, at a minimum, include:

- *Business and Systems Linkage.* The issues here were discussed in Chapter 3. The main one is to assure that resource commitments are in concert with the business missions and objectives established for each SBU.
- *Alternatives Assessment.* Have all options been considered, beginning with the buy or build decision? If it is to be bought, has the selection process been thorough? Have contract terms and conditions been resolved? Is the hardware and software compatible with existing architecture? If it is to be built, are the resources available? If there is a shortfall, how is it to be made up (new hires, transfer, contract help)? Have architectural bridges to other systems been identified?
- *System Objectives.* Is it a new or replacement system? What type of system is it (i.e., customer, management, or operations)? Productivity-oriented systems (OSS) are usually of low interest to market-driven SBUs. LEAD mission SBUs generally focus on customer systems (CSS). Conversely, CSSs are often too risky for control-oriented managers; therefore, HARVEST mission SBUs usually focus on operating systems (OSS).
- *Risk Analysis.* Does management understand the risk associated with the project? Risk refers to the likelihood of overrun (time, money, or both) in completing the project. A simple risk assessment technique (Figure 10.12) is what I call the "Bo Derek System," because it measures risk on a scale of 1 to 10. For each project, have three experienced systems people familiar with the project judgmentally rate the three risk dimensions of size (man-months), structure (precise or unstructured), and technology (new or old) of the project on a scale of 1 to 10, with 10 being most risky. Then average the composite scores of the three raters to get the project's risk profile. This simple technique

	Low risk				Medium risk			High risk			Composite	Average
	1	2	3	4	5	6	7	8	9	10		
Project size					x	x	x				18	6
Project structure						x	xx				20	6.6
Project technology			xx	x							10	3.3
Total												15.9

Overall risk rating: 5.3 (15.9/3) = MEDIUM

Figure 10.12. Project risk analysis.

alerts management to the likely precision of the numbers; that is, riskier projects are more likely to experience overruns.

- *Economic Analysis.* A standard cost–benefits analysis (CBA) worksheet should be devised so that the IRM committee has an easier time passing on projects that are all calculated in a similar manner; that is, ROI means the same for every project.

   An example taken from my previous book is shown in Figure 10.13. In this example, the cost of the present operation is compared to the cost of the proposed operation to get the annual projected gain or loss. The one-time costs of systems development are then factored in and an after-tax cash flow is calculated. Capital investments (equipment, etc.) are added to produce the total cash flow over the life of the system, which is then discounted to present value and the return of investment (ROI) is calculated. If the ROI covers the company's cost of capital (hurdle rate) for new investments, the project is cost-justified. While this is a good technique for CSS and OSS developments, it short-changes MSS projects because their benefits are usually qualitative rather than in hard dollars. For these we need a different treatment. We can provide a VOI (value of information) on such projects, which works like this: Assume your company's "hurdle rate" (desired ROI) is 15% after taxes. Determine what revenue is needed to cover the system project's costs and also provide a return on investment of 15%. Plug that amount into the cost–benefit analysis worksheet as the quantified value of the qualitative benefits of the new system. In other words, the amount needed to justify the project is the "value" of the information processed. For instance, if $50,000 of annual revenue would produce an acceptable ROI, include it in the CBA and explain: "If you believe that the qualitative benefits (value of information) of this system are worth $50,000 a year, the project is worth doing. (This is what the last box in Figure 10.12 means.) You will be pleasantly surprised at how often this procedure "sells" a project that cannot otherwise be cost-justified.

Project Management. Once a project is approved, the architectural issues center around the implementation process. A clear understanding of the roles of the various parties involved, adherance to corporate systems standards, and project assurance activities are some of the activities to be followed.

- *Development Roles.* Systems development should always be a joint process between users and systems staff. One faction without the other delivers half a product. All users and no systems may produce an effective system, but it is unlikely to be efficient; conversely, all systems and no users usually produces an efficient but ineffective system. Together, the twin goals of efficiency and effectiveness are more likely

	Period 0	Year 1	Year 2	Year 3	Year 4	Year 5	Year 6	Year 7
1. Present Operation Income Expenses Net operational result								
2. Proposed Operation Income Expenses Net result								
3. Projected Gain (Loss)								
4. Project Costs (One-time) IM charges User time Computer development Package cost Consulting fees Site costs Other								
5. Cash Flow Less taxes @ 55% Less tax return on depreciation Less ITC Net cash flow								
6. Capital Investments								
7. Total Cash Flow Discount factor (15%) Present value Cumulative net present value								

8. Return on investment
(ROI)
(Check one)
☐ Net benefits discounted at 15% after taxes produces a payback in _____ years and a return on investment of _____ %.
☐ In order to achieve a 15% after tax return over the life of the system, the non-quantified system benefits must have a value of $_____ annually.

Figure 10.13. Costs–benefits analysis. (From W. R. Synnott and W. H. Gruber, Information Resource Management, Wiley, New York, 1981, p. 309.)

to be realized. In addition, more and more companies have a central DA function to oversee the database design aspect of new systems projects. This group can also play a valuable role in helping to create a data model of the system to be built, to create the data dictionary, and to assist in the logical and physical database design.

- *Corporate Standards.* The minimum architectural standards needed are systems development life cycle and database design standards. While these are necessarily customized to each firm, guideline standards obtained from trade organizations, consultants, or "methodology" vendors can often be helpful in getting started. Adherance to such standards helps to assure consistency in systems architecture across the corporation. By making the development of such standards a collaborative process between line and staff groups, everyone has input to the process, making it more likely that the standards will be reasonable and thus followed.

- *Project Assurance.* A formal project control system is needed for all systems projects to track programs over the project life cycle. Not only does this allow the capture of hours spent by whom on the project but, if properly designed, will give early warning to possible overruns, either in time, money, or both. The use of modern tools such as online programming, computer-aided design (CAD) workstations, fourth-generation languages, and other productivity aids also helps project assurance. The use of prototyping as discussed in Chapter 7 is another possibility. The role of the project manager versus the CIO in providing a quality assurance role also needs to be resolved, that is, what oversight role does the CIO have over project development? In some organizations, it may be none, putting all responsibility on the project managers; in others, it will be milestone reviews of major projects only; in still others, it will be close monitoring of all systems projects. Finally, the company should have a policy on post-audits. Are they to be done on all projects or selected projects, and by whom?

Systems Support

OPERATIONAL

IW 62—SYSTEMS SUPPORT Maintaining existing information systems.

When systems are decentralized, the ongoing maintenance and support of in-place systems is strictly a SBU responsibility. The main role of the corporate CIO is to understand the architectural makeup of the systems portfolio, to track the architectural impacts, if any, of major systems enhancements, and to monitor adherence to policies and standards.

Profile of Applications Systems. As stated previously, the architectural starting point of all information resources is an inventory of what is in place. In this case, the resultant systems portfolio profile serves as an excellent base reference point for systems planning. At a minimum, the systems profile data includes an analysis of the total investment in systems, systems interface requirements, age analysis, types of systems, architecture, development/maintenance ratios, and a value analysis.

- *Investment.* The total investment in systems is the cumulative cost of acquisition/development over the life of the systems. It is useful to know the total value of the systems software asset (usually several times more than the investment in hardware), but it is probably more useful to focus on current annual spending, broken down by SBU and by expense category. The first helps management to see if systems support is appropriate to the contribution of the SBU; the second is helpful in observing trends and making comparisons to industry averages.
- *Interfaces.* In Figure 10.14, we see an example of an inventory of applications systems together with their interdependencies—System A receives feeds from systems D and B and, in turn, sends updated output to system D. As new systems come on board, it is easy to add to this list so the architect can track "bridge building." (A corporate policy could require that all bridges to other systems are the responsibility of the new system builder.)
- *Age.* The age composition of the portfolio is important from a planned replacement point of view. Typically, systems have a useful life of

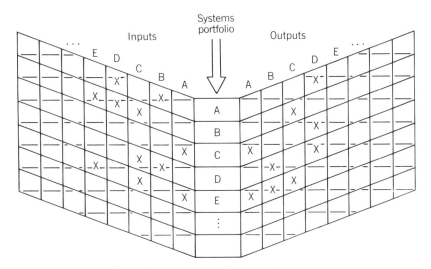

Figure 10.14. Inventory of systems interfaces.

around 10 years but, also typically, a quarter of the portfolio may be over 10 years old. An aging portfolio spells trouble. Obsolete systems generally do not support the business well, hinder modern data management, represent a major backlog of work, and impact architecture negatively. Therefore, the age mix is a most important piece of information.

- *Systems Types.* How are the systems divided between OSS, MSS, and CSS? Typically, the profile is pyramidal in shape, with the bulk of the systems on the bottom being operations support, a smaller group in the middle representing management support, and a small fraction at the top of the pyramid classed as customer, or market-driven, systems. The bulk of the operational systems have been automated in most organizations, as have probably half of the potential management systems. But there remains a huge potential for customer systems. Information on the types of systems servicing the various business units can help to focus future development along more competitive lines (perhaps turning the pyramid upside down).
- *Architecture.* Systems can also be classified as to their general architecture, that is, mainframe, mini, or micro systems; batch, online, or database systems; sequential file or random access; packages or in-house developed. If the pattern does not show a strong and steady trend toward state-of-the-art architecture, corrective action may be indicated.
- *Development/Maintenance.* The ratio of new and old is important. The industry norm is 40:60, that is, 40% of systems resources are devoted to new development and 60% to maintaining existing systems. Abnormal ratios bear closer examination but, more importantly, management needs to understand that to be competitive with systems technology, it is vital that the percentage devoted to new development be maintained, or even increased. To do that requires continued investment in systems, because over time maintenance will increase at the expense of development, as depicted in figure 10.15. Old systems will require more maintenance and new systems will require maintenance that did not exist before. Managers who freeze systems budgets fail to recognize this. The result could be to put themselves right out of the systems business—and the competitive race.
- *Value Analysis.* The actual value of the systems portfolio in terms of its efficiency and effectiveness can be measured as described in the section on Automation Penetration in Chapter 7. Systems that are not measuring up, whether old or new, need attention. Fine tuning, modifications, rewrites, or replacement may be in order to bring systems support up to snuff.

The Monitoring Role. The role of the CIO in overseeing the ongoing systems process is quite different when systems are decentralized, and

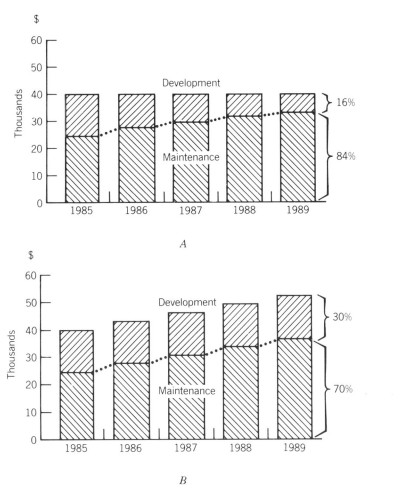

Figure 10.15. System Development versus Maintenance: (A) Scenario 1—Flat total budget squeezes out development. (B) Scenario 2—Level development causes annual budget growth.

very much a matter of corporate preference. Three monitoring tasks persist, however, regardless of who does the monitoring. These are a project-tracking system, development standards, and post-audits:

- *Project Tracking.* A project-tracking system provides automatic monitoring over the life of a project, not just development, but ongoing maintenance. This enables potential overruns to be detected early. It also helps the CIO to track architectural impacts, such as major enhancements to in-place systems that affect other systems. There are a number of good project-control systems on the market. (The *ICP Quarterly* software service, for example, lists a number that are cheap enough so that no organization can really afford to be without one.)

The wide variety of reports available from such systems permit easy project tracking of systems, by whoever is doing the monitoring.

- *Development Standards.* Policies are generally developed individually, but standards are usually cumulative, collecting into a comprehensive manual on a subject. The particular standards of interest here are systems development, database design, and computer security. These may be combined into a single manual, or they may be separate manuals. It is not usually necessary to write these from scratch as there are many organizations (vendors, consultants, software houses, trade groups) that have already developed generic manuals. These can often be used as is, or can be easily modified to fit the environment, at a fraction of the work effort needed to develop them in-house. For example, DBMS, Inc. (Ann Arbor, Michigan) sells a "Standards, Procedures, and Guideline" manual for IDMS users that comprehensively covers both systems development and database design activities.

- *Post-Audits.* Most companies perform post-audits on selected (usually major) projects following implementation. These after-the-fact evaluations offer several important benefits: we learn from mistakes; the quality of future work is improved, evaluation leads to better future utilization of resources; and the success of a project is communicated to management. Credibility is enhanced if the post-audit is conducted by a team representing diverse interests, such as the project manager, a high-level user representative, an audit representative, and the CIO (or his delegate). The object is to determine if objectives were met, if predicted savings materialized, the reason for overruns, if any, and so on. Post-audits of major projects work better if they are a matter of corporate policy rather than choice. This, again, is the CIO's job.

References

1. 1985 Seminar: *Integrated Office Systems: User Needs and Vendor Responses,* A. D. Little, New York, April 1985.

2. *Information Week,* 10/7/85, p. 20.

3. *The Professional Automation Report,* Forrester Research, Cambridge, MA, Sept. 1985.

4. As reported by Lou Bartnick, Pacific Bell, at an IDC Conference, New Orleans, Nov. 1985.

5. *The Wall Street Journal,* 8/20/84; *ICP Business Software Review,* April–May 1985; *Information Systems News,* 11/29/82, respectively.

PART IV

CHANGE MANAGEMENT

11

ENGINES OF CHANGE

Change takes place no matter what . . . . There must be measured,
laborious preparation for change to avoid chaos.

PLATO

We are struggling today through a period of wrenching discontinuities.
Discontinuity means change, and effective "change management" will be
the key to success in the 1990s.

In this book I have advanced several notions dealing with the changes
being brought about by the transformation from the Computer Era of the
past to the Information Era of the future. Four of the discontinuities, or
engines of change, that are impacting information management are discussed below, along with some observations on how the IW planner can
capitalize and manage these engines of change to positive advantage.

First, there is the evolution from an industrial to an information society,
and the growing importance of information to an information economy.
Second, the maturation of information technology has enabled it to
emerge from the back office to become a significant competitive force in
the marketplace. Third, we realize that information is a valuable corporate
asset that must be managed intelligently, through a philosophy of information resource management that harnesses and synergizes the information power of the enterprise. Fourth, the new role of the emerging chief
information officer can and will become the technological engine of change
driving the other three trends toward increased business growth and profitability in the 1990s.

ENGINE 1: THE INFORMATION REVOLUTION

I began this book with the statement that the information age is upon us.
There is no question that with two-thirds of the population of the United
States now working in information-related jobs, we are, indeed, an infor-
mation society. The services sector is driving the demand for information

services, because service companies (e.g., government, education, financial, the professions) depend largely on information for their survival. The services sector, in turn, is highly competitive and subject to rapid change. This creates a profound impact on business organizations because change is primarily brought about through reorganization. Organizational change, then, is also a driver of change. It not only results in new structures, but often in new management as well, thus fostering new cultures (beliefs) and goals that further promote change. The current drive for corporate entrepreneurship is, in turn, fanning the flames of decentralization, as corporations strive to create relative autonomy and freedom of action through decentralized "accountability" structures.

These developments of the information revolution are profoundly affecting information management. The metamorphosis from the Computer Era of the past to the Information Era in which we embarked today has already been dramatic. Information management has moved from a technocratic back-room operation to a market-driven competitive force; it has migrated from centralized data processing to decentralized information resource management; it has changed from a cost-cutting function to a revenue-generating business. All of this has not just been due to the information revolution; it has been fueled by the technology revolution as well. Technology itself has made great strides; it is cheap and pervasive; it is easy to use; and it is the cause of great discontinuities as technological waves of change continue to sweep across the business landscape.

Consider the business impact of these technological waves of change:

- Mainframe computing power, as measured in MIPS (millions of instructions per second), is growing at the rate of 45% per year. The 1984 IBM 3081K computer was a 14 MIPS machine; the 1986 Sierra series of machines offer up to 100 MIPS per machine. Growth and price/performance gains in computing power is providing tremendous economies of scale to "big iron" users, and with it, significant competitive advantages.

- Personal computing is an even greater wave of change. The PCs represent an unprecedented invasion of the office, from 100,000 installed in 1977 to 60 million predicted for 1987. Here is a $20 billion business that did not even exist 10 years ago! And consider the growth in power. From early 64K floppy disk machines we now have 1 MIPS, 3-megabyte desktop machines with 40 megabytes of hard disk storage. Ten years ago we would have called that a data center. As managers rise up the computer literacy curve, research-based (analytical) management will add to intuitive-based management, creating a new and integrated style of management aided by technology.

- Software is still the name of the game, despite hardware growth. It is the software that creates value, not hardware. We produce more hardware than we can use today, so the need is to dramatically increase software productivity (i.e., automate the software creation process). Developments in computer-aided software engineering (CASE), Expert Systems (the robotics of the office), micro-code, and end-user computing software are all great inroads.

- Telecommunications is fast becoming the key information resource, the link between all others. Satellites, fiber-optics, and other developments will eventually have as potent an impact on communications costs as chip technology has had on computing costs. Satellite communications will open up worldwide markets and new business opportunities. Network management will likely be the dominant responsibility of tomorrow's CIO as the investment in networks grow to 10 or 20 times what they are today. Communications will be the key to the "electronic" information society.

- Distributed processing will be the wave of the future as minis and micros that are spread all over the corporation are shared and linked to one another. Users will run computers, not computer professionals. Just as the telephone company solved its telephone operator shortage by turning us all into operators through direct dialing, so we will solve the programmer shortage by turning computing over to users. The goal of the CIO in the future will be to manage the information function rather than the resources, to forge distributed information resources into a coherent and integrated information delivery system rather than decentralized technical chaos. The mandate is clear; the execution is less so, but the challenge is evident.

- Office automation is expanding to cover white-collar workers from clerks to presidents. Everyone in the office is being impacted by office automation ranging from simple word processing, to electronic mail, personal computing, advanced workstations, and communications to internal and external databases. Although the productivity payoff is hard to measure, the potential is enormous. There are 55 million white-collar workers in the United States today. At an average cost of $30,000 per year per worker, we are looking at $1.5 trillion dollars. A productivity gain of 10% would represent annual savings of $150 billion to American business. That's worth going after.

The information revolution will continue to foster change. But how one deals with change makes the difference. Most managers assume the status quo will continue; at best, they react to change (often resisting it) negatively. The managers who not only recognize the changes that are taking place around them but are able to adapt positively to those changes, who in fact become leaders of change, will be the winners in the Information Era. As someone once observed: "Without the courage to change, there is not growth."

ENGINE 2: INFORMATION AS A COMPETITIVE WEAPON

The vision of competitive IT is not really a dream in leading-edge information companies, because these companies are not just thinking about it, they are doing it. Companies like American Hospital Supply, McKesson, American Airlines, Citicorp, Bank One, Dun & Bradstreet, Federal Express, United Air Lines, Merrill Lynch, and the USSA Group[1] are already reaping the benefits of technological one-upmanship.

Nonetheless, we would still have to call this a vision, because such technology leaders are in the minority. The vast majority of companies still view IT as a back-office accounting or operations support function, or, even if they intellectually believe in the vision, have done nothing about it, perhaps because they don't know *how* to exploit its competitive potential. The CIO can help by proposing frameworks, such as the IW model, for generating ideas, but to do this he/she must be part of the strategic planning process, corporate strategy must be communicated and understood broadly in the organization, and the corporate environment must be favorable and encouraging to the use of information technology for competitive advantage.

There are also the "doubting Thomases." Some industry observers have, in fact, suggested that the promise of IT has greatly exceeded benefits, that in spite of all the talk, many companies have not been able to demonstrate the value-added of technological development. One reason for this might be explained by looking once again at the evolution of systems. The primary application of computers over the last 30 years has been to back-shop operations, the operations support systems (OSS). These were mostly initially justified by productivity gains through labor reductions. Once in place, however, future costs are seen only in data processing, whereas ongoing benefits inure to the user beneficiaries. This is often lost on management, who see only the rising DP budget without obvious offsetting benefits, the traditional dilemma of DP. True productivity due to automation is often hard to demonstrate and often is not even attempted, leading to the erroneous belief that productivity has, in fact, not occurred. Management support systems (MSS) are even worse. These are rarely cost-justified with hard-dollar savings because benefits are usually qualitative. Once again, management sees the costs, but benefits are hard to prove; it's largely a matter of subjective judgment. Finally, customer support systems (CSS) are relatively new, so there are limited examples to draw on to demonstrate their profit potential. This book has attempted to document many of these to help planners see the potential and find their own information weapons.

Perhaps this will be the ultimate answer to the critics. Information systems in the past have been cost centers; in the future, they will be profit

[1]The 10 companies identified by a panel of experts convened by *Information Week* as those most successfully utilizing competitive systems (1).

centers. Successful information weapons will not save money so much as they will make money, increase share of market, and beat the competition. This is the potential of the information weapon vision: to hit management where it counts—in the bottom line!

The information weapon model presented in this book is meant only as a framework for thinking; a way to help managers search for technological opportunities within their product/service lines or to develop new lines. The strategies and case examples discussed in the chapters on innovation, information services, and productivity were designed to help IW planners build bridges to customers while simultaneously creating barriers to competitors. Historically, the sequential evolution of IT has been OSS, followed by MSS, and now CSS. In the future, IW systems will look for all three functions. Not all systems will provide all three, but by looking for them, the IW planner will find more competitive opportunities than otherwise would be the case. In the past, IT impacted mostly employees; in the future, customers will be heavily impacted, if not by you, then by your competition. That is why business managers will have no choice but to act (lead) or react (follow), or risk losing business to their more technology-enlightened competitors.

Many managers grasp the information weapon conceptually, but do not know how to move it forward. Information weapon planning is not a task for the traditional long-range planning committee; it is usually too cumbersome and too slow. Such planning is better performed by a small and diverse group representing differing viewpoints, for example, a product manager, a marketing representative, strategic planner, and a CIO (or other systems representative). Michael Vitale of the Harvard Business School even has labels for such a planning group: the wizard (computer researcher), the weed puller (the judge of whether an idea has value), the teacher (he who explains the innovations of the wizard), and the marriage broker (the intermediary between the user and the wizard) (1).

The key is to keep such planning groups small, diverse, dynamic, and unfettered in their thinking. It must be recognized, however, that there are two kinds of information weapons: planned and unplanned. Many of the best-known case examples achieved competitive advantage by accident. American Hospital Supply started out to move their back-shop operations to the customer to cut costs; the American Airlines reservation system started as a transaction processing DP system. When it works, we say it was planned that way. Planning can help identify opportunities, of course, but unplanned accidents will happen. Often one can be a leader through planning, and a follower through copying the "accidental" advantages achieved by competitors.

As we stand on the brink of realizing the true power of the computer in the Information Era—the power of the information weapon—the potential for leveraging the enterprise has never been greater. Those who seize the opportunity to exploit the true potential of the firm's information resources will be able to clearly demonstrate the return on the technological investment, will see their companies excel in the 1990s, and will beat their own path to the executive suite in the process. To those with vision will go the corporate laurels.

ENGINE 3: INFORMATION RESOURCE MANAGEMENT

Information is not only an important corporate asset, it is a dispersed asset; that is, information is in every nook and cranny of the firm. Likewise, the technology resources that manage, process, move, and manipulate that asset around the corporation are also dispersed throughout the organization, often in decentralized organization structures. Therefore, information resource management in the future will not just be a matter of managing information assets; it will involve managing information assets that are under the control of decentralized organizations. Thus IRM in the 1990s will require a completely different mind set and management style than in the past. The information resource manager, or CIO, of the future will have two main roles in the organization: (1) to bring *value* to the corporation through the harnessing of IT to help reach corporate and business unit goals, and (2) to ensure a unified underlying technology *structure* that serves as a support foundation to business plans for the corporate "house" that rests on that foundation.

The *value* role requires business skills—knowledge of the business, ability to work with managers at all levels, an executive "presence"—in other words, an IRM manager that is as comfortable with ROI, SOM, and EPS as with MIPS, COBOL, and X.25. The effective planning of information weapons requires a total integration of the systems process with the business process. In most organizations today, this is not the case. If the information systems function is involved at all it is usually in a reactive, not proactive, way. Not only does this suggest that business/information planning must be integrated, but business/systems people must also be integrated. The continued decentralization of systems resources into user areas will facilitate this integration process in the 1990s. This will also create the small group alliances needed to do the IW planning, as suggested in Engine 2. The *structure* role requires technical skills—a broad knowledge of diverse technologies, an awareness and understanding of important technical trends and their likely impact on the organization, a "big picture" mentality (not someone who is lost in the bits and bytes). The structure role is the architectural planner, ensuring that all the parts come together to form a whole that functions as a single, unified system, a holistic structure rather than a collection of unrelated parts.

Business managers (and top management) today are crying for better information to help them run their businesses. As important as that is, it only affects the bottom line indirectly. Tomorrow, managers will be crying for the information technology needed to win in the marketplace. This *is* the bottom line. If information managers find themselves under fire for better information management today, wait until tomorrow. Those who can't or don't produce the information weapons will likely find themselves working for someone who does.

If it is important for the IR manager to understand this dual *value and structure* role, it is doubly important that senior management understand it; otherwise, the IR manager could very well find him/herself functioning solely as a technology architect, not involved in the strategic planning process at all and not involved in IW planning. The education of management to the changing world of IRM is made more difficult because most busy senior managers can't afford to devote the time needed to thoroughly understand it. The CIO's task is to take the entire field of IRM and present it in a highly condensed, yet cogent, fashion to senior management. There is nothing new in this, as all managers from other disciplines necessarily do the same. The difference is that top managers usually have a grounding and familiarity with sales, marketing, finance, and other general business disciplines, whereas this is seldom the case with technology. This challenge requires that the CIO must also be an excellent corporate teacher, with a thorough understanding of IRM and where it is going, and the ability to communicate this succinctly and clearly to a management with very little time to spare.

The information manager of the future will not only have to manage decentralized resources, but his/her job will likely be dramatically changed as a result of decentralization. The information manager will change from a management style that has total control over resources and decisions regarding those resources, to partial control at best, with decisions either made jointly with user management, or by user management alone. The planning and control of information resources architecture in such an environment requires a management style that is consultative, participative, influential—a leader, not a controller. Managing things they don't control will affect many information managers adversely. In fact, many will lose their jobs, as *Information Week* notes: "During the next five years, as many as 50% of the corporate MIS directors of large decentralized corporations will change jobs over the issue of decentralization." (2) This statement means that they will either find their new role to be too watered down in authority and responsibility and will resign, or they will be unable to adapt to the new demands for extensive business (as well as technical) knowledge and they will be fired.

Change management is complexity management; IRM means managing change, so IRM is complexity management. There is too much technology and too many options. Complexity management involves choosing among alternatives that best fit the environment at the time and under the circumstances. When this is documented and supported by corporate policies and standards, we have a technology architecture. When that architecture is used to support business planning, we have strategic systems planning. When we have strategic systems planning *and* an architectural plan, we have an information resource management program. Organizations such as the U. S. Government, the World Bank, the State of South Carolina, and Bank of Boston have instituted formal IRM programs. The future will see many more joining the bandwagon because of the competitive necessity to harness decentralized information resources to avoid chaos.

ENGINE 4: THE CHIEF INFORMATION OFFICER

To be an engine of change, the information manager must also change. The traditional role of the DP/MIS manager of the past will not suit the information company of the future. A higher-level role is needed, an executive role that fits between top management and the DP/MIS professionals. In the last 5 years, many companies have recognized the need for, and have appointed, CIOs in their organizations. This is not because it is the latest fad, or a new name for the MIS manager. It is because of *change*. The rising investment in technology, the critical reliance on computers, the pervasiveness of technology in business, and the increasing awareness of IT as a competitive weapon, have all contributed to a rising awareness of the need for a higher-level computer executive, a CIO, to bridge management and technicians, business and technology, strategy and computers.

The CIO role also holds out an opportunity to information managers to rise up and contribute at a higher level in the organization, to bring information technology into the mainstream of the business, and to find new and rewarding challenges in turning IT loose on the competitive marketplace. It is an exciting time for information managers, after years in the back room, to come out of the dark and into the sunlight of business activity (mushrooms to flowers).

But the CIO role is still evolving. There is great confusion and misunderstanding about the CIO role, not just among CEOs, but among MIS managers themselves. Many have taken to calling themselves the CIO even though their job and responsibilities have not changed. A CIO is not just another name for an MIS manager; it is a different function. The CIO functions at a higher executive level of management because the tasks performed are at a higher level. The traditional roles of DP operations, systems development, and technical services are delegated to others. The CIO concentrates not on daily activities but on long-range planning, both strategic and architectural. The CIO is involved in corporate strategy, in technical trends, and in the competitive use of technology in the industry and by competitors. The CIO, more and more, is a staff person, often with a small but elite staff of planners, forging direction, creating corporate policy for the technology architecture, and coordinating the work of line groups to assure technological optimization. Companies need a CIO who can bring the vision of the information weapon to reality, who can cut through the complexities of technology to bring order to information management, who can manage and make sense out of decentralized information resources not necessarily under his/her direct control, and who is as comfortable in the executive suite as in the computer room. Such individuals are rare today. Those who have it are in great demand and are rewarded handsomely.

This will be doubly true in the decade ahead as technology becomes even more imbedded in business. There is little question that the CIO is real, and that the role will continue to emerge and take root in corporate America. Technology is too important to business for this not to happen. In the 1990s, computers will be so absorbed into the business fabric that business and computing will be inseparable. Computer literacy among users and managers will grow to the point where all managers and staff will use and rely heavily on computing support. This will not mean that a CIO is no longer needed. On the contrary, the greater the penetration of computers in the organization, and the greater computer literacy grows, the further technology will advance and the more planning, leadership, and education will be needed from the CIO. It is not a question of if, but of who? Who will occupy this vital executive role in American business in the next decade? Will information managers, business executives, or others fill this role? The future leaders are being identified now.

CHANGE MANAGEMENT

IW 63—CHANGE MANAGEMENT
Harnessing the forces of change to positive advantage.

The function of a manager is to manage. And if change is the order of the day, then the function of the manager is to manage that change. (3)

So say authors Burack and Torda in *The Manager's Guide to Change*. I would go one step further. It is not enough to manage change; we must *lead* change in order to be successful in the 1990s. Some people are aware of change, others adapt to it, and others manage it, but few have the vision to lead change. In the words of Nicholas Murray Butler:

People, it has been said, can be placed in three classes, the few who make things happen, the many who watch things happen, and the overwhelming majority who have no idea what has happened. (4)

The few who will make things happen in the Information Era will be those who can not only manage change, but lead change. To manage is to direct and control; to lead is to guide and show the way. When I served in the Korean conflict in 1952, the motto of my 116th Engineer Combat Battalion was "Prepare the Way." That pretty well sums up what is required. The change agent, or leader, must have a beckoning vision and then prepare the way to lead others to that vision. Change is inevitable. Therefore, the choice is not whether to change, but how to lead it. Change agents anticipate it, plan it, and turn it to positive competitive advantage. They don't just watch things happen, they make things happen. They influence the future, they don't just wait for it.

The impact of change on business in the Information Era is almost overwhelming. Quotes *Management Review:* "Businesses are caught in a maelstrom of evolving technologies, international competition, organizational restructuring, and shifting values on a scale unprecedented since the dawn of industrialism, or even civilization for that matter." (5)

The reason information managers, CIOs, and IW planners are change agents is because their tool in trade is technology, and technology is one of the great creators of change. In a recent survey, the American Management Association questioned 400 of its advisory council members on what they felt would be the issues of greatest concern to corporations of the future. The two highest ratings went to technology and global business developments (6). It is clear that technology is now at a point where it can change the way a business is run, not just support it. In many cases, technology is the driving force of the business, if not the business itself.

Organizational structures are also changing. The forces of this change include the drive for corporate entrepreneurship that is creating decentralized organizations, technological change that is changing the way work is done and products are delivered to the marketplace (e.g., global electronic delivery), and the evolution from an industrial to a service economy. Stanley M. Davis, management consultant, asks us to consider the following syllogism:

> Major Premise. The United States has a post industrial service-based economy.
> Minor Premise. All the models we have for managing and organizing service-based organizations in our economy were developed in, by, and for industrial organizations.
> Conclusion. We are using the wrong models for managing most of the organizations and corporations in our society." (7)

Dr. Davis suggests that traditional management models suffer from what he calls the "either/or" syndrome, that is, headquarters *or* field, strategy *or* operations, corporate *or* individual. The old industrial-based paradigm would say that you can't have both, but, in fact, that is exactly what is needed in a service-based organization, a set connected by *and* rather than *or*, that is, centralization *and* decentralization (controlled autonomy), computers as productivity tools *and* competitive weapons, a CIO that provides both value (strategic planning) *and* structure (architectural planning), management styles that depend on both analytic *and* intuitive thinking. We need to get away from the "mutually exclusive" binary way of thinking. Strategic thinking includes both. And the information revolution is helping to create strategic thinking. Instead of thinking of customers as individuals *or* masses, of goods as standardized *or* customized, of product delivery as local *or* global, information technology is making it possible to deliver standardized and customized goods, to individuals on a mass scale, delivered electronically on a local and global basis.

For business to change, people must change. Many workers and managers consciously or unconsciously resist change. It is not enough to create change, one must foresee the impact of planned change on the organization and manage through it. Understanding the forces behind such resistance can be helpful to the change agent in minimizing problems. Burack and Torda identified at least four resistive forces at work, loosely translated as follows:

- *Predictability.* The ability to predict cause-and-effect connections is important to people. Change introduces uncertainty into the cause-and-effect relationship, creating stress, and thus resistance to change.
- *Inconvenience.* People do not like to disturb what is comfortable. How often have you heard the expression: "It's worked that way for 20 years. Why change it?"
- *Skepticism.* Some people genuinely believe that the change proposed is not as good, let alone better, than the status quo.
- *Confused goals.* Unclear, misunderstood, or poorly stated goals result in people pulling in different directions.

All of these resistance forces can be minimized with good training and salesmanship up-front. Training breeds familiarity and thus removes the fear of the unknown. And slow introduction of change provides time for assimilation, for adaptation. Ripples are better than tidal waves. Clearly expressed goals and reasons for change, especially as they may benefit the changes, can also do a lot to soften resistance. These and other strategies are needed to prepare the human resource for change, often a very neglected part of change introduction.

The change agent needs to be able to see the organization as a whole, in order to see and understand how change will affect the whole. At the same time, he/she needs to understand *structure;* that is, how the whole is divided into parts, and the relationships between the component parts. This kind of broad "systems" thinking is something that information managers are accustomed to, for it is the very essence of systems development, that is, seeing the big picture, breaking it down into its subcomponents, building each from the ground up, and integrating all into the whole. Applying this same systems thinking to how change will affect the organization as a whole, as well as the impact on the various parts, is vital to anticipating and dealing with organizational problems related to change.

But before technology can create change and therefore affect organizations and people, there must be commitment to the vision of IT as a competitive weapon. As suggested earlier, the vision must be shared to be real. This not only requires capturing the CEO's attention, but his time as well—not an easy task, as Richard Foster suggests in *Innovation:*

> Everybody's advice to the CEO about every function—operations, law, planning, marketing, distribution, finance—is that he has to pay more attention to it. But if technology is the key to continued corporate success, the case for CEO involvement in technology is stronger than it is in other areas. The CEO has a unique role to play either as the architect of his company's strategy or the maestro who orchestrates its development. (8)

That may be, but getting the CEO and other top managers to spend the time necessary to learn about information technology and the information weapon vision, to understand why it is important to the company's future, and why failure to provide the necessary support could result in lost business to competitors who *do* share the vision, is difficult. Among the reasons for this are (1) top managers generally do not understand enough about technology and particularly its potential for competitive advantage, (2) information managers often do not know enough about the business and its products to identify information weapon opportunities, and (3) a strategic bridge between the two factions is lacking in most organizations owing to the historic tradition, culture, and organization of the information function within the corporate hierarchy.

An IW vision, by itself, will not work. It must be shared. But in order for it to be shared, there must be a receptive climate, a corporate culture that supports technological innovation. In some organizations this simply will not happen until or unless the corporate culture is changed, perhaps by an organizational restructuring and a change in management. These organizations suffer from the "transition mismatch" phase of the period of discontinuity between the Computer Era and the Information Era described in Chapter 2 (see Figure 2.2). In many companies, the strategic bridge between these discontinuous eras is still missing.

It is my hope that this book might help in one small way to build this bridge by painting a picture of some of the major changes that are going on around us, by classifying the respective roles and responsibilities of the different management factions (top management, user management, systems management) in managing that change, and by facilitating the search for competitive information weapons.

The search for competitive advantage, according to researchers at MIT's

Sloan School of Management, generally takes three forms: case examples, planning frameworks, and management techniques (9). Some present case examples of firms that have achieved competitive advantage through IT with the expectation that the reader will be able to relate to and create something that works in his/her own environment from the ideas presented. Others provide frameworks for thinking about how to go about identifying strategic systems opportunities in their organizations. The third form focuses on how to manage in the Information Era to prepare for the exploitation of IT.

In this book I attempted to present all three: a number of case examples were cited to illustrate a variety of IW strategies used by many companies in diverse (though largely *service*) industries; several frameworks for planning were introduced, especially the strategic planning frameworks in Chapter 3, the information weapon model in Chapter 4, and the architectural planning model in Chapter 8; finally, information resource management "how to's" were liberally spread throughout the book as a guide to change agents in managing (and leading) the changes brought on by the discontinuities of the Information Era. If only one or two of these ideas take hold, the effort will have been worthwhile.

INVENTORY OF INFORMATION WEAPONS

In all, 63 information weapon strategies are presented in this book. In Chapter 1, I promised to present a compilation of these strategies as a handy reference source to IW planners. Here is that list, presented in order of presentation in the book with page numbers for easy lookup references.

Information Weapon	Page Number

References

1. *Information Week*, 5/26/86, p. 27.

2. *Information Week*, 6/2/86, p. 6.

3. Elmer H. Burack and Florence Torda, *The Manager's Guide to Change*, Lifetime Learning Publications, Belmont, CA, 1979.

4. Nicholas Murray Butler, publication unknown.

5. *Management Review,* July 1986, p. 16.

6. Ibid., p. 61.

7. Stanley M. Davis, "Management Models for the Future," *New Management*, Spring 1983.

8. Richard Foster, *Innovation*, Summit Books, New York, 1986, p. 241.

9. Michael E. Treacy, "Toward a Cumulative Tradition of Research on Information Technology as a Strategic Business Function," CISR WP # 134, MIT Sloan School of Management, Mar. 1986.

Challenge is the core and mainspring of all human activity.
If there's an ocean, we cross it,
If there's a record, we break it,
If there's a mountain, we climb it.

JAMES RAMSEY ULLMAN

INDEX

325